TEXAS BUCKET LIST TRAVEL GUIDE

The Must-Have Handbook with Lots of Practical Tips for Planning Breathtaking Experiences and Make Unforgettable Memories

Forrest R. Cowan

© *Copyright 2023 by Forrest R. Cowan - All rights reserved.*

The content contained within this book may not be reproduced, duplicated or transmitted without direct written permission from the author or the publisher. Under no circumstances will any blame or legal responsibility be held against the publisher, or author, for any damages, reparation, or monetary loss due to the information contained within this book. Either directly or indirectly.

Legal Notice:
This book is copyright protected. This book is only for personal use. You cannot amend, distribute, sell, use, quote or paraphrase any part, or the content within this book, without the consent of the author or publisher.

Disclaimer Notice:
Please note the information contained within this document is for educational and entertainment purposes only. All effort has been executed to present accurate, up to date, and reliable, complete information. No warranties of any kind are declared or implied. The content within this book has been derived from various sources.
By reading this document, the reader agrees that under no circumstances is the author responsible for any losses, direct or indirect, which are incurred as a result of the use of information contained within this document, including, but not limited to, errors, omissions, or inaccuracies.

DISCLAIMER: Verifying the coordinates before using them for navigation is recommended, as they may not always be completely accurate. Additionally, it's important to note that the address or name of the location may have changed over time. So, double-checking before using the coordinates with a GPS device or mapping software is a good idea.

I'm an independent publisher, and I'm not affiliated, sponsored, associated, authorized, endorsed by, or in any way officially connected; I've no partnerships with any company, agency, or government agency named in this book. All names are the property of their respective holders. Mention of them does not imply any affiliation with or endorsement by them.
The information and opinion in this guide are provided "as is" without any representations or warranties, express or implied.

Cover Image by Shutterstock/ID 676407478 by ducu59us edited and modified by Forrest R.Cowan

"The Stars at Night are Big and Bright,
Deep in the Heart of Texas

The Prairie Sky is Wide and High,
Deep in the Heart of Texas

The Sage in Bloom is Like Perfume,
Deep in the Heart of Texas

Reminds Me of the One I love
Deep in the Heart of Texas."

From the Lyrics "Deep in the Heart of Texas"

TABLE OF CONTENTS

INTRODUCTION	6

TOP-RATED TOURIST ATTRACTIONS

The Alamo	10
San Antonio River Walk	12
Big Bend National Park	14
Palo Duro State Park Canyon	16
South Padre Island National Seashore	18
Dallas Arboretum and Botanical Garden	20
Fort Worth Stockyards	22
Texas State Capitol	24
National Ranching Heritage Center	26
Buddy Holly Museum	28
Tube The Comal River	30
Bat Watching in Austin Under Congress Bridge	32
Nacogdoches Visitor's Center	34
Menil Collection in Houston	36
Rothko Chapel in Houston	38
Hermann Park in Houston	40
Houston Museum of Natural Science - Hmns	42
Houston Museum of Fine Arts - Mfah	44
1892 Bishop's Palace in Galveston	46
Gruene Hall-Texas' Oldest Dance Hall	48
Dallas Museum of Art	50
Austin City Limits Music Festival - Acl	52

ROMANTIC GATEWAYS

Texas Rose Festival in Tyler	54
The Seawall in Galveston	56
Willow City Loop Near Fredericksburg	58
Scenic Drive - Overlook	60
Inner Space Cavern	62

Nasher Sculpture Center	64
Gerald d. Hines Waterwall Park	66

BEST NATIONAL PARKS AND NATURAL LANDMARKS

Enchanted Rock State Park and Natural Area	68
Garner State Park	70
Chisos Mountains	72
Boquillas Canyon	74
Fort Davis National Historic Site	76
Guadalupe Mountains National Park	78
Amistad National Recreation Area	80
Natural Bridge Caverns	82
Sea Rim State Park	84
South Llano River State Park	86
Big Thicket National Preserve	88
Lake Meredith National Recreation Area	90
Cedar Hill State Park and Lake Joe Pool	92
Balcones Canyonlands National Wildlife Refuge	94
Lady Bird Lake Hike-and-Bike Trail	96
Barton Springs Pool	98
Longhorn Cavern State Park	100
Fossil Rim Wildlife Center	102
Santa Elena Canyon	104
Rockport Beach	106
White Rock Lake Park	108
Cascade Caverns	110
Pedernales Falls State Park	112

HISTORICAL SITES

San Fernando Cathedral	114
San Antonio Missions National Historical Park	116
Goliad State Park & Historic Site	118
San Jacinto Monument	120
Uss Lexington in Corpus Christi	122

Mcnay Art Museum	124	Ocean Star Offshore Drilling Rig & Museum	188
Lyndon B. Johnson National Historical Park	126		
Bob Bullock Texas History Museum	128	**BEST FAMILY-FRIENDLY ATTRACTIONS TO GO WITH KIDS**	
President George H. W. Bush Museum	130	Houston Space Center	190
		Moody Gardens in Galveston	192
The National Museum of the Pacific War	132	Fort Worth Museum Of Science And History	194
LBJ Presidential Library	134	Houston Zoo	196
Dealey Plaza National Historic Landmark District	136	Fort Worth Zoo	198
		San Antonio Botanical Garden	200
Top O'Hill Terrace	138	Landa Park	202
Majestic Theatre in San Antonio	140	Perot Museum of Nature and Science	204
King Ranch Visitor Center	142	McDonald Observatory	206
King William Historic District	144	Kimbell Art Museum	208
Texas Ranger Hall of Fame and Museum	146	Sundance Square	210

HIDDEN GEMS AND LITTLE-KNOWN PLACES		**A JOURNEY THROUGH THE LONE STAR STATE**	212
Lost Maples State Natural Area	148	**CONCLUSION**	223
Caverns of Sonora	150		
Eight Wonders of Port Aransas	152	**PLACES BY REGION AND ALPHABETICAL ORDER**	224
Grapevine Historic Main Street District	154		
Blue Hole in Wimberley	156		
Devil's Sinkhole Natural Area	158		
Gorman Falls	160		
Westcave Preserve	162		
Malaquite Beach	164		
Jacob's Well in Wimberley	166		
Japanese Tea Garden	168		

WEIRD PLACES IN TEXAS-AS STRANGE AS THERE CAN BE

Marfa Prada Store	170
Marfa Lights Viewing Center	172
Cadillac Ranch	174
The Ghost Town of Terlingua	176
Sparky Pocket Park in Austin	178
Cathedral of Junk in Austin	180
Barney Smith's Toilet Seat Art Museum	182
Hueco Tanks in El Paso	184
National Museum of Funeral History	186

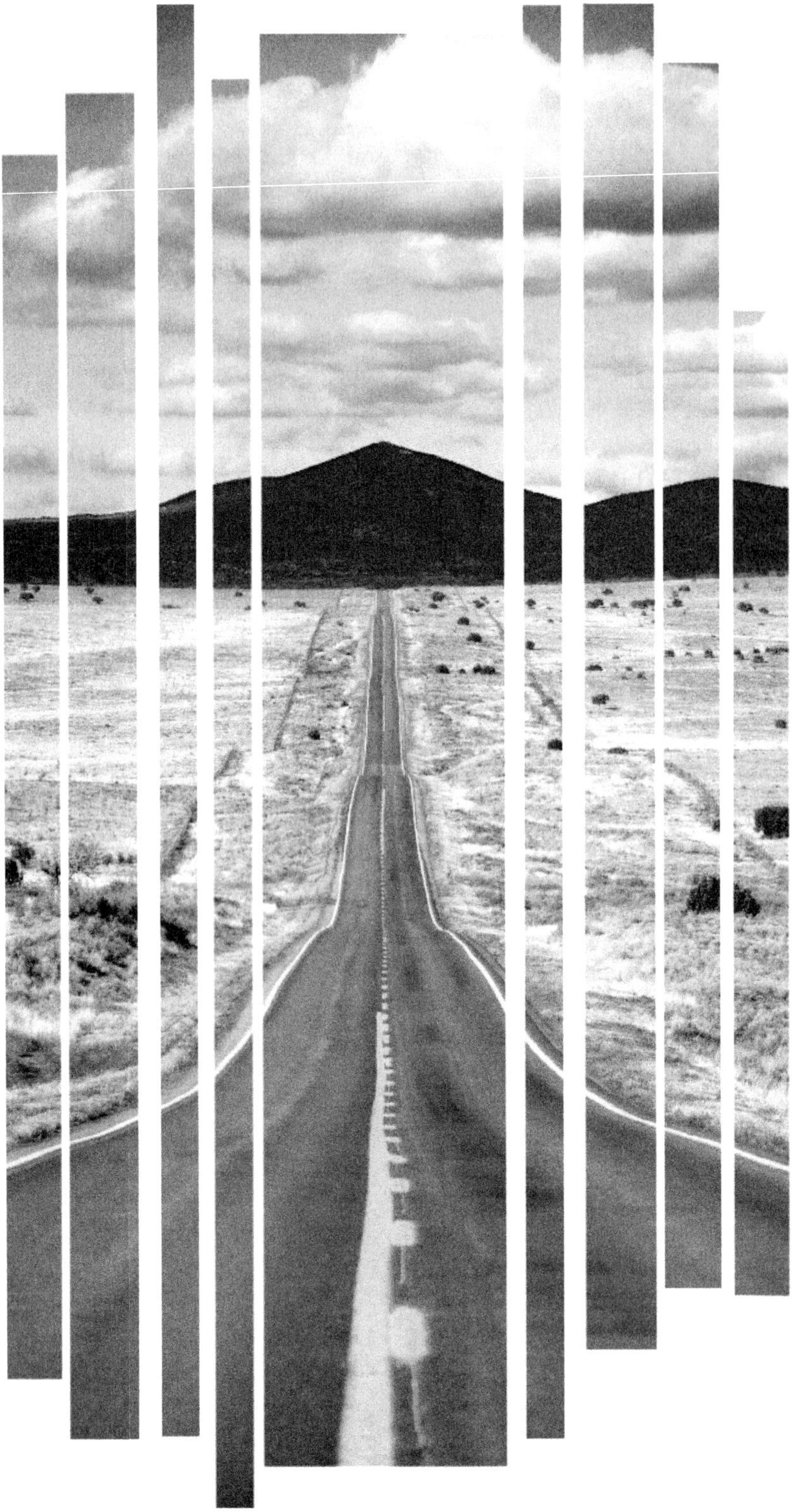

INTRODUCTION

Texas – The Lone Star State

Welcome to the great state of Texas, where the skies are big, and the landscapes are even bigger. From the rugged mountains of the west to the sandy beaches of the Gulf Coast, Texas is a land of contrasts and diversity. This guidebook will take you on a journey through the diverse regions of Texas, showcasing the best that this great state has to offer.
Discover Texas's rich history and culture by visiting iconic landmarks such as the Alamo in San Antonio, the San Jacinto Monument in Houston, and the State Capitol in Austin. Explore the state's natural beauty by visiting Big Bend National Park, the Hill Country, and Padre Island National Seashore. And, of course, no trip to Texas would be complete without experiencing the legendary cowboy culture of the state, which can be found in places like the Fort Worth Stockyards and the National Cowgirl Museum and Hall of Fame.
My name is Forrest R. Cowan, and I have had the pleasure of calling this wonderful state my home for more than 60 years. I have been fortunate enough to travel and explore every corner of Texas, and I am excited to share my knowledge and experiences with you.
As a lifelong Texan, I have seen this state change and evolve over the years. Still, one thing that has remained constant is the spirit and energy of the people who call it home. I deeply appreciate Texas's rich history and culture and am always in awe of its natural beauty. I hope my guidebook will give you a true sense of the diversity and beauty of this state and that it will inspire you to come and see it for yourself.
Whether you're a first-time visitor or a returning traveler, this guidebook will help you plan the perfect trip to Texas. So, grab your cowboy boots and explore Lone Star State!

The Story Behind Texas' Nickname, "The Lone Star State"

The origin of the name Texas is a topic of much debate and speculation. According to historical accounts, this state was once a province of Mexico known as Coahuila y Tejas. The region that is now the state of Texas was part of this larger territory. It is believed that the flag of this land featured two gold stars on a background of red, green, and white stripes, similar to the flag of Mexico. The exact etymology of the name "Texas" is unknown. Still, it is thought to have originated from the indigenous people of the region.

The state's history is deeply rooted in its fight for independence from Mexico in the 1830s. This struggle created a new flag for the newly independent Republic of Texas, featuring a lone star symbolizing defiance, pride, and independence. Texas officially joined the Union in 1845 as the 28th state, but its residents still take pride in their independent spirit. In 1889, an artist named Peter Krag was commissioned to design a new flag for Texas featuring the iconic lone star, which is still the official flag today

A Look at the Organization of My Book

Texas is a state rich in natural beauty and cultural heritage. From picturesque small towns to bustling cities, the Lone Star State offers visitors a wide range of attractions. From scenic mountains and deserts to lush forests and pristine beaches, it is home to some of the most breathtaking sights in the country. National, state, and local parks, ocean beaches, lakes, canyons, caves, theaters, antique shopping, restaurants, food trailers, architectural tours, F1 auto races, horse races, professional sporting events, golf courses, rodeos, universities, two Presidential libraries, museums, Blue Bonnet ...

People often ask me, "If you were to recommend one place to see while in Texas, what would it be?"

This book is a collection for tourists interested in exploring Texas' natural beauty, history, and culture, to adventure seekers looking for unique experiences. It caters to solo travelers, couples, families with children, groups of friends, and those who want to experience the spirit of Texas.

Texas is incredible, and there are many things to see and do! Don't know where to start?

In my guide, I have selected the most fascinating places for you to visit, expressing honest opinions on what I liked or disliked about them.

By reading this book, you'll discover:

- Top-Rated Tourist Attractions: Explore the iconic landmarks and must-see destinations that make Texas a top destination.
- Romantic Gateways: Find your perfect romantic escape in Texas, from charming small towns to scenic nature getaways.
- Best National Parks and Natural Landmarks: Discover the stunning natural beauty of Texas, with breathtaking landscapes, rare wildlife, and endless adventure opportunities.
- Historical Sites: Step back in time and immerse yourself in the rich history of Texas, from the Alamo to the battlefields and historic districts.
- Hidden Gems and Little-Known Places: Go off the beaten path and discover Texas's hidden gems and best-kept secrets, from quirky roadside attractions to natural wonders.

- Weird Places in Texas - As Strange As There Can Be: Embrace the weird and wacky side of Texas with some of the state's quirkiest and most unusual attractions.
- Best Family-Friendly Attractions to Go with Kids: Plan a fun-filled family vacation in Texas with a wide range of kid-friendly attractions and activities, from waterparks and amusement parks to zoos and museums.
- And Much More!

In this guide, you'll discover detailed maps with clear directions to each location, ensuring you won't miss a fantastic spot in this great state.

Plus, this book serves as a bucket list, inspiring you to visit all these beautiful locations and make the most of every moment. The vivid descriptions will motivate and encourage you to step out of your comfort zone and create memories that will last a lifetime.

Additionally, each place listed has a section for you to record your cherished memories and experiences during your visits.

Get ready to fall in love with the beauty of this state and indulge in hours of dreams and imagination. Whether as a gift for a special occasion or for yourself, this book will prepare you to embark on an adventure of a lifetime exploring the diverse and breathtaking sights Texas offers.

BONUS GIFT!

**Open your phone camera app and point the QR Code.
You will have access to interactive maps of each location described in the book to seamlessly navigate your way through hidden gems, local favorites, and must-see landmarks, enriching your travel experience with every step**

(Remember to check your e-mail spam folder)

THE ALAMO

The famous 18th-century mission in San Antonio, Texas, where a small group of Texan soldiers fought a 13-day battle against the Mexican army in 1836.

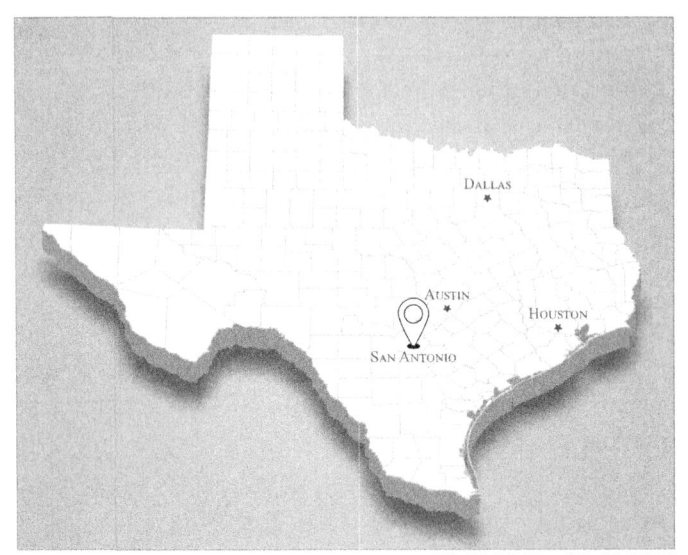

29.425840, -98.486560

WHAT'S ABOUT?:

The Alamo, located in San Antonio, Texas, is one of the state's most famous and historically significant tourist attractions.

The Alamo was originally built as the Misión San Antonio de Valero in 1718 and served as a Spanish mission and fortress. However, it is most famously known for the Battle of the Alamo, which took place in 1836.

During the Texas Revolution, a small group of Texan soldiers, including famous figures like Davy Crockett and Jim Bowie, defended the Alamo against the much larger Mexican army for 13 days. The battle ended in defeat for the Texan soldiers. However, their bravery and sacrifice have been celebrated as a symbol of Texan independence and spirit.

Today, the Alamo is a museum and historic site open to the public. Visitors can explore the mission grounds, see the Alamo church, and learn about the history of the battle through exhibits and presentations.

The Alamo is also surrounded by the Alamo Plaza Historic District, a UNESCO World Heritage site that includes other historic buildings and missions, such as the San Antonio Missions National Historical Park

WHERE IS?
The Alamo is in the heart of downtown San Antonio, on Alamo Plaza. It is bordered by Crockett, Houston, Alamo, and Commerce streets. It is approximately a 15-minute walk from the River Walk, a popular tourist destination in San Antonio. Additionally, the Alamo is about 8 miles from San Antonio International Airport if you travel by car.

WHAT'S GOOD/WHAT'S BAD:
Visiting the Alamo was indeed an unforgettable experience. I highly recommend reserving a spot (which is free) to tour the main building and stroll around the grounds. A visit to the Alamo can be completed in roughly an hour, including taking in the exterior grounds; guided tours are also available for purchase. Additionally, there is a seating area that features a TV playing the History Channel's production of the Alamo's history, which is also free, and I would highly recommend watching it. As I walked through the church and main building, I couldn't help but feel a sense of reverence and awe, similar to when I visited Pearl Harbor. It was truly awe-inspiring to be standing on such historically significant grounds. During my visit on a Friday, the crowds were minimal, and I had the opportunity to learn more about the cannons from a knowledgeable volunteer.

The Alamo is a must-see destination for any history buff or anyone looking to better understand the past.

DATE(S) VISITED:

WEATHER CONDITIONS:

ACCOMODATIONS:

WHAT WAS THE BEST PART OF TODAY?

SPECIAL MEMORIES:

SAN ANTONIO RIVER WALK

A network of walkways along the San Antonio River in the heart of downtown San Antonio.

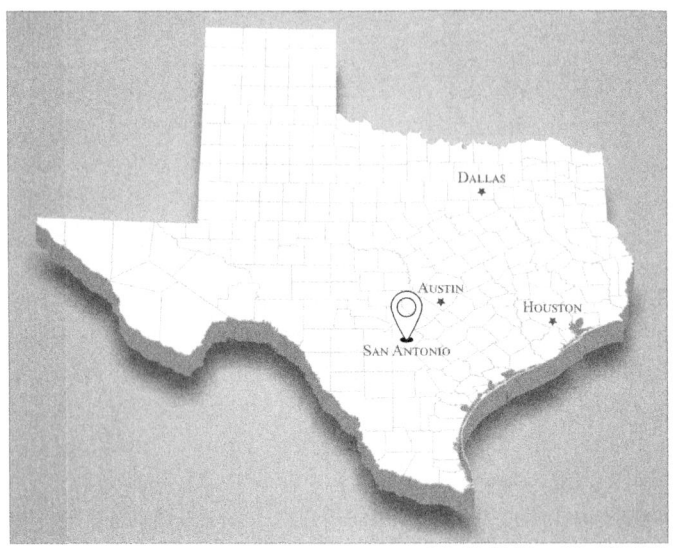

29.424358, -98.485103

WHAT'S ABOUT?:

The San Antonio River Walk, also known as the Paseo del Rio, is a network of walkways along the San Antonio River that winds through downtown San Antonio, Texas.

The River Walk is a popular tourist destination, offering visitors a unique perspective of the city and its rich cultural heritage. In addition, the River Walk has shops, restaurants, bars, and hotels, providing plenty of opportunities to explore, dine, and relax.

One of the River Walk's main attractions is the five Spanish colonial missions that make up the San Antonio Missions National Historical Park, including the Alamo. These UNESCO World Heritage sites offer a glimpse into the history of the city and the people who lived here. Visitors can also enjoy the lush greenery and landscaping along the river and the colorful public art displays.

The River Walk is also home to several annual events, including the Ford Holiday River Parade, the Texas Cavaliers River Parade, and the Luminaria Arts Festival. These events feature floats, live music, and other entertainment, making them a great way to experience the River Walk's festive atmosphere.

The River Walk is easily accessible by foot, bike, or boat.

There are several options for guided tours, including boat and Segway tours.

WHERE IS?
The San Antonio River Walk is a 15-mile-long waterway that runs through the heart of downtown San Antonio for about 5 miles. It does not have a specific address; for navigation, you can use the Shops at Rivercenter address on the River Walk at 849 E. Commerce Street, San Antonio. The River Walk is open year-round and is accessible to visitors via several entry points throughout downtown San Antonio. If you're planning to drive to the River Walk, remember that over 2,000 parking meters are available, typically enforced from 8AM to 6PM on weekdays and Saturdays. However, parking is complimentary outside these hours and at city-operated garages and lots during "Downtown Tuesday," which occurs most Tuesdays after 6 PM.

WHAT'S GOOD/WHAT'S BAD:
The San Antonio River Walk is a picturesque destination for a leisurely stroll and a great spot to unwind, grab a bite to eat or a drink, and people-watch. The crowds can be heavy depending on the day and time.

The variety of restaurants is astounding, with options for Mexican, German, Italian, seafood, and steaks. The River Walk is a bright and lively spot with eclectic music and entertainment options. While you're there, be sure to take a River Tour on a colorful barge, which offers a history commentary and is best done at night to enjoy the sparkling lights. It's a unique experience, reminiscent of Venice, and not to be missed. Remember to wear comfortable walking shoes as the River Walk winds through the city, and the cobblestone paths can be tiring.

DATE(S) VISITED:

WEATHER CONDITIONS:

ACCOMODATIONS:

WHAT WAS THE BEST PART OF TODAY?

SPECIAL MEMORIES:

BIG BEND NATIONAL PARK

A rugged wilderness area in far West Texas that offers hiking, camping, and backpacking opportunities.

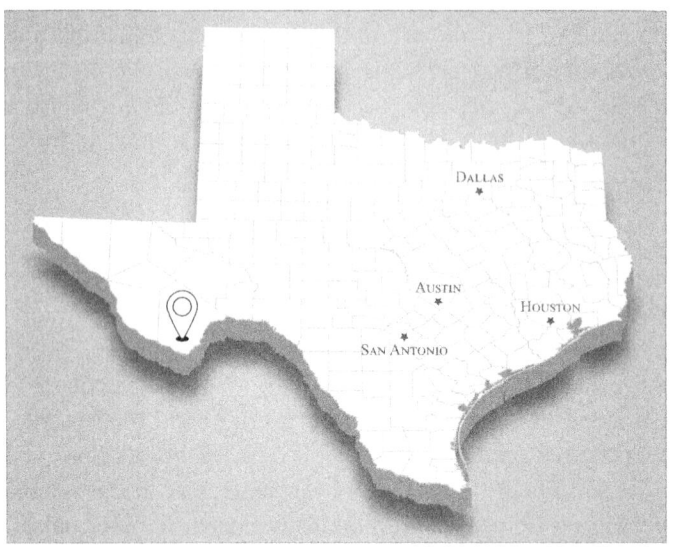

29.301090, -103.507515

WHAT'S ABOUT?:

Big Bend National Park is a nature lover's paradise in the far west of Texas. The park covers over 800,000 acres of a rugged desert landscape and boasts some of the state's most diverse and unique terrain. The park is home to various plant and animal life, including over 450 species of birds, deer, mountain lions, and black bears.

One of the most popular attractions in the park is the Chisos Mountains, a range of peaks that rise over 7,000 feet above sea level. Visitors can hike to the summit of Emory Peak, the highest point in the park, for breathtaking views of the surrounding desert. The park also features several trails for hikers and backpackers of all skill levels, including the South Rim Trail, which offers a challenging and scenic hike to the top of the Chisos Mountains.

The park is also home to the Rio Grande, which forms the park's southern boundary and provides visitors with opportunities for rafting, kayaking, and fishing. The Rio Grande Wild and Scenic River is a great place to explore the park's rugged terrain and enjoy the area's natural beauty.

Big Bend National Park is also home to several historic sites, including the ruins of the Castolon Historic District, which was once a thriving community of settlers and traders. Visitors can also tour the park's historic buildings, including the Chisos Mining Company, which was once the largest mining operation in the park.

WHERE IS?

Big Bend National Park is located in the far western region of Texas, near the border with Mexico, in Brewster County, approximately 4.5 hours southeast of El Paso and 5 hours southwest of Midland. The park covers over 800,000 acres of rugged terrain, including the Chisos Mountains, the Chihuahuan Desert, and the Rio Grande River. The park is also around 3 hours east of the city of Marfa and approximately 3.5 hours west of the city of Del Rio. Midland and El Paso are the closest airports; the nearest major city is Alpine.

WHAT'S GOOD/WHAT'S BAD:

It's a fantastic National Park, and I recommend visiting during the early spring or late fall, as it can get quite hot. Being off the beaten path only adds to the appeal of this National Park. With countless canyons and trails to explore, it offers a stunning and untamed escape from bustling city life. If you're seeking solitude, you can spend days in the park without encountering more than a few individuals. The Chisos Mountains, which form the core of Big Bend National Park, are one of the most breathtaking places on earth. Make sure to witness the beauty of the Chihuahuan Desert and, if possible, embark on a hike along the Lone Mountain Trail. Take the Ross Maxwell Scenic Drive to see two of the park's most magnificent sights, from the Chisos Mountains to Santa Elena Canyon. Also, consider exploring these great sites: the compact botanic garden at the Panther Junction Visitors Center, the nature trail showcasing flora and fauna at Dugout Spring, and the desert hike at Lone Mountain Trail. All three offer an incredible experience!

DATE(S) VISITED:

WEATHER CONDITIONS:

ACCOMODATIONS:

WHAT WAS THE BEST PART OF TODAY?

SPECIAL MEMORIES:

PALO DURO STATE PARK CANYON

A breathtaking park known for its towering red-hued cliffs and deep canyons, which provide a breathtaking contrast against the blue skies above.

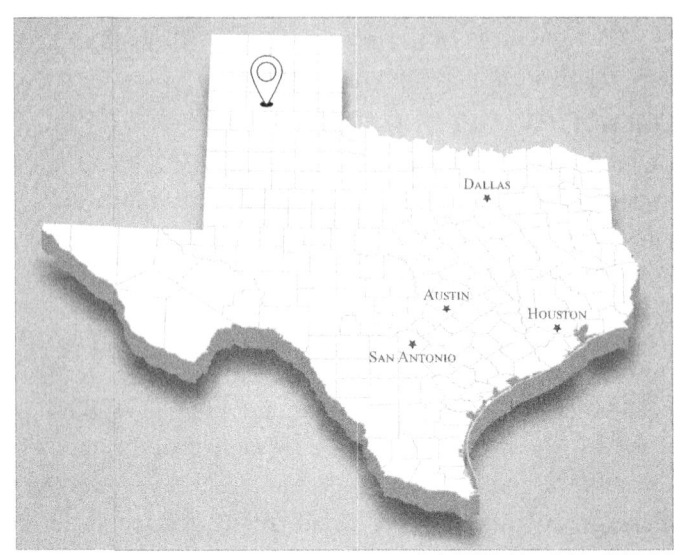

34.971941, -101.678232

WHAT'S ABOUT?:

Palo Duro State Park Canyon is a stunning natural attraction in the Texas Panhandle. The park encompasses over 29,000 acres of rugged terrain, with diverse landscapes including prairies, mesas, and canyons.

Visitors can explore the park's numerous hiking trails, including the Lighthouse Trail, which takes visitors to the top of a towering mesa for panoramic views of the surrounding landscape.

Palo Duro Canyon is also popular for outdoor recreational activities like horseback riding, mountain biking, and rock climbing. In addition, the park is home to an equestrian center, where visitors can rent horses and explore the trails on horseback. The park also offers a variety of educational programs and events, such as ranger-led hikes, campfire programs, and guided stargazing events.

Visitors can also enjoy camping, from primitive campsites to RV sites with full hookups.

The park has several picnic areas, a restaurant, and a gift shop.

Overall, Palo Duro State Park Canyon is a must-visit for nature lovers, outdoor enthusiasts, and anyone seeking a unique and memorable experience in Texas.

With its stunning natural beauty and wealth of recreational opportunities, this park is a true gem of the Lone Star State.

WHERE IS?
Palo Duro Canyon is in the Texas Panhandle region of the state, about 26 miles southeast of Amarillo. It is primarily situated in Randall County but also extends into Armstrong County. From Amarillo, the distance is approximately 30 miles; from Lubbock, it is about 140 miles. The park is also about 200 miles from Oklahoma City, Oklahoma, and 300 miles from Dallas.

WHAT'S GOOD/WHAT'S BAD:
It was a beautiful and majestic experience. I wish I had more time to explore! The trails were great, with many possibilities, from a short, easy, flat hike to a full-day hike with great canyon views. The rangers were friendly and helpful. The Lighthouse trail was the thing to do here, 6 miles out and back. It was an easy, long hike until the last part, where I had to start climbing. There were beautiful views and photo spots all around. There was also incredible history to learn about. I highly recommend doing a 1-hour jeep tour at Palo Duro Ranch before starting the hike for an introduction to the area and its history. The roads in the park were easy to access. I wish more van tour hours were available. The canyon was beautiful, but I underestimated the heat, so be prepared for the weather.

DATE(S) VISITED:

WEATHER CONDITIONS:

ACCOMODATIONS:

WHAT WAS THE BEST PART OF TODAY?

SPECIAL MEMORIES:

SOUTH PADRE ISLAND NATIONAL SEASHORE

Discover a 70-mile barrier island boasting miles of untouched beaches, ample birdwatching opportunities, and the chance to witness sea turtles nesting.

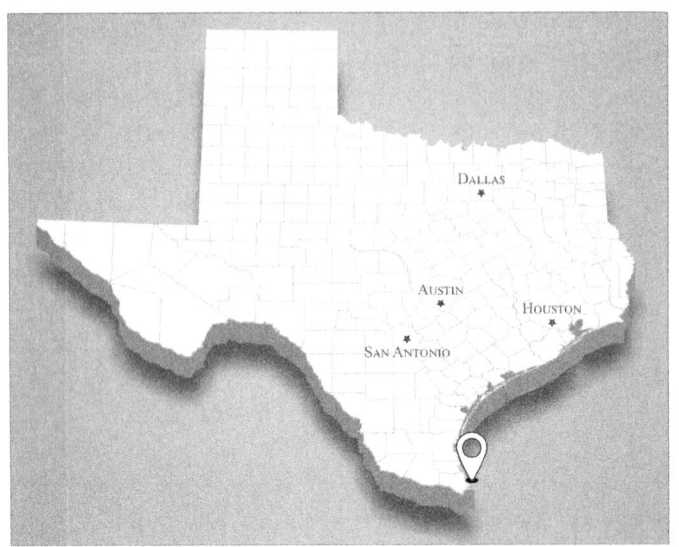

27.424389, -97.299810

WHAT'S ABOUT?:

South Padre Island National Seashore is a barrier island in the Gulf of Mexico on the coast of Texas. The island spans 70 miles and offers pristine beaches, allowing visitors to enjoy the sun, surf, and sand.

The area is a haven for birdwatchers, with diverse species in the dunes and tidal flats, including pelicans, herons, and spoonbills. The coastline is also a popular nesting site for sea turtles, with several species of turtles coming to lay eggs on the beaches each year.

The island's protected natural habitats make it an ideal place for wildlife observation and outdoor recreation.

In addition to its wildlife and breathtaking views, the seashore offers visitors a range of recreational opportunities, including fishing, hiking, and beachcombing. Visitors can also take a stroll along the miles of unspoiled beaches, swim in the warm waters of the Gulf, and explore the nearby dunes and tidal flats.

The South Padre Island National Seashore is a must-visit destination for anyone looking to experience the beauty and wildlife of the Gulf of Mexico.

WHERE IS?
South Padre Island National Seashore is located on the Gulf of Mexico coast in Cameron County. It is approximately 35 miles south of Port Isabel and 50 miles south of Brownsville. The seashore is 60 miles from South Padre Island, a popular tourist destination. The nearest major city to the seashore is Corpus Christi, which is approximately 165 miles to the north. The seashore provides a natural barrier between the Gulf of Mexico and the mainland.

WHAT'S GOOD/WHAT'S BAD:
I visited great beaches in front of condos, hotels, and beach bars. Alternatively, I went farther north and found secluded beaches with medium surf for body surfing. Compared to the East Coast's famous beaches, it was more laid back, people were more friendly, and the beach and waves were more gentle. I enjoyed 120 miles of joy. The lovely long beaches were immaculate. The parts near the hotels can get busy, but I took a short drive, either on the road or on the beach, and it was lovely and peaceful. It was great for just taking a stroll. I noticed it was also dog-friendly. I made sure to bring plenty of sunscreens. The food and choices for dinner were pretty impressive.

DATE(S) VISITED:

WEATHER CONDITIONS:

ACCOMODATIONS:

WHAT WAS THE BEST PART OF TODAY?

SPECIAL MEMORIES:

DALLAS ARBORETUM AND BOTANICAL GARDEN

A beautiful garden showcasing a variety of stunning blooms, gardens, and landscapes that offers seasonal displays and educational programs.

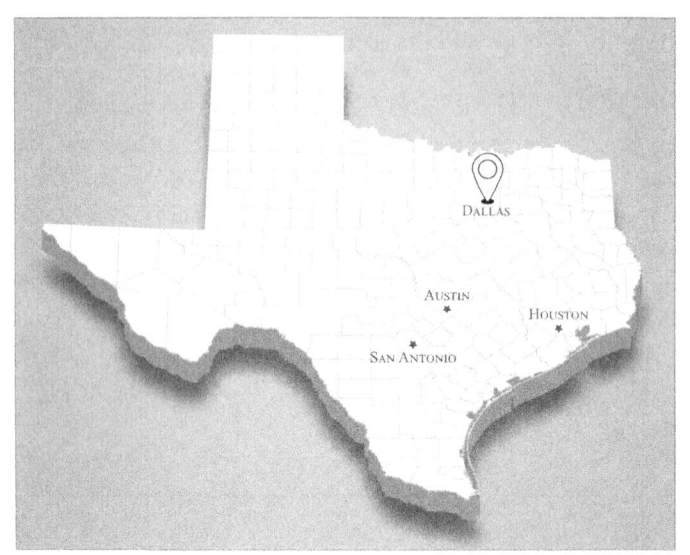

32.824590, -96.715116

WHAT'S ABOUT?:

The Dallas Arboretum and Botanical Garden is a 66-acre public garden on the southeastern shore of White Rock Lake in Dallas, established in 1984.

The park boasts a stunning collection of floral displays and botanical specimens, including seasonal flower gardens, heritage rose gardens, and specialty gardens dedicated to ferns, herbs, and perennials.

Visitors can stroll through the lush gardens, offering breathtaking lake and city skyline views.

Highlights of the arboretum include the two-acre DeGolyer Garden, featuring a wide range of plants and flowers and a stunning array of sculptures and fountains. The Rosine Smith Sammons Butterfly House and Insectarium offers a close-up look at some of nature's most fascinating creatures, from colorful butterflies and moths to giant stick insects.

In addition to its botanical displays, the Dallas Arboretum and Botanical Garden also features a variety of educational programs, including classes and workshops, guided tours, and seasonal events, such as holiday-themed light displays. So whether you're a seasoned gardener or appreciate the beauty of nature, the Dallas Arboretum and Botanical Garden is a must-visit destination for anyone in the Dallas area.

WHERE IS?
The Dallas Arboretum and Botanical Garden is situated near the neighborhood of East Dallas. The Dallas Arboretum is located about 8 miles northeast of downtown Dallas. It is easily accessible from major highways, including I-30, I-35E, and US-75. The nearest major airport is Dallas Love Field, approximately 15 miles from the Arboretum. In addition, the city of Dallas offers a variety of public transportation options, including buses and the DART Light Rail system; these make it easy to reach the Arboretum and other popular destinations in the city.

WHAT'S GOOD/WHAT'S BAD:
I loved the time spent here! I highly recommend taking the golf cart tour with a guide for an immersive experience. The natural settings of trees, bushes, and flowers are simply stunning. The walkways, water fountains, and falls are set against beautiful flora and fauna, and the lake adds to the peaceful ambiance. There are spectacular views everywhere you look! It's a perfect place to unwind and immerse oneself in nature. Although the customer service could improve, I highly recommend this place to everyone.

DATE(S) VISITED:

WEATHER CONDITIONS:

ACCOMODATIONS:

WHAT WAS THE BEST PART OF TODAY?

SPECIAL MEMORIES:

FORT WORTH STOCKYARDS

Step back in time and experience the iconic cowboy culture of Texas at a historic cattle district.

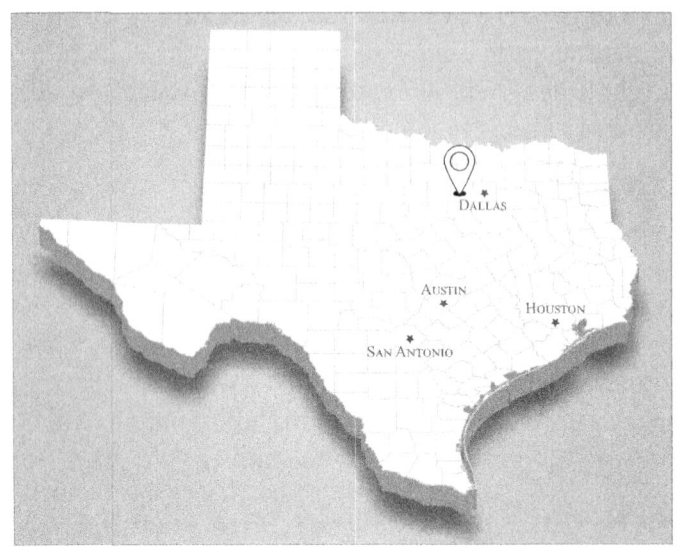

32.789419, -97.347315

WHAT'S ABOUT?:

The Fort Worth Stockyards is a historic district in Fort Worth that celebrates the city's rich cowboy heritage.

This iconic attraction is a popular destination for visitors looking to immerse themselves in the spirit of the old West.

The Stockyards offers a unique blend of shops, restaurants, entertainment venues, and museums that all come together to create an authentic Wild West experience.

One of the main attractions of the Stockyards is the twice-daily cattle drive, where longhorn cattle are driven through the district's streets. This event is a nod to Fort Worth's history as a significant stop on the Chisholm Trail and is a must-see for visitors of all ages.

Another popular stop is the Stockyards Museum, which showcases the history of Fort Worth and its role in the cattle industry.

Visitors to the Fort Worth Stockyards can also enjoy various other activities, including horseback rides, rodeo shows, and live music performances. The district is also home to shops selling Western wear and cowboy gear, making it a popular destination for souvenir shopping. In addition, the Stockyards is known for its delicious cuisine, serving classic Texan dishes like barbecue and chili.

Whether you're a history buff, a fan of the Wild West, or just looking for a unique experience, the Fort Worth Stockyards is a must-visit destination. So, go and experience the spirit of the old West in one of the most authentic places in Texas!

WHERE IS?

Fort Worth Stockyards is located in the Fort Worth area of North Central Texas, in Tarrant County. It is about 30 miles west of downtown Dallas and 20 miles east of downtown Fort Worth. The Fort Worth Stockyards National Historic District is easily accessible from major highways, including I-30, I-820, and Loop 820. From Dallas, the drive to the Stockyards takes approximately 30 minutes, while from Fort Worth, it is a 20-minute drive. The Stockyards are also served by the Fort Worth Intermodal Transportation Center, providing access via Amtrak trains and local and regional bus lines.

WHAT'S GOOD/WHAT'S BAD:

I had a beautiful and scenic adventure into the western past! The lovely parade of longhorns twice a day was a sight to behold; they were huge! It was amazing to get up close and personal with these beauties. There's a petting zoo, kiddie attractions, a rodeo arena, and many shops and restaurants to visit. If you like history, this place is fantastic. The Longhorn cattle drive was impressive as well. The shopping and restaurants were galore. The steak smells will attract you even if you are not hungry! There were tons to do and see and eat here. I highly recommend it for a good time with good country music, a family atmosphere, and phenomenal stores.

DATE(S) VISITED:

WEATHER CONDITIONS:

ACCOMODATIONS:

WHAT WAS THE BEST PART OF TODAY?

SPECIAL MEMORIES:

TEXAS STATE CAPITOL

Discover the Heart of Texas Politics: Explore the Majestic Texas State Capitol Building.

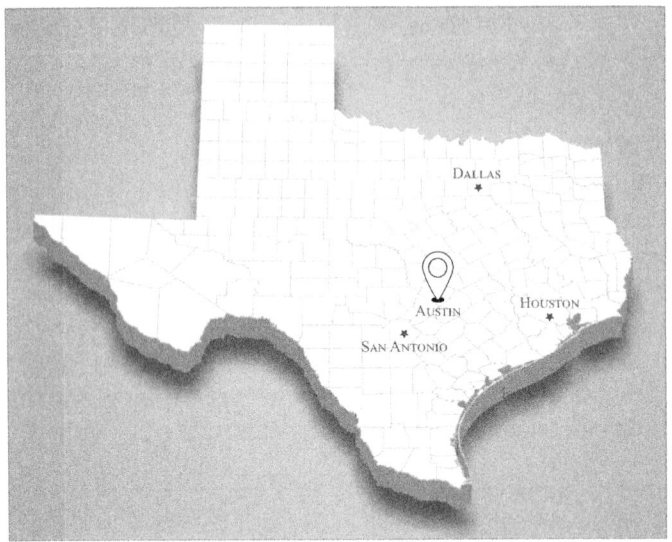

30.272814, -97.741028

WHAT'S ABOUT?:

The Texas State Capitol is a magnificent building in the heart of Austin. It serves as the state government's headquarters, symbolizing the state's rich history and political power.

Built in 1888, the Texas State Capitol is a National Historic Landmark. It is widely considered one of the most beautiful capitols in the United States. The building is made of pink granite and mixes Renaissance Revival and Victorian styles. It stands 308 feet tall, making it one of the tallest state capitol buildings in the country. The interior of the Texas State Capitol is just as impressive as the exterior, with its ornate decorations, marble staircases, and colorful stained glass. Visitors can explore the rotunda and see the four historical paintings depicting significant events in Texas history. They can also visit the House of Representatives and Senate chambers and see the Governor's Office, which is located on the second floor. One of the highlights of a visit to the Texas State Capitol is the observation deck, which provides breathtaking views of Austin. Visitors can also take guided tours of the building, which offer a deeper understanding of the history and architecture of the Texas State Capitol. The building is open to the public every day except for major holidays, and admission is free.

Whether you're a history buff, an architecture enthusiast, or simply someone who loves beautiful buildings, visiting the Texas State Capitol is a must. It symbolizes the state's proud history and a testament to the power of Texas' democracy.

WHERE IS?
The Texas State Capitol Building is located in Austin, the capital of Texas, in Travis County, about 140 miles from San Antonio, 240 miles from Houston, and 190 miles from Dallas. The Texas State Capitol Building is a historic and significant landmark in the city. It is easily accessible by car and public transportation.

WHAT'S GOOD/WHAT'S BAD:
I was amazed by the grandeur of the Texas Capitol Building; just as they say, everything is bigger in Texas! The history and architecture of this building are truly fascinating. I found it easy to park in the area and suggest starting at the Visitors Center before exploring the Capitol. The Capitol's grounds are adorned with several monuments and statues you can appreciate before embarking on a guided or self-guided tour. You must go through security before entering, but the staff is friendly and efficient. If you have mobility issues, elevators can access the different building floors. Overall, it's an experience worth having, especially for history buffs and those who appreciate architecture.

DATE(S) VISITED:

WEATHER CONDITIONS:

ACCOMODATIONS:

WHAT WAS THE BEST PART OF TODAY?

SPECIAL MEMORIES:

NATIONAL RANCHING HERITAGE CENTER

Uncover the rich history and culture of the American West at the National Ranching Heritage Center, where cowboy traditions come to life in stunning exhibits.

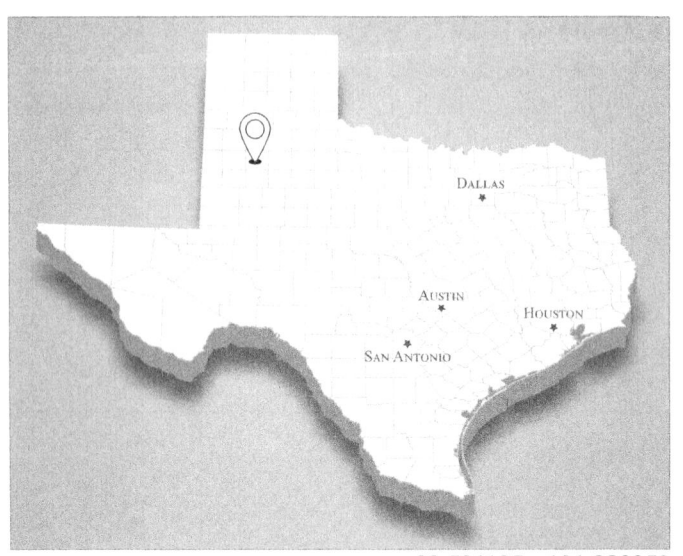

33.591195, -101.883959

WHAT'S ABOUT?:

The National Ranching Heritage Center is a museum that showcases the rich history and culture of the American West and its significance in the development of the state of Texas and the nation. The center was established in 1974 and housed on the Texas Tech University campus. It features over 50 original structures, including homes, barns, and other buildings, relocated from different parts of the state and reassembled on the museum grounds. The center's goal is to preserve the history and traditions of the American West and educate visitors about the vital role of ranches and cowboys in shaping the region. Visitors can explore a variety of exhibits and hands-on activities, including interactive displays and multimedia presentations that bring the history of the American West to life. One of the highlights of the National Ranching Heritage Center is the XIT Ranch Museum, which showcases the history of one of the world's largest and most successful ranches. Visitors can also explore the El rancho Blanco exhibit, which displays the history of one of the most famous Mexican ranches in the state. The White Buffalo exhibit showcases the history of the buffalo trade and its impact on the West.

The National Ranching Heritage Center is a must-visit for anyone interested in the history and culture of the American West. It offers a unique opportunity to learn about the region's heritage and traditions. Whether you are a history buff or simply looking for a fun and educational experience, the center is the perfect place to spend a day exploring the rich history of the American West.

WHERE IS?
The National Ranching Heritage Center is located in Lubbock, Texas, in Lubbock County. It is approximately 259 miles from Austin, the capital of Texas, and 240 miles from Dallas, one of the largest cities in Texas. The center is located on the campus of Texas Tech University. It is dedicated to preserving and showcasing the rich history and cultural heritage of ranching in the American West.

WHAT'S GOOD/WHAT'S BAD:
I had a great time experiencing the history of ranching in Texas. The authentic buildings are arranged in a clear chronological path, and the signage at each stop provides interesting information, making it a delightful walking tour. In addition, the ranch buildings are easily accessible, and special events throughout the year make it worth the trip. My favorite stops were the Barton House, the train station, and the recently added Church. I highly recommend this experience to people of all ages.

DATE(S) VISITED:

WEATHER CONDITIONS:

ACCOMODATIONS:

WHAT WAS THE BEST PART OF TODAY?

SPECIAL MEMORIES:

BUDDY HOLLY MUSEUM

Discover the rock 'n' roll legacy, where music history comes alive with exhibits and interactive experiences that honor the life of the influential musician.

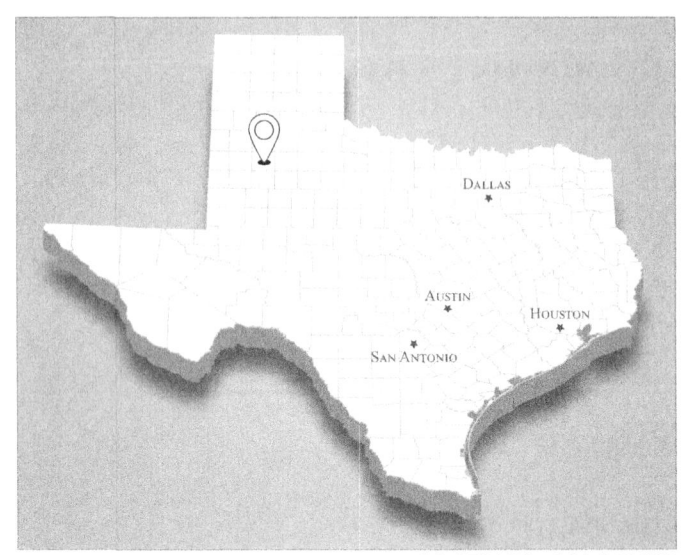

33.578408, -101.842692

WHAT'S ABOUT?:

The Buddy Holly Museum in Lubbock is a tribute to the legendary musician who revolutionized the rock and roll genre in the 1950s.

Through various exhibits and displays, this museum showcases the life and career of Buddy Holly, born in Lubbock in 1936, whose real name was Charles Hardin Holly.

Visitors can learn about Holly's upbringing in Lubbock, early musical influences, rise to fame, and lasting impact on the music industry.

The museum features original artifacts and memorabilia, including Holly's signature glasses, stage outfits, and musical instruments.

Visitors can also listen to recordings of Holly's hit songs, such as "Peggy Sue," "That'll Be the Day," and "Everyday."

The museum also highlights the contributions of Holly's fellow musicians, including The Crickets, who performed and recorded with him.

In addition to its exhibits, the Buddy Holly Museum offers educational programs and events, including live performances, film screenings, and special presentations.

This museum is a must-visit destination for fans of Buddy Holly, music lovers, and anyone interested in the rich history of rock and roll.

WHERE IS?
The Buddy Holly Museum is located in Lubbock County in the northwestern part of the state. It is approximately 200 miles west of Fort Worth and 300 miles south of Amarillo.

WHAT'S GOOD/WHAT'S BAD:
I had a great time exploring this small museum, filled with fascinating information about one of the greatest singer-songwriters ever. It's a fun part of Lubbock's history and is located in the historic downtown area. Their exhibits are fascinating and conveniently located next to the iconic West Texas Cafe, Cast Iron Grill. Here you can try delicious home-style food and meet some characters. Unfortunately, no photographs are allowed, but the 15-minute movie is worth seeing. After visiting the museum, I walked to the park to see the Buddy Holly sculpture and the wall of fame plaques, which was a great experience. The gift shop had so many unique souvenirs that I got a lot for myself.

DATE(S) VISITED:

WEATHER CONDITIONS:

ACCOMODATIONS:

WHAT WAS THE BEST PART OF TODAY?

SPECIAL MEMORIES:

TUBE THE COMAL RIVER

Experience the thrill of floating down the crystal-clear waters of the Comal River in a tube, surrounded by scenic beauty and opportunities for adventure in Texas.

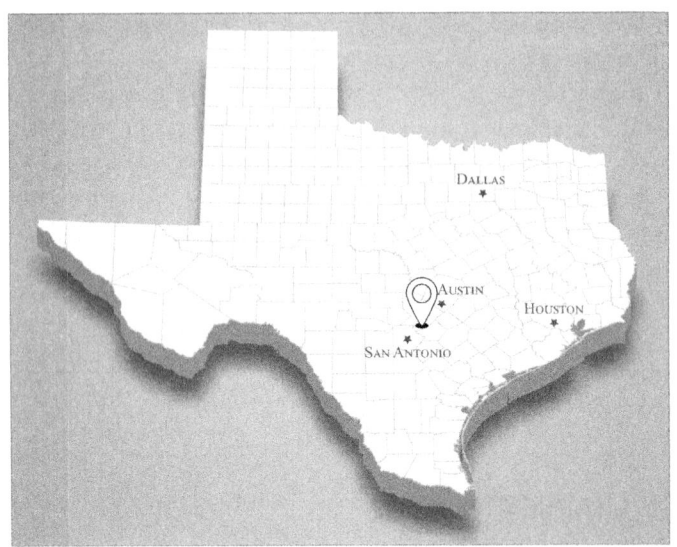

29.707519, -98.126743

WHAT'S ABOUT?:

The Comal River in Texas is a popular destination for water activities, especially tubing. The clear and calm waters of the Comal River make it an ideal place for floating on a tube and taking in the scenic beauty of the surrounding hills and countryside. The river also offers plenty of opportunities for fishing, kayaking, and canoeing. The tubing experience on the Comal River is a unique and fun way to enjoy the Texas summer with family and friends. Visitors can rent tubes, life jackets, and other equipment from local outfitters and then float down the river at their own pace.

The Comal River is a popular summertime destination, so it's best to plan and make a reservation to ensure a spot on the river. The Comal River is not just a place for tubing; it is a popular recreational area in Texas with a rich history and a thriving ecosystem. The river is surrounded by lush vegetation and wildlife, including various species of birds, fish, and other wildlife, making it an ideal spot for nature lovers and bird-watchers.

The Comal River is also steeped in history. It has been used by the indigenous people of Texas for centuries as a source of water and food. In addition, the river has played an essential role in developing the city of New Braunfels and the surrounding areas. Its significance has been recognized by establishing Landa Park and Comal Springs. Visitors can take guided tours of the springs, where they can learn about the history and ecology of the area.

WHERE IS?
The Comal River is the shortest navigable river in the world. It is located in New Braunfels, in Comal County, approximately 35 miles northeast of San Antonio and around 60 miles southwest of Austin. New Braunfels is known for its German heritage. Many events and attractions reflect this cultural influence, such as the Wurstfest festival, held each November.

WHAT'S GOOD/WHAT'S BAD:
Floating down a river with good company is the ultimate way to enjoy a warm summer day. The Comal River is fed by a cool spring, so the water stays refreshing and clear even when the southeast Texas sun is scorching. Except for the occasional crowds and party floats, expect a relaxed two-mile trip with a couple of exciting chutes. After the first chute, you may get lucky and find The Float In, a riverside eatery, open for business.

DATE(S) VISITED:

WEATHER CONDITIONS:

ACCOMODATIONS:

WHAT WAS THE BEST PART OF TODAY?

SPECIAL MEMORIES:

BAT WATCHING IN AUSTIN UNDER CONGRESS BRIDGE

Experience the magic of a prime location for bat-watching where hundreds of thousands of bats emerge from under the bridge in a thrilling display of nature.

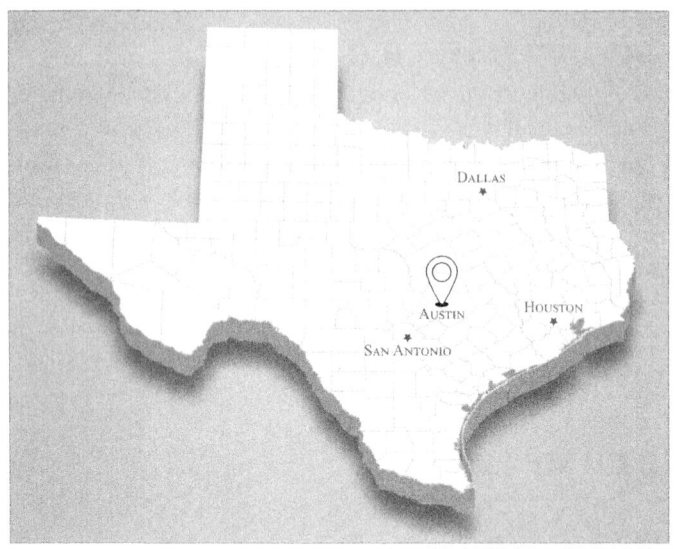

30.259925, -97.745606

WHAT'S ABOUT?:
WHAT'S ABOUT?

The experience of seeing bats at the Congress Bridge in Austin is not to be missed. This natural phenomenon attracts thousands of visitors yearly as hundreds of thousands of bats take flight from under the bridge in a stunning display. It is best to visit the bridge between May and October, in the summer, to witness this incredible spectacle when the bats are most active.

Visitors can expect to arrive early in the evening, around dusk, to secure a good spot along the bridge or on the river bank. Many locals and tourists gather here to watch the bats take flight, so planning and arriving well before sunset is advisable. In addition, several boat tour operators offer guided bat-watching trips, which provide a unique and up-close perspective of the bats.

Before heading out to see the bats, it's essential to remember that the Congress Bridge is a busy location, so be prepared for crowds and allow extra time for parking. Additionally, be mindful of the bats and the environment by keeping noise levels low and avoiding disturbing the bats or their habitat.

The Congress Bridge bat-watching experience is a must-see event for anyone visiting Austin. With its beautiful setting, awe-inspiring wildlife, and vibrant community, it is an unforgettable experience that combines the best of Austin's natural beauty and rich culture.

WHERE IS?
The Congress Avenue Bridge spans the Colorado River. It is in downtown Austin, near several other popular attractions, such as Lady Bird Lake, the Texas State Capitol, and the Ann W. Richards Congress Avenue Bridge Bats Observation Deck.
If you're in Austin and want to get to the Bridge, there are several ways:
- Drive: You can drive to the bridge, with nearby parking options.
- Bus: Austin has a comprehensive bus network, and several bus routes serve the area near the bridge. You can check the Capital Metropolitan Transportation Authority website for more information.
- Bike: Austin is known for its bike-friendly culture, and you can rent a bike from one of several locations around the city to reach the bridge.
- Walk: If you're staying in the downtown area, you can easily walk to the bridge, which is located just a few blocks from the central business district.

WHAT'S GOOD/WHAT'S BAD:
I had no idea there were so many bats in one place until I saw it myself. Witnessing the bats emerge from under the bridge was indeed an unforgettable experience. There were so many of them; it was mesmerizing. Then, watching them fly into the sunset was simply amazing. The sunset bat tour on the river was a great way to experience this natural wonder. The glow paddle up the Colorado and Barton Creek was just as incredible. It's definitely a must-see attraction in Texas.

DATE(S) VISITED:

WEATHER CONDITIONS:

ACCOMODATIONS:

WHAT WAS THE BEST PART OF TODAY?

SPECIAL MEMORIES:

NACOGDOCHES VISITOR'S CENTER

Nacogdoches, the oldest town in Texas, is a vibrant blend of history, outdoor recreation, and cultural diversity that promises a unique and captivating adventure.

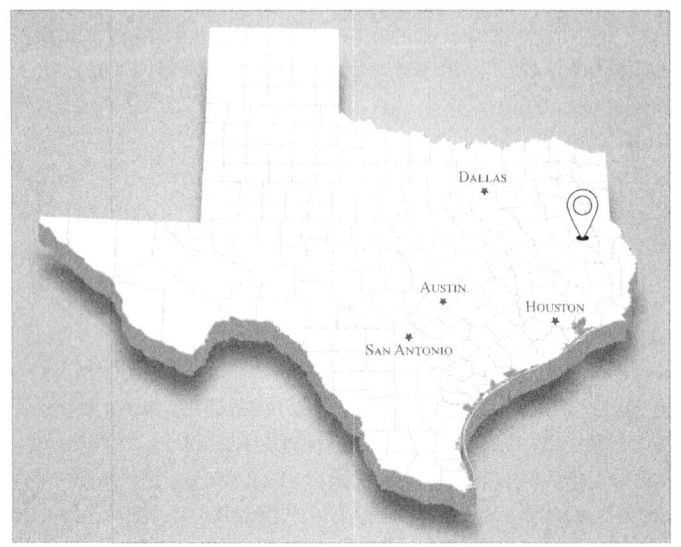

31.603032, -94.654945

WHAT'S ABOUT?:

The Nacogdoches Visitor's Center is located in the heart of Nacogdoches.
It is a hub for visitors looking to explore all the town offers. As the oldest town in Texas, Nacogdoches has a rich history and unique culture that visitors can learn about and experience through various attractions, events, and tours.
At the Nacogdoches Visitor's Center, you can glimpse the town's past and present through interactive exhibits and displays showcasing the area's rich heritage. The center's knowledgeable staff can also help visitors plan their itineraries and provide recommendations for local restaurants, shops, and other points of interest. In addition to providing information and resources for visitors, the Nacogdoches Visitor's Center also serves as a gathering place for locals and tourists alike. Something exciting is always happening at the center, from community events and festivals to guided tours of the town's historic sites.
Whether you're a first-time visitor to Nacogdoches or a lifelong resident, the Nacogdoches Visitor's Center is the perfect starting point for discovering all the town has to offer.

WHERE IS?

Nacogdoches is a city located in Nacogdoches County. It is about 160 miles southeast of Dallas, 165 miles northeast of Houston, and 160 miles west of Shreveport, Louisiana. To get to Nacogdoches, you can fly into Nacogdoches Airport, just outside the city. You can also drive using significant highways such as US Highway 59, US Highway 84, or Texas State Highway 7. For example, moving from Houston, you can take US Highway 59 North to reach Nacogdoches. If coming from Dallas, you can take US Highway 59 South to get to Nacogdoches.

WHAT'S GOOD/WHAT'S BAD:

As I walked into this place, I immediately felt welcomed by the friendly staff. The visitor center has been carefully restored and meticulously maintained. The museum inside highlighted the visit with its collection of historical guns and photos. I was amazed to see the oldest rifle ever made. The video showcasing the town's history was informative and engaging. The staff helped direct me to other points of interest in the city, conveniently located just a short walk from the visitor center. The town center is lined with charming shops and restaurants and dotted with statues that transport you back to over a century ago. It's fascinating to imagine what life was like in those days. Overall, this is a really cool place that I highly recommend visiting.

DATE(S) VISITED:

WEATHER CONDITIONS:

ACCOMODATIONS:

WHAT WAS THE BEST PART OF TODAY?

SPECIAL MEMORIES:

MENIL COLLECTION IN HOUSTON

Discover a world-renowned collection of art and artifacts, where a diverse range of pieces awaits your exploration and intrigue.

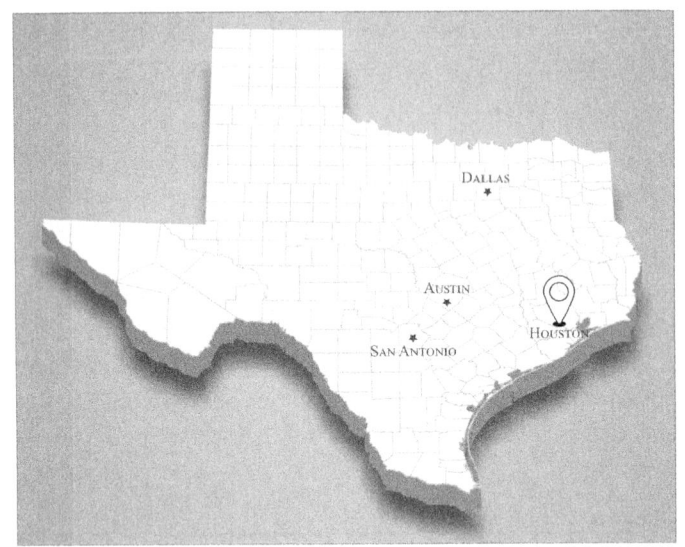

29.736902, -95.398539

WHAT'S ABOUT?:

The Menil Collection in Houston is a world-renowned art museum that houses an extensive modern and contemporary art collection.

Housed in a series of minimalist buildings designed by architect Renzo Piano, the museum is known for its stunning architecture and carefully curated exhibitions. Visitors can view works by some of the most influential artists of the 20th and 21st centuries, including Pablo Picasso, Max Ernst, René Magritte, and Cy Twombly, among many others.

The museum's permanent collection is accompanied by rotating exhibitions, ensuring there is always something new to discover and explore. In addition to the exhibitions, the Menil Collection offers a variety of public programs, including lectures, films, and concerts, making it a vibrant cultural hub in Houston.

The Menil Collection also features several historic homes, a park, and a Byzantine Chapel, which make it an interesting and eclectic destination for art lovers and history buffs alike.

Additionally, the museum is free to the public, making it accessible to everyone. The surrounding neighborhood of Montrose is a vibrant and eclectic area with its own distinct character.

Whether you are an art lover or simply looking to spend a few hours surrounded by beauty and inspiration, the Menil Collection is a must-visit destination in Houston.

WHERE IS?
The Menil Collection is located in the Houston neighborhood of Montrose, at 1533 Sul Ross Street, Houston, Texas 77006. To get there, you can drive and park in the museum's parking lot or take the METRORail to the Museum District stop and walk 10 minutes to the museum. You can also take a taxi or rideshare service like Uber or Lyft to the museum.

WHAT'S GOOD/WHAT'S BAD:
I was impressed by the Menil Collection. The art pieces were beautifully displayed, with plenty of space for the art to stand out. The private collection was eclectic but well-curated, with a good mix of works from major artists like Rouault, Leger, and Bacon. The exhibition space was excellent, with a simple, airy, and discreet design that blended well with the surrounding neighborhood. The staff was friendly and helpful, but be aware that guards are in every room, so it's best to be on your best behavior. Overall, it's an excellent museum; the best part is that it's free to enter.

DATE(S) VISITED:

WEATHER CONDITIONS:

ACCOMODATIONS:

WHAT WAS THE BEST PART OF TODAY?

SPECIAL MEMORIES:

ROTHKO CHAPEL IN HOUSTON

The Rothko Chapel in Houston is a meditative space offering a serene escape from the city's bustle and a thought-provoking experience for visitors.

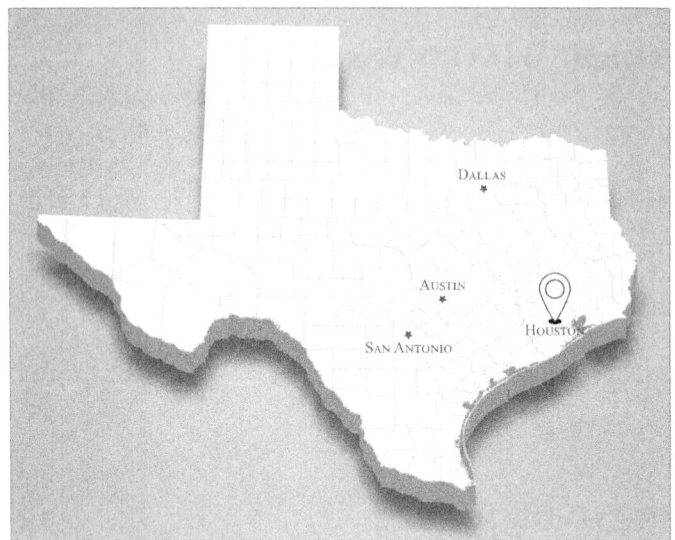

29.736959, -95.396206

WHAT'S ABOUT?:

WHAT'S ABOUT?

The Rothko Chapel in Houston is a non-denominational chapel founded by philanthropists John and Dominique de Menil in 1971.

The chapel is famous for its series of 14 large-scale murals by Abstract Expressionist artist Mark Rothko, specially commissioned for the space.

The Chapel is considered one of the most important works of 20th-century art and is renowned for its serene, meditative atmosphere. Visitors to the Rothko Chapel are often struck by the powerful and emotional impact of the art. The Chapel, in fact, has been designed to evoke a sense of peace and contemplation.

The Chapel is open to the public daily and offers free admission.

It is a must-visit destination for art lovers, spiritual seekers, and anyone looking for peace and reflection in the city's heart.

In addition to its influential art, the Rothko Chapel is known for its strong commitment to human rights and social justice.

The chapel has hosted numerous events and exhibitions that address critical social and political issues and has been a gathering place for activists and communities working for change.

Whether you are an art lover, a spiritual seeker, or an activist, the Rothko Chapel is a truly unique and inspiring place to visit in Houston.

WHERE IS?
The Rothko Chapel is located in Houston's Midtown neighborhood, near the Museum District and the Menil Collection. Visitors can take the METRORail Red Line to the Montrose Boulevard station and walk a short distance to the chapel.

WHAT'S GOOD/WHAT'S BAD:
Although not everyone may appreciate art, the Rothko Chapel is an incredible and significant work. It isn't easy to fully describe or put into words the emotions and thoughts that arise from being inside the chapel. As a fan of Rothko's art, I thoroughly enjoyed my visit here. The large, dark paintings offer a contemplative and sobering experience. However, I understand that others may have different opinions. My wife, an art fan, found the atmosphere quite depressing. If you are a fan of Rothko's work, then this is definitely a place you shouldn't miss. Additionally, it is worth noting that admission to the chapel is free.

DATE(S) VISITED:

WEATHER CONDITIONS:

ACCOMODATIONS:

WHAT WAS THE BEST PART OF TODAY?

SPECIAL MEMORIES:

HERMANN PARK IN HOUSTON

A lush, urban oasis offering breathtaking views and a variety of recreational activities that intrigue visitors to relax and enjoy nature in the heart of the city.

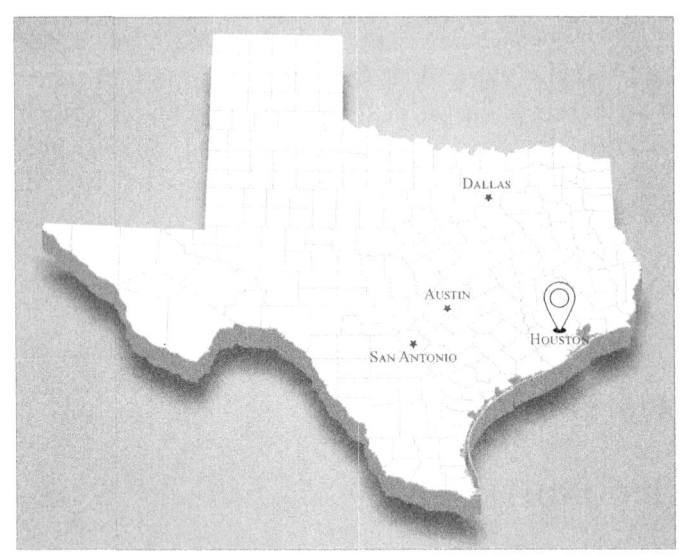

29.715334, -95.389138

WHAT'S ABOUT?:

Hermann Park is a lush, sprawling urban park in the heart of Houston.
It covers over 145 acres and is a popular destination for visitors and residents. The park has several notable attractions, including the Houston Zoo, the Gerald D. Hines Waterwall Park, and the Japanese Garden.
Additionally, there are several walking and biking trails, picnic areas, and a golf course for visitors to enjoy.
One of Hermann Park's main draws is its natural surroundings' peacefulness and beauty.
The park is home to numerous species of trees, flowers, and wildlife, making it a perfect place to escape from the hustle and bustle of the city.
The park also has several scenic lakes and water features, adding to its serene atmosphere.
Visitors can also learn about the history of Houston and its development as a city by exploring the park's many monuments and memorials. For example, a statue is dedicated to Sam Houston, the city's namesake and another monument is dedicated to the soldiers who fought in World War I.
Whether you're looking for a quiet place to relax and enjoy nature or you're interested in exploring Houston's rich history, Hermann Park is a must-visit destination. So be sure to add this beautiful park to your itinerary!

WHERE IS?

Hermann Park is located in the heart of Houston. The park is easily accessible by car and near the Texas Medical Center and the Museum District. The park is at 6001 Fannin St, Houston, TX, 77030, USA. If you're driving to the park, several parking options are available, including a free parking lot on the south side and a paid parking lot on the north side. To get there by public transportation, you can take the METRORail Red Line and get off at the Hermann Park/Rice U station. From there, it's just a short walk to the park.

WHAT'S GOOD/WHAT'S BAD:

As a nature enthusiast, I highly recommend this park, which is also great for families. It's a unique city park with a lot of history, featuring a train ride and a zoo. Children can access pedal boats and beautiful gardens, pools, and lakes. The park even has an open-air theatre. A tram-train ride is offered to visitors, a great way to experience the park's vastness. I walked to the Japanese garden, the biggest one I have ever seen. Paddle boats are available for rent, and we enjoyed observing the variety of geese and ducks. I think the city of Houston should promote this park more, as it's truly a gem.

DATE(S) VISITED:

WEATHER CONDITIONS:

ACCOMODATIONS:

WHAT WAS THE BEST PART OF TODAY?

SPECIAL MEMORIES:

HOUSTON MUSEUM OF NATURAL SCIENCE - HMNS

A treasure trove of fascinating exhibits and interactive displays, offering a glimpse into the wonders of the natural world that will leave you in awe and intrigue.

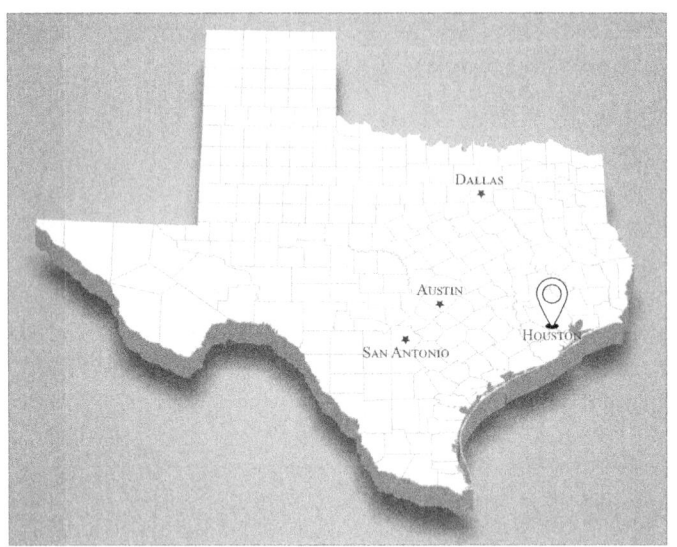

29.721757, -95.388838

WHAT'S ABOUT?:

The Houston Museum of Natural Science is Houston's leading educational and cultural institution. With a mission to inspire and educate people of all ages about the natural world and its wonders, the museum offers a wide range of fun and educational exhibits and programs. From its vast collection of dinosaur fossils and other prehistoric specimens to its interactive displays on astronomy, space science, and earth science, the Houston Museum of Natural Science is a must-visit destination for anyone interested in natural history and the natural world.

One of the museum's most popular features is its IMAX theater, which offers visitors the chance to experience the beauty and majesty of nature in high-definition and surround sound. The museum also features a Planetarium, which offers shows and educational programs on astronomy and space science. There is also a Butterfly Center where visitors can experience the beauty and diversity of butterfly species worldwide.

In addition to its many exhibits and programs, the Houston Museum of Natural Science is also home to several research facilities and institutes, including the Paleontology Research Laboratory, the Center for Space Science, and the Institute for the Advancement of Science. So whether you're a student, a scientist, or just someone who loves nature and the natural world, the Houston Museum of Natural Science is an experience you won't soon forget.

WHERE IS?
The Houston Museum of Natural Science is located in the Museum District at 5555 Hermann Park Dr, in the heart of Houston. To get there, you can take the METRORail Red Line and get off at the Museum District/Hermann Park Station, or take a bus, ride a bike, or drive and park in the museum's parking lot. The museum is also easily accessible from major highways, including I-45 and US-59.

WHAT'S GOOD/WHAT'S BAD:
I had a great time visiting this museum! The atmosphere was welcoming, and the staff was very informative and helpful. I enjoyed viewing the exhibits, particularly the King Tut/Egyptian floor, the mineral/gem area, and the Energy Exhibit on the 4th floor. To fully explore the museum, I recommend allowing at least 3 hours. Parking costs $30; additional fees may apply for movies or special exhibits. However, the well-designed and high-quality displays offer a great learning experience. It's best to book early or arrive first thing in the morning to avoid crowds and ensure availability for the tram tour.

DATE(S) VISITED:

WEATHER CONDITIONS:

ACCOMODATIONS:

WHAT WAS THE BEST PART OF TODAY?

SPECIAL MEMORIES:

HOUSTON MUSEUM OF FINE ARTS - MFAH

Discover a world of art where masterpieces from around the globe await to captivate your imagination and awaken your senses.

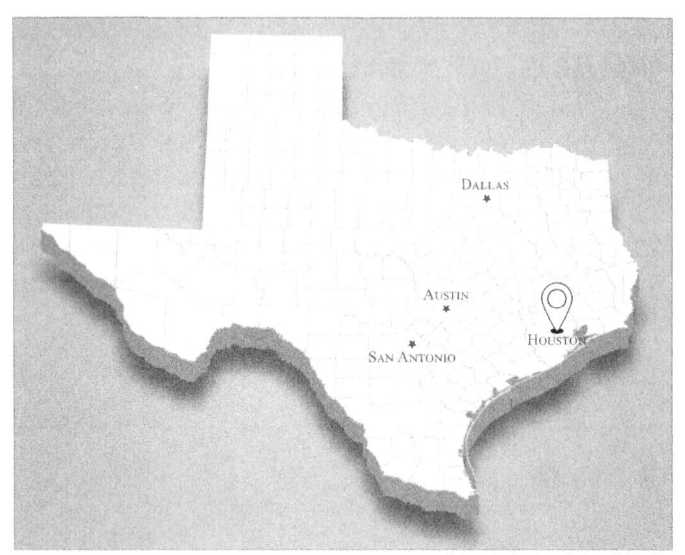

29.725745, -95.389702

WHAT'S ABOUT?:

The Houston Museum of Fine Arts (HMFA) is a world-renowned art museum in Houston.

The museum showcases an extensive collection of art worldwide, ranging from ancient artifacts to contemporary masterpieces.

The museum has over 70,000 works of art, including paintings, sculptures, decorative arts, photography, and more. One of the most notable features of the HMFA is its extensive collection of American art, including works by famous artists such as Winslow Homer, John Singer Sargent, and Georgia O'Keeffe.

In addition to its permanent collection, the museum hosts numerous special exhibitions throughout the year, featuring works from renowned artists and showcasing the latest trends in the art world.

Visitors to the Houston Museum of Fine Arts will be surrounded by an impressive collection of works housed in a beautiful, spacious building.

The museum also has an enormous auditorium where lectures, concerts, and other cultural events are held, making it a hub of artistic activity in Houston.

For art lovers, the Houston Museum of Fine Arts is a must-visit destination, offering an unparalleled opportunity to view and experience some of the world's greatest works of art. If you're interested in art, culture, or history, the Houston Museum of Fine Arts is a fascinating and inspiring place to visit.

WHERE IS?
The Houston Museum of Fine Arts (HMFA) is in the Houston Museum District at 1001 Bissonnet Street. It can be easily accessed by car or public transportation. In addition, the museum is close to several other cultural institutions, such as the Children's Museum of Houston and the Buffalo Soldiers National Museum. To get to the Houston Museum of Fine Arts, take the METRORail Red Line to the Museum District Station or park at the museum's parking garage at 5101 Montrose Boulevard. Visitors can also use the METRO bus line and various taxi and ride-sharing services.

WHAT'S GOOD/WHAT'S BAD:
I was pleasantly surprised by the quality and size of the art museum. The extensive collections in all three buildings were impressive, from daggers and swords from the Islamic world to impressionist paintings. The museum's underground tunnels connecting each building were a unique and enjoyable feature. Navigating and enjoying the collections was easy, with direct access from the parking garage to the museum buildings. I spent about five hours there, so wear comfortable shoes. Regardless of your preferred type of art, there is something for everyone, covering every period of human history. The expansive layout may be slightly confusing, but the museum's quality pieces and extensive collections made it a worthwhile visit.

DATE(S) VISITED:

WEATHER CONDITIONS:

ACCOMODATIONS:

WHAT WAS THE BEST PART OF TODAY?

SPECIAL MEMORIES:

1892 BISHOP'S PALACE IN GALVESTON

A stunning architectural wonder that invites visitors to step back in time and explore the grandeur of Victorian-era opulence.

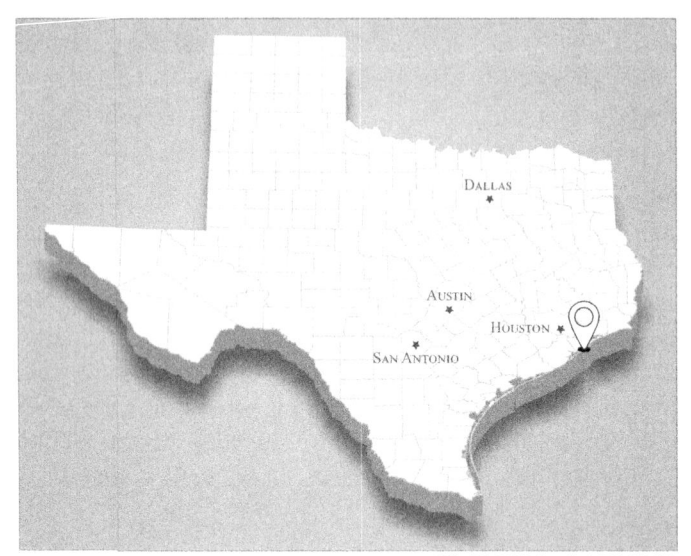

29.302884, -94.782082

WHAT'S ABOUT?:

Bishop's Palace, located in Galveston, was built in 1886 and is a stunning Victorian-style home that showcases the architectural prowess of the late 19th century. This majestic structure was commissioned by wealthy businessman and philanthropist Colonel Walter Gresham. It was designed by prominent architect Nicholas Clayton.

Bishop's Palace is considered one of the most significant and well-preserved Victorian homes in the United States. It is a popular tourist attraction in Galveston. It is open to the public as a museum.

Visitors can tour the palace's interior and learn about its history, architecture, and the family who once lived there. Guided tours are available, and the palace is also open for self-guided tours. Admission fees apply, and hours of operation may vary, so it is advisable to check the official website or contact the visitor center for more information before planning your visit.

Galveston, the island city on the Gulf of Mexico, attracts millions of visitors annually. It is known for its rich history, stunning beaches, and vibrant cultural scene. The city dates back to the 1800s and has numerous historical landmarks and museums, including the Galveston Historical Foundation and the Moody Mansion Museum.

Galveston is also known for its vibrant arts and culture scene. Its numerous theaters, galleries, and museums glimpse the city's creative spirit.

WHERE IS?
Galveston is a coastal city located in Galveston County. It is about 50 miles southeast of Houston and about 165 miles northeast of Corpus Christi. The city is accessible by car, with the main highway being I-45, which connects Galveston to Houston and other cities in Texas. Galveston is also accessible by plane, with William P. Hobby Airport located about 40 miles away and George Bush Intercontinental Airport approximately 60 miles away. Additionally, Galveston is accessible by ferry from the mainland, with several ferry services running between Galveston Island and the mainland.

WHAT'S GOOD/WHAT'S BAD:
As I arrived at this museum, I was immediately captivated by the striking beauty of the house. Every inch of the place exudes elegance, from the magnificent windows to the intricate woodwork and design. The tour was impressive, and I couldn't help but be amazed by the sheer beauty of the home. The house is immaculate, and self-guided audio tours are available for a small fee and provide extra information for the tour. The gift shop is decent. Although the home was once luxuriously opulent, it now requires a bit of TLC. Visitors can leave donations to help with its upkeep. The free parking is also a plus. I highly recommend this museum to anyone visiting the area, as it is truly a sight.

DATE(S) VISITED:

WEATHER CONDITIONS:

ACCOMODATIONS:

WHAT WAS THE BEST PART OF TODAY?

SPECIAL MEMORIES:

GRUENE HALL - TEXAS' OLDEST DANCE HALL

Step back in time and experience live music like never before, where legends like Willie Nelson and Lyle Lovett have graced the stage.

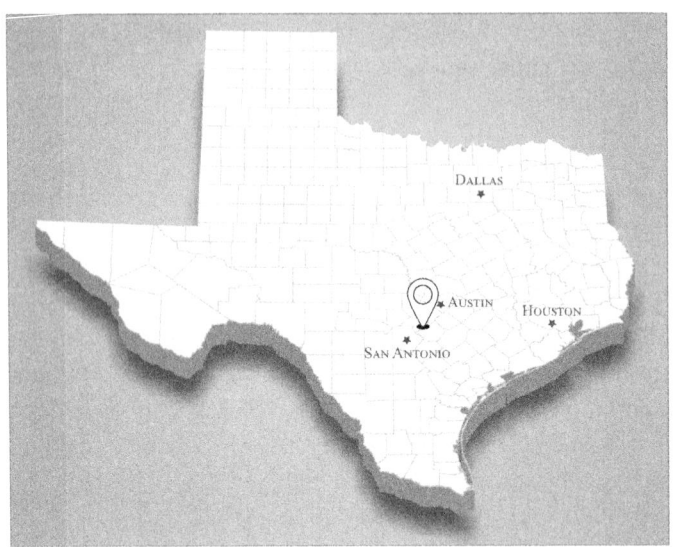

29.738374, -98.104220

WHAT'S ABOUT?:

Gruene Hall, located in the small town of New Braunfels, is the state's oldest dance hall. This historic venue was built in 1878 and has seen its fair share of legendary country music performers. It has been a staple in Texas music culture for over 140 years. The hall is a simple wooden structure with a classic Western style. It features a raised stage and a spacious dance floor, making it a perfect place to kick up your boots and dance the night away.

One of the most exciting things about Gruene Hall is its longevity. Despite being over 140 years old, the hall has remained unchanged, maintaining its original charm and character. It is a testament to the hall's rich history and cultural significance, and visitors can feel the sense of history as soon as they step inside.

Gruene Hall is not only a place for dancing but also for live music. It has hosted countless legendary musicians, including Willie Nelson, George Strait, and Lyle Lovett. It continues to bring in top acts to this day. So whether you're a country, blues, or rock fan, you will find a show that will make your night at Gruene Hall unforgettable.

So if you're ever in the area and looking for an authentic Texas experience, stop by Gruene Hall and enjoy a night of live music and dancing. You'll be stepping back in time and experiencing a piece of Texas history that will leave a lasting impression.

WHERE IS?
Gruene Hall is located in the small town of Gruene in Comal County, Texas, about 30 minutes south of New Braunfels and 45 minutes southeast of Austin. To get there, one can take I-35 to exit 191, follow Gruene Road for about 2.5 miles, and turn left onto Hunter Road. Gruene Hall is located on the right-hand side. Alternatively, following the directions above, one can take US-281 South from San Antonio and exit Gruene Road in New Braunfels.

WHAT'S GOOD/WHAT'S BAD:
Stepping into Gruene Hall is like stepping back in time. It's an authentic Texas dance hall with a ton of history. The atmosphere is relaxed, with country, and daily music, including daytime bands. It's the perfect spot for music lovers. However, they only accept cash for drinks and souvenirs, so come prepared. Unfortunately, there's no food available inside, but you're right downtown, and plenty of quaint shops and restaurants are nearby.

DATE(S) VISITED:

WEATHER CONDITIONS:

ACCOMODATIONS:

WHAT WAS THE BEST PART OF TODAY?

SPECIAL MEMORIES:

DALLAS MUSEUM OF ART

A diverse collection of over 24,000 works of art spanning from ancient civilizations to contemporary art, a must-visit destination for art enthusiasts in Texas.

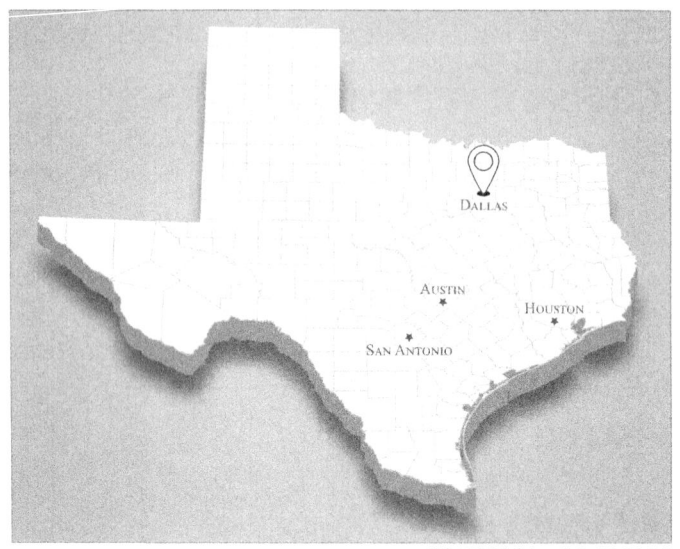

32.788331, -96.801920

WHAT'S ABOUT?:

The Dallas Museum of Art (DMA) was established in 1903. It is located in the heart of the city's Arts District and is one of the largest art museums in the country, with a collection that spans thousands of years and a wide range of cultures.

The museum's mission is to inspire, engage and educate by providing public access to its collections, exhibitions, and programs.

The museum's extensive collection includes everything from ancient Greek and Roman art to Renaissance masterpieces, to contemporary works, with a particular emphasis on American and European art from the 19th and 20th centuries.

One of the museum's most popular exhibitions is the Thannhauser Collection, which features works by some of the biggest names in modern art (including Pablo Picasso, Vincent van Gogh, and Henri Matisse).

The museum also offers a range of educational programs, including art classes and workshops for children and adults, as well as lectures, films, and special events.

It is an iconic city landmark and a cultural hub that attracts thousands of visitors annually.

The museum is open seven days a week, and admission is free.

With its impressive collection and commitment to education and accessibility, the Dallas Museum of Art is an important destination for art lovers and culture enthusiasts.

WHERE IS?
The Dallas Museum of Art is located in the Arts District of downtown Dallas, Texas, in Dallas County. It is located approximately 15 miles from Dallas/Fort Worth International Airport. It is near several major highways, including Interstates 35E, 30, and 45. Visitors can drive and park in the museum's underground garage or take public transportation, including the DART Light Rail and the M-Line Trolley, to get to the museum. The museum is also within walking distance of several downtown hotels and restaurants.

WHAT'S GOOD/WHAT'S BAD:
I highly recommend visiting this art museum when in Dallas. The museum has beautiful art pieces and stunning views. Most areas are free, but some exhibits are paid for. The museum has impressive galleries with a wide variety of art, making it easy to spend several hours viewing. The staff was helpful with navigation and keeping guests safe from the artwork. While the parking garage charged $15, I was lucky enough to find a spot right in front of the museum for only $.95 for two hours. It was an incredible experience and definitely worth a visit.

DATE(S) VISITED:

WEATHER CONDITIONS:

ACCOMODATIONS:

WHAT WAS THE BEST PART OF TODAY?

SPECIAL MEMORIES:

AUSTIN CITY LIMITS MUSIC FESTIVAL - ACL

An annual celebration of music, art, and culture featuring a diverse lineup of over 125 acts across multiple stages, attracting music lovers from all over the world.

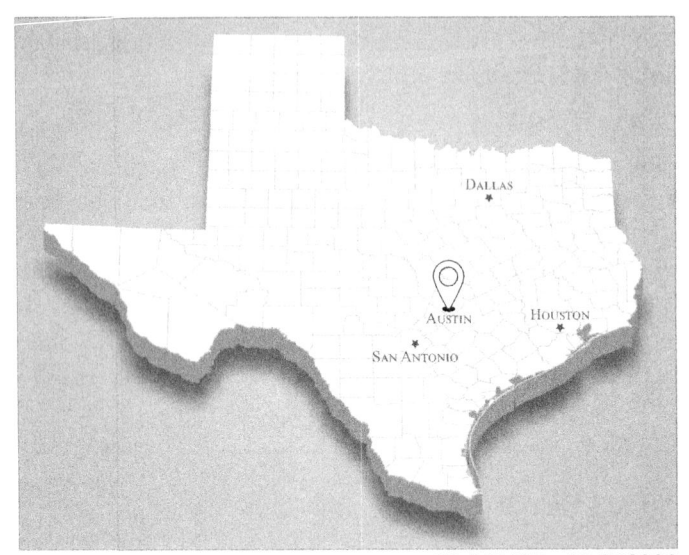

30.266435, -97.768828

WHAT'S ABOUT?:

The Austin City Limits (ACL) Music Festival is an annual music festival held in Austin, featuring a diverse lineup of musical acts and performances. With a history dating back to 2002, the festival has become one of the most famous music events in the United States, attracting hundreds of thousands of visitors yearly.

The festival takes place over two weekends in the fall and is held at Zilker Park, a large urban park in the heart of Austin. The park provides a beautiful backdrop for the festival, with its sprawling lawns, trees, and natural scenery. During the festival, multiple stages are set up for performances and various food and beverage vendors, merchandise stands, and other attractions.

The ACL Music Festival features various musical acts, including established artists and up-and-coming performers. Past performers have included the likes of Kendrick Lamar, The Black Keys, Radiohead, and many more. The festival is known for its eclectic mix of musical styles, with genres ranging from indie rock and hip hop to country and electronic dance music.

In addition to the music, the ACL Music Festival is also a celebration of Austin's vibrant culture and unique atmosphere. With its laid-back vibe, delicious food, and thriving music scene, Austin is one of the most popular destinations in Texas. The ACL Music Festival provides an excellent opportunity to experience the city's unique energy.

WHERE IS?

Zilker Park is easily accessible by car and just a few miles from downtown Austin. The park borders Barton Springs Road to the north and Lady Bird Lake to the south. The easiest way to get to the park is by car, but it's also accessible by bike, bus, and foot. There's ample parking available in the surrounding area for those driving to the park. Once in Zilker Park, several paths and trails lead to the Austin City Limits Music Festival, making it easy for festival-goers to navigate the park. Additionally, shuttle services provide transportation to and from the festival grounds.

WHAT'S GOOD/WHAT'S BAD:

I had an amazing time at this event - definitely one of the best of its kind that I have been to. So many people were in attendance, and the music was great all day. The food was delicious, and an impressive selection of beer was available. The event was well organized, with plenty of restrooms and friendly staff constantly cleaning up and recycling. I noticed plenty of water stations everywhere to ensure that everyone stayed hydrated. The main sponsor did an exceptional job, and there were no long lines anywhere. Security was also perfect without being invasive, and medical tents and hydration stations were located throughout the event. The swag was great, and the event being held in the heart of a fantastic city made it even better.

DATE(S) VISITED:

WEATHER CONDITIONS:

ACCOMODATIONS:

WHAT WAS THE BEST PART OF TODAY?

SPECIAL MEMORIES:

TEXAS ROSE FESTIVAL IN TYLER

Discover the beauty and charm of the Lone Star State with the annual Texas Rose Festival, a celebration of all things roses in the historic city of Tyler.

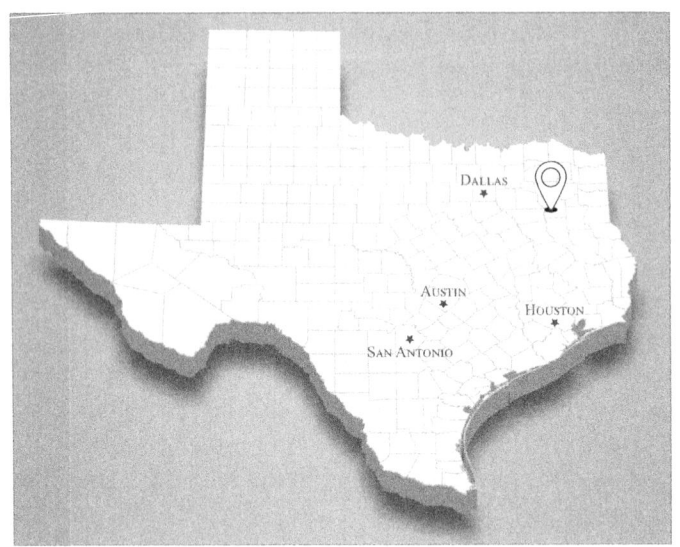

32.345290, -95.322834

WHAT'S ABOUT?:

The Texas Rose Festival in Tyler was first established in 1933. It is an annual event held in October to celebrate the blooming of rose plants and the history of Tyler as the "Rose Capital of the Nation."

The festival features a variety of events, including a Rose Show, where thousands of rose blooms are displayed and judged for their quality. There is also a Rose Parade featuring decorated floats, a Queen's Coronation, where a young woman is crowned as the festival's queen, and various other activities such as live music performances, food vendors, and children's games.

It is a family-friendly event and a significant event in Tyler. It attracts thousands of visitors annually, making it a considerable part of the city's cultural heritage and celebrating its connection to the rose industry.

In addition to the Rose Festival, some other popular places to visit include:
- Tyler State Park: a beautiful park that offers a lake, hiking trails, picnic areas, and fishing opportunities;
- The Caldwell Zoo: a family-friendly zoo that is home to over 2,000 animals from all over the world;
- The Tyler Azalea Trail: a scenic trail that showcases the city's blooming azalea bushes and historic homes.

Whether you are a history buff, an outdoor enthusiast, or just looking for a relaxing day out, Tyler has something for everyone.

WHERE IS?
Tyler is located in Smith County in the East Texas region of Texas. It is approximately 100 miles east of Dallas, Texas, and 100 miles west of Shreveport, Louisiana. Tyler is the largest city in Smith County and is the county seat.

WHAT'S GOOD/WHAT'S BAD:
The Texas Rose Festival in Tyler left a lasting impression on me. The garden was a sight to behold, with vibrant colors and a mesmerizing fragrance. I took my time strolling through the garden, admiring each unique rose.

One of the highlights of the festival was the parade. The floats were spectacularly adorned with fresh roses, and the town was awash with hues of pink and red. It created a cheerful atmosphere that was infectious.

I enjoyed exploring the different vendors and sampling the delicious food and drinks. The gift shop was a hit, with their rose-scented soap being the show's star. A great place to find unique and fragrant souvenirs.

DATE(S) VISITED:

WEATHER CONDITIONS:

ACCOMODATIONS:

WHAT WAS THE BEST PART OF TODAY?

SPECIAL MEMORIES:

THE SEAWALL IN GALVESTON

Experience the scenic views of the Gulf of Mexico and enjoy a refreshing sea breeze on this expansive waterfront promenade.

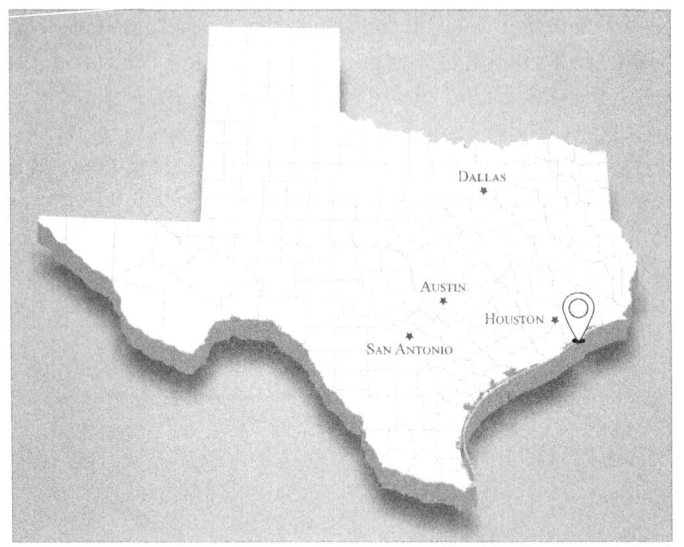

29.266449, -94.826241

WHAT'S ABOUT?:

The Seawall in Galveston is a popular and scenic spot stretching miles along the Gulf of Mexico.

Completed in 1904, the Seawall was built to protect the city of Galveston from the devastating effects of hurricanes. It has become a symbol of the resilience of the town.

The Seawall offers stunning views of the Gulf, making it a popular destination for locals and tourists.

It is a perfect spot for taking a romantic walk with a loved one or enjoying the ocean breeze.

The Seawall features several beaches where couples can relax and spend a day in the sun, building sandcastles or just listening to the sound of the waves.

In addition to the beautiful ocean views, the Seawall boasts various restaurants and shops, making it a perfect spot for a romantic dinner or shopping excursion.

The Galveston Island Historic Pleasure Pier at the end of the Seawall offers exciting rides and games, making it an excellent spot for a fun-filled date.

Overall, the Seawall in Galveston is a picturesque and romantic destination where couples can spend a day enjoying the beauty of the Gulf and each other's company.

WHERE IS?
The Seawall in Galveston is located along the coast of the Gulf of Mexico and stretches for about 10 miles. It can be reached by car, bike, or on foot, and several parking options are available nearby.
The nearest cities to Galveston are Texas City, La Marque, Dickinson, and League City. Houston is also nearby, located about 50 miles to the north.

WHAT'S GOOD/WHAT'S BAD:
I had a wonderful time walking along the seawall in Galveston. The beach is stunning, and there are many bars, hotels, and restaurants to stop at. The area is immaculate, and I enjoyed people-watching as I walked. The trolley is a great option, with a low fare of just $1.00 for adults, and it even includes a transfer to the downtown area. I appreciated the history of Galveston that was available to read on benches throughout the walk. The only downside was crossing the road - heavy traffic and some people weren't very cautious. Also, watching out for young children in the area is essential.

DATE(S) VISITED:

WEATHER CONDITIONS:

ACCOMODATIONS:

WHAT WAS THE BEST PART OF TODAY?

SPECIAL MEMORIES:

WILLOW CITY LOOP NEAR FREDERICKSBURG

25 TEXAS

A scenic drive offering breathtaking views of the Texas Hill Country, perfect for an adventurous and nature-filled road trip experience.

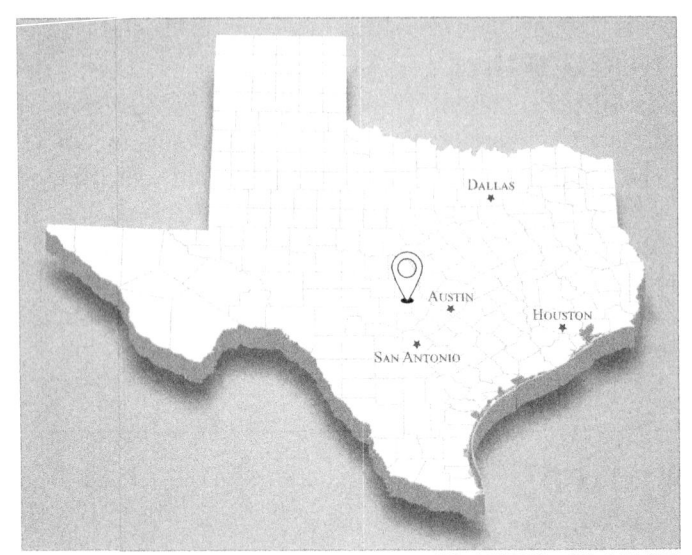

30.445088, -98.663580

WHAT'S ABOUT?:

The Willow City Loop is a scenic 13-mile drive near Fredericksburg, Texas. It winds through the beautiful Texas Hill Country. It is known for its stunning views of rolling hills, bluebonnets, and other wildflowers in the spring.

Bluebonnets are a species of wildflowers native to Texas, specifically the prairies and woodlands of the state. They are the state flower of Texas known for their vibrant blue petals and delicate appearance. Bluebonnets typically bloom in late March to early April, and their blooming season can last up to a month. This timing makes them a popular springtime attraction for tourists and locals alike, who flock to see the fields of blue stretching out before them. Bluebonnets are often seen along Texas highways and in rural areas. They have become a symbol of the state's natural beauty.

The Willow City Loop is popular among tourists, nature lovers, and photographers looking to capture the area's breathtaking beauty. The road is a mix of twists and turns, with scenic vistas around every bend, making it an excellent option for a leisurely drive or a scenic motorcycle ride. Some popular stops along the way include the Willow City Loop Park, which offers picnic areas and a fishing pond, and the Willow City General Store, which sells souvenirs, snacks, and cold drinks. Overall, the Willow City Loop is a must-visit destination for anyone in the Fredericksburg area looking to experience the natural beauty of the Texas Hill Country.

WHERE IS?
Willow City Loop is a panoramic route in the Texas Hill Country near Fredericksburg. It is in Gillespie County, approximately 65 miles from San Antonio and 85 miles from Austin. To get there, you can take Ranch Road 1323 from Fredericksburg and follow the signs for Willow City Loop.

WHAT'S GOOD/WHAT'S BAD:
I had an incredible experience riding on one of the most scenic routes in Texas. The roads were well-maintained, and the view was stunning throughout the 13-mile loop. The best time to visit is in spring when the wildflowers are in full bloom, filling the entire area with various colors. The picturesque ranches and creeks are an added bonus to the already breathtaking view. It was a peaceful ride with barely any traffic, a perfect getaway if you enjoyed the serenity of nature. However, I've heard it can get very crowded during bluebonnet season, so be sure to plan accordingly.

DATE(S) VISITED:

WEATHER CONDITIONS:

ACCOMODATIONS:

WHAT WAS THE BEST PART OF TODAY?

SPECIAL MEMORIES:

★26 SCENIC DRIVE - OVERLOOK
TEXAS

Marvel at stunning panoramic views of the surrounding landscape from a unique vantage point, providing a breathtaking experience that will leave you in awe.

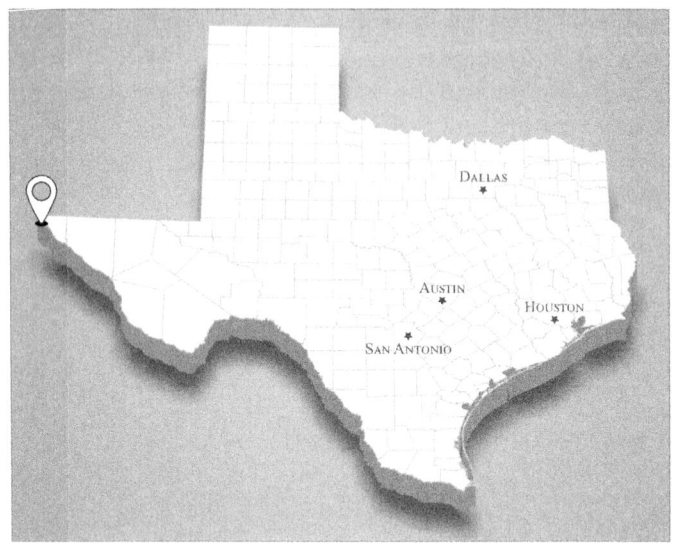

31.782661, -106.480001

WHAT'S ABOUT?:

The Scenic Drive is a must-visit destination in El Paso. As the name suggests, it's a scenic drive to take visitors on a picturesque journey showcasing the area's natural beauty. This 7-mile route offers some of the best views of El Paso and the surrounding mountains. The overlook provides stunning panoramic views that are sure to take your breath away.

Scenic Drive is sometimes called "Lovers Lane" because of its romantic views and reputation as a popular spot for couples to watch the sunset. In fact, the drive is top-rated during sunset hours, as the sky is painted with pink, purple, and orange hues, making the scenery even more dramatic and romantic. It's an ideal location to take your significant other on a romantic date or to enjoy some quiet time together. In addition to the scenic views, visitors can find walking and hiking trails leading to other overlooks and viewing spots. The fresh air, picturesque scenery, and mountain landscapes make it an ideal location for a long, leisurely walk with your partner. The overlook is located in the historic neighborhood of Sunset Heights, which is known for its charming and well-preserved bungalow-style homes. It was built in the 1930s as part of the New Deal, a series of programs and policies President Franklin D. Roosevelt implemented to help the United States recover from the Great Depression.

The drive up to the overlook is a winding road that offers a fun and adventurous driving experience, perfect for car enthusiasts.

WHERE IS?
The Scenic Drive-Overlook is located in El Paso. To reach it, take Interstate 10 to the Executive Center Blvd exit, then head north on Executive Center Blvd until you reach Scenic Drive. The overlook has a parking area, but it can get crowded on weekends and holidays, so arriving early is recommended. There is also street parking available nearby.

WHAT'S GOOD/WHAT'S BAD:
I had a fantastic experience at lookout point. The view of El Paso and Ciudad Juárez is just breathtaking. The road leading to the lookout point is wide enough to drive on, and though it's a bit windy, it's manageable. There are several beautiful parks that I stopped at along the way. The view from the lookout point is surreal and peaceful and goes on for miles and miles. I thoroughly enjoyed every moment of it. There are various lookout points, each with a different level of view. One can easily make this a quick trip or take some time to enjoy the view and watch the sunset. It's an excellent way to get a glimpse of the city and its surroundings, especially during the holiday season, to see the beautiful Christmas lights.

DATE(S) VISITED:

WEATHER CONDITIONS:

ACCOMODATIONS:

WHAT WAS THE BEST PART OF TODAY?

SPECIAL MEMORIES:

INNER SPACE CAVERN

Explore a hidden world beneath the surface and discover the secrets of our planet's natural history.

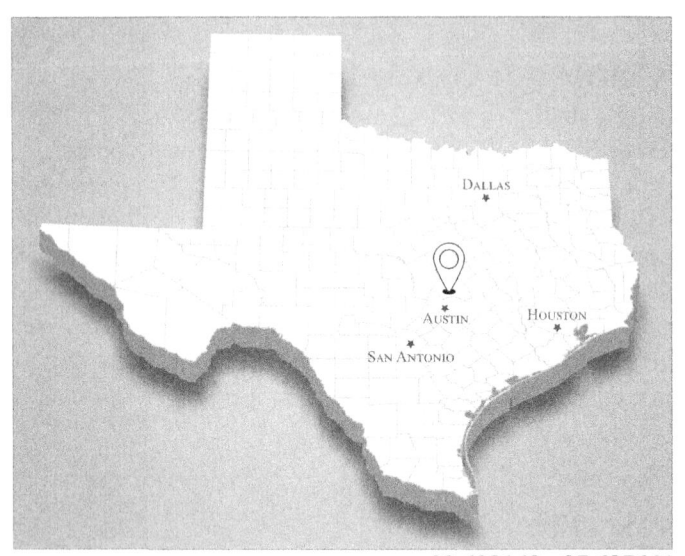

30.608168, -97.687664

WHAT'S ABOUT?:

Located in the heart of the Texas Hill Country, the Inner Space Cavern, discovered in 1963, is a fascinating underground world that will take visitors on a journey through time. The cavern is believed to be over 10,000 years old. It features a range of stunning geological formations such as stalagmites, stalactites, and columns. Visitors can tour the cavern's three levels, each showcasing unique and breathtaking formations. The tour offers an informative and educational experience as knowledgeable guides share the history and geology of the cave. In addition to the natural formations, visitors can learn about the various archaeological discoveries made in the cave, including prehistoric animal remains.

The Inner Space Cavern is also home to various underground creatures, such as the Texas cave salamander and the blind Mexican Tetra fish. Visitors can also enjoy a gift shop and a mining exhibit, where they can learn about the history of mining in the region.

The cavern's unique and awe-inspiring atmosphere makes it an excellent destination for couples looking for a romantic and adventurous date. With its outstanding acoustics, the dimly lit cavern offers a memorable experience for visitors of all ages.

The Inner Space Cavern is easily accessible to visitors. The cavern offers ample parking space, a picnic area, and a shaded pavilion for visitors to relax and enjoy the surrounding natural beauty.

WHERE IS?
The Inner Space Cavern is located in Georgetown, about 30 miles north of Austin. The address is 4200 S. I-35, Georgetown, TX 78626. It can be reached by taking I-35 and exiting at exit 259, with signs for the cavern. There is parking available on site.

WHAT'S GOOD/WHAT'S BAD:
I had an entertaining adventure exploring this place! The tour guide was fantastic and provided informative and amusing commentary throughout the tour. The gift shop was also a fun place to browse. A few different tour options were available, with some requiring advance reservations. During our time, we descended 70 feet into the cave's depths. I recommend wearing good shoes, as the ground can be damp and slippery. Handrails are provided in most places, but it's not an ideal activity for very young children or older adults. The walk is quite lengthy, but the stunning natural beauty of the cave is definitely worth the effort!

DATE(S) VISITED:

WEATHER CONDITIONS:

ACCOMODATIONS:

WHAT WAS THE BEST PART OF TODAY?

SPECIAL MEMORIES:

NASHER SCULPTURE CENTER

Discover an exquisite collection of contemporary sculptures that will capture your imagination and leave you in awe of the artists' creativity.

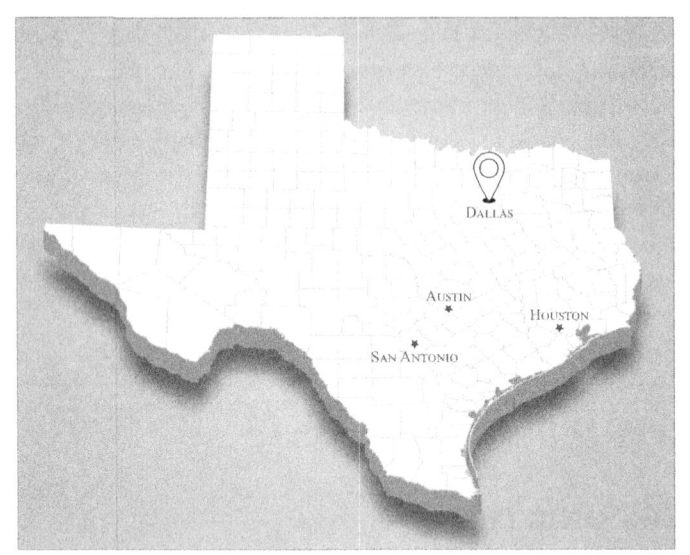

32.788748, -96.800769

WHAT'S ABOUT?:

The Nasher Sculpture Center is a stunning museum in Dallas that houses a world-class collection of modern and contemporary sculptures.

The museum's serene and intimate outdoor garden is a romantic destination, featuring numerous sculptures from renowned artists. Couples can stroll hand-in-hand through the beautifully landscaped garden, enjoying the lush greenery and stunning sculptures that evoke a sense of peace and harmony. The indoor galleries offer an equally impressive collection of contemporary art, emphasizing sculptural works, including pieces by masters like Matisse, Calder, and Rodin. In addition, the museum offers a range of programs and events, including tours, talks, and workshops, providing a wealth of opportunities for art lovers and couples to engage with the art and artists.

For couples, the Nasher Sculpture Center is an ideal destination for a romantic day out. The peaceful and contemplative atmosphere of the museum's garden provides a perfect backdrop for a romantic stroll or a picnic.

The indoor galleries offer an equally impressive collection of contemporary art, giving plenty of opportunities for couples to immerse themselves in the beauty and creativity of the art world. Whether exploring the galleries or relaxing in the garden, the Nasher Sculpture Center is a must-visit destination for art lovers and couples seeking a unique and inspiring experience.

WHERE IS?
The Nasher Sculpture Center is located in the Arts District of downtown Dallas, at 2001 Flora Street. It is easily accessible by car or public transportation. The closest DART rail station is the St. Paul Station, a short walk from the museum. There are also several bus stops in the area, and many visitors choose to walk or bike to the museum. The center has a parking garage on-site and several other nearby parking lots and garages.

WHAT'S GOOD/WHAT'S BAD:
I had a great experience at this modern sculpture museum. Although it may not be the most significant or extensive, it's well-organized. I was impressed by the airy and open indoor spaces. The outdoor garden was a beautifully structured oasis offering a peaceful break from the outside city. It's a great place to stroll, appreciates fantastic art, and relax. The tour doesn't take long, and friendly docents can answer any questions. The garden-level cafe is a nice touch, too. Overall, it's definitely a museum worth visiting and supporting.

DATE(S) VISITED:

WEATHER CONDITIONS:

ACCOMODATIONS:

WHAT WAS THE BEST PART OF TODAY?

SPECIAL MEMORIES:

GERALD D. HINES WATERWALL PARK

An impressive water feature in a lush green oasis with a stunning architectural design that mesmerizes visitors.

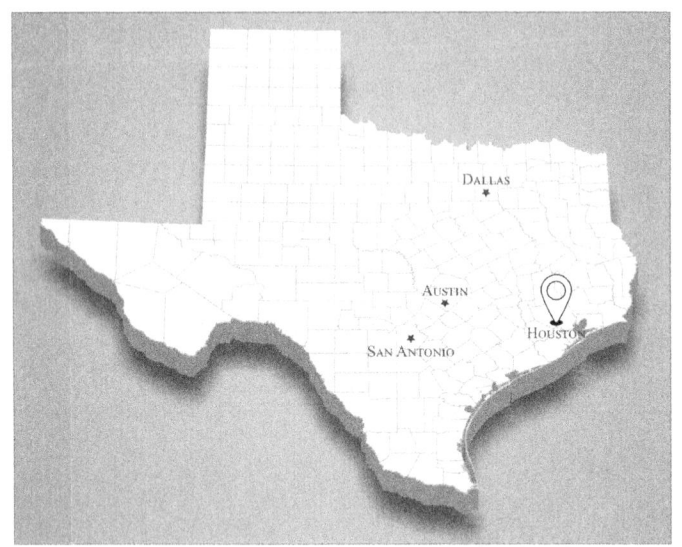

29.736134, -95.461312

WHAT'S ABOUT?:

The Gerald D. Hines Waterwall Park is a stunning oasis in the heart of Houston that will captivate any visitor. The park's highlight is an impressive 64-foot-tall semi-circular fountain, which creates a majestic waterfall effect that cascades down to a shallow pool at the base. The soothing sound of the falling water, the lush greenery, and the peaceful atmosphere make it an ideal spot to unwind and take a break from the hustle and bustle of the city.

Waterwall Park is a popular destination for couples, with plenty of benches and picnic tables scattered throughout the park and a small amphitheater that often hosts live music and other performances. The beautiful setting and romantic ambiance make it a perfect place to spend time with your significant other.

In addition to its romantic appeal, Waterwall Park is a popular destination for families and tourists, with walking paths, gardens, and plenty of photo opportunities.

The Gerald D. Hines Waterwall Park is one of the most photographed sites in Houston and has been featured in several TV shows and movies. In fact, it has appeared in the opening credits of the TV show "The Good Place" and the movie "Rushmore."

The park was also the site of a historic moment in 1991 when former South African president Nelson Mandela visited and addressed a crowd of over 75,000 people.

Additionally, the park has hosted several events, including concerts, weddings, and even yoga classes.

WHERE IS?
The Gerald D. Hines Waterwall Park is in Houston, specifically in the Uptown area. It is situated at Post Oak Boulevard and Hidalgo Street, across from The Galleria shopping mall. The park is easily accessible by car and public transportation, with multiple bus stops and a nearby metro station. In addition, there is a parking lot available for visitors and nearby street parking.

WHAT'S GOOD/WHAT'S BAD:
Visiting this place is a must when traveling to Houston and staying near the Galleria area. It's beautiful and mesmerizing but tends to get crowded due to the many visitors. If you want to take photos without anyone in the background during peak hours, try taking them from the sides rather than the front. There is paid street parking available, but I recommend parking in the mall's parking garage 2 blocks away. Look for signs about Macy's or Nordstrom; you'll know you're in the right place.

DATE(S) VISITED:

WEATHER CONDITIONS:

ACCOMODATIONS:

WHAT WAS THE BEST PART OF TODAY?

SPECIAL MEMORIES:

ENCHANTED ROCK STATE PARK AND NATURAL AREA

Discover the ancient mystery and natural beauty, where towering granite rock formations beckon adventurers and serene picnic spots.

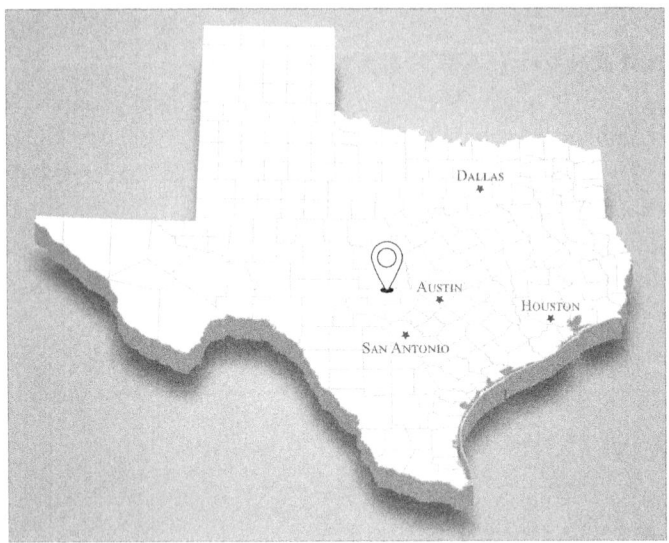

30.495032, -98.819896

WHAT'S ABOUT?:

Enchanted Rock State Park is a unique natural wonder. It is a massive pink granite dome that rises 425 feet above the surrounding landscape and covers 640 acres of rolling hills and towering rock formations. The park offers a variety of outdoor activities for visitors, including hiking, camping, rock climbing, and stargazing. Hikers can climb to the top of the dome for breathtaking views of the surrounding countryside. The park also has various wildlife, including deer, turkeys, and bird species. It is also known for its unique geology and is considered one of the most important geological sites in Texas, with rock formations that date back over one billion years. A long-standing legend surrounding the park says the rock is enchanted and that, at night, it glows and hums with a mysterious energy. According to local folklore, Native American tribes believed the rock was inhabited by spirits, and they would hold ceremonies there to honor these spirits and the powerful energy of the rock. The strange noises and lights reported over the years have only added to Enchanted Rock's mystery. Despite the lack of scientific evidence to support these claims, many visitors to the park still feel a sense of awe and wonder as they explore the unique landscape. As a result, many continue to believe in the enchantment of Enchanted Rock.

Enchanted Rock State Park and Natural Area is a must-visit destination for outdoor enthusiasts, history buffs, and anyone looking to escape the city and experience the beauty of the Texas Hill Country.

WHERE IS?
The Enchanted Rock State Natural Area is in the Texas Hill Country, near Fredericksburg in Gillespie County. The park is 85 miles west of Austin and 65 miles north of San Antonio. You can take State Highway 16 from Fredericksburg or U.S. Highway 87 from Llano to get there. You can access the park by car, and parking is available onsite. The park is open from 8 a.m. to 10 p.m. every day.

WHAT'S GOOD/WHAT'S BAD:
The trails in this park are incredible and offer stunning views of the local cacti. It's an absolute must-see for nature lovers. Unfortunately, the hike to the top of the rock is relatively short. Still, the panoramic view of the Texas Hill Country is absolutely breathtaking. This park is ideal for outdoor activities with family and friends, such as hiking. The camping facilities are excellent, although the campsites are pretty close, with little privacy or separation. I recommend making reservations months in advance to ensure you get a spot. If you're not camping, arriving early in the morning is best, as the park can fill up quickly, and you may be turned away at the entrance.

DATE(S) VISITED:

WEATHER CONDITIONS:

ACCOMODATIONS:

WHAT WAS THE BEST PART OF TODAY?

SPECIAL MEMORIES:

GARNER STATE PARK

A scenic retreat offering endless outdoor adventures and a mesmerizing view of the Frio River, tempting visitors with its breathtaking beauty.

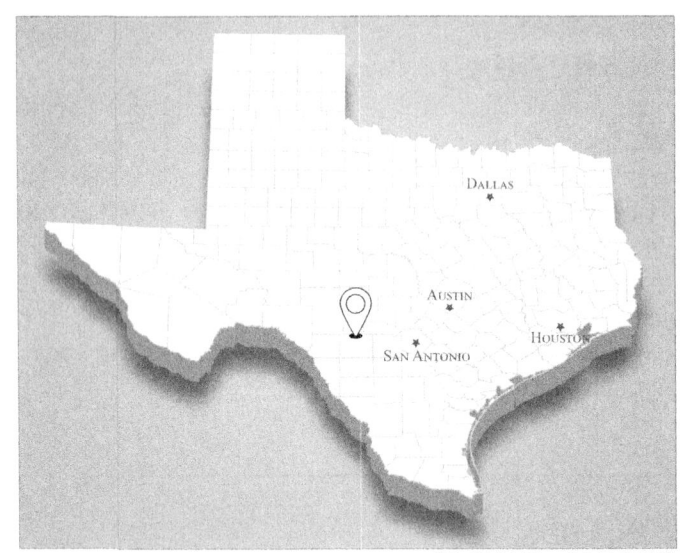

29.599123, -99.743769

WHAT'S ABOUT?:

Garner State Park is a stunning natural area in the heart of the Texas Hill Country. It is known for its scenic beauty, recreational opportunities, and rich history.

This 1,774-acre park is nestled on the banks of the Frio River and is surrounded by towering cliffs and panoramic views.

Visitors to the park can enjoy various activities, including camping, hiking, swimming, fishing, and much more. One of the most popular activities at Garner State Park is floating down the Frio River on inner tubes. This tradition has been enjoyed by generations of visitors.

Additionally, the park features several scenic hiking trails that wind through the lush landscape and offer breathtaking views of the surrounding area.

Garner State Park is home to diverse wildlife, including white-tailed deer, squirrels, raccoons, armadillos, and various bird species such as great blue herons, roadrunners, and many species of songbirds.

The park also provides a habitat for various reptiles, including snakes and turtles. Visitors to the park may spot these creatures on their hikes or while relaxing along the river.

The park is also home to many bat populations, seen at night flitting across the sky in search of insects.

Overall, Garner State Park is a must-visit destination for anyone looking to explore the beauty of the Texas Hill Country.

WHERE IS?
Garner State Park is located in Uvalde County. It is about 80 miles west of San Antonio and about 100 miles northwest of San Antonio. You can take US Highway 83 to Concan, then follow Park Road 62 for about 10 miles to the park entrance. The park is easily accessible by car and offers ample parking.

WHAT'S GOOD/WHAT'S BAD:
This is a stunning park with plenty to do, especially for families. It's a popular spot, so expect it to be busy on weekends. Many activities exist, from strenuous hiking to relaxing in the clear river. Next time, I'll remember to bring hiking boots or trail shoes to better grip some more challenging trails. Don't miss the opportunity to hike to Old Baldy for breathtaking views. I was impressed by the variety of fascinating animals I saw up close. Remember that this park gets crowded on weekends and holidays, so plan accordingly and book early to secure your spot.

DATE(S) VISITED:

WEATHER CONDITIONS:

ACCOMODATIONS:

WHAT WAS THE BEST PART OF TODAY?

SPECIAL MEMORIES:

CHISOS MOUNTAINS

Discover the breathtaking beauty of the Chisos Mountains, where the rugged terrain and diverse wildlife offer a unique and adventurous escape.

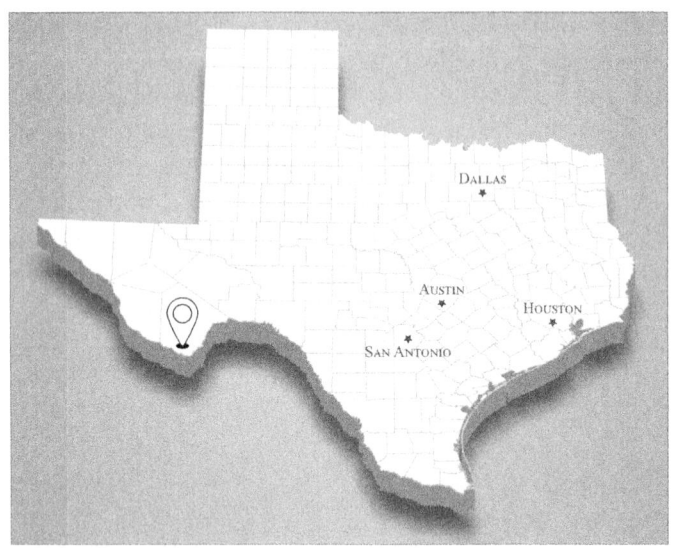

29.270053, -103.300338

WHAT'S ABOUT?:

The Chisos Mountains are a breathtaking natural landmark in Big Bend National Park in West Texas.

The mountains rise dramatically from the surrounding desert, forming the park's heart and offering spectacular views of the surrounding landscape. The Chisos Mountains are a visual wonder and a hub for outdoor recreation, providing a range of hiking, camping, and birdwatching opportunities.

They have been considered a sacred place for Native American tribes such as the Apache and Comanche for many generations. The mountainous region provided a natural fortress that was essential to the survival of these tribes. The remote location and rugged terrain offered a refuge from their enemies and an ideal place to hold spiritual ceremonies and rituals. The natural beauty and serenity of the Chisos Mountains inspired feelings of reverence and awe among the Native American tribes. They believed that the area was home to powerful spirits that could be invoked for guidance, protection, and healing. Many Native American tribal members still view the Chisos Mountains as sacred, and many consider it one of the world's most spiritual and powerful landscapes.

The park offers a range of activities, including guided hikes and ranger-led programs, making it the perfect destination for nature lovers and outdoor enthusiasts of all ages. Explore the rugged terrain, take in the breathtaking views, or immerse yourself in the nature of Chisos Mountains!

WHERE IS?
The Chisos Mountains are located in the Big Bend National Park. The park is in Brewster County, in the southwestern part of the state. The nearest major city to Chisos Mountains is El Paso, which is about 140 miles to the northwest. To get to the Chisos Mountains, you can drive to the park and then take a scenic drive to the Chisos Basin area, which is the location of the Chisos Mountains. The park is accessible via Route 118 and Route 385 and offers many scenic drives, hiking trails, and picnic areas.

WHAT'S GOOD/WHAT'S BAD:
I had an amazing experience at the heart of Big Bend National Park, undoubtedly one of the most beautiful places on earth. The drive into the mountains is simply stunning. It provides a welcome respite from the heat, cooling everything down in a truly fantastic way. There's a straightforward walk that I'd highly recommend as the views are simply superb. There's also a small visitors' center and a little supermarket where you can grab a bite to eat and admire the scenery. However, be aware that there aren't many lodging options near the park, and the distances to and within the park are pretty substantial. As a result, I'd strongly suggest staying inside the park at the lodge or campground to minimize driving time. While the lodging inside the park is essential, it's quite adequate. It will provide you with everything you need for a comfortable stay.

DATE(S) VISITED:

WEATHER CONDITIONS:

ACCOMODATIONS:

WHAT WAS THE BEST PART OF TODAY?

SPECIAL MEMORIES:

BOQUILLAS CANYON

A breathtaking natural wonder in Texas, where the Rio Grande winds its way through towering cliffs and lush vegetation.

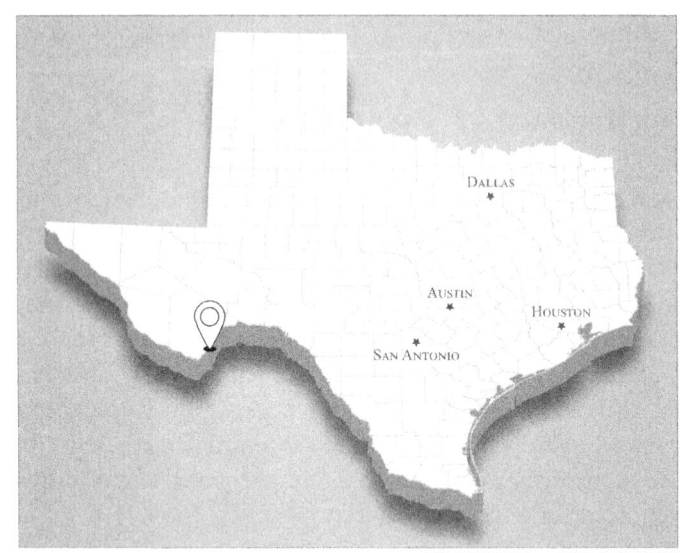

29.185198, -102.961989

WHAT'S ABOUT?:

Boquillas Canyon is a stunning natural wonder in Big Bend National Park in Texas. The canyon, formed by the Rio Grande River, offers breathtaking views of towering cliffs and lush vegetation.

The canyon is home to various animals, including white-tailed deer, javelinas, black bears, and multiple species of birds, including the striking roadrunner, the Peregrine Falcon, and the endangered Golden Eagle.

The canyon has a rich cultural history, with Native American petroglyphs and evidence of ancient mining operations. In addition, the Rio Grande river that flows through the canyon has played an essential role in the lives of the region's people, providing irrigation and transportation.

One of the most intriguing features of Boquillas Canyon is the opportunity to explore and experience the unique culture of the Mexican border town of Boquillas del Carmen, accessible by crossing the river by boat.

The town offers a glimpse into the traditional way of life, with a local restaurant, artisans selling handcrafted goods, and friendly residents eager to share their culture with visitors.

However, it is essential to note that crossing into Mexico requires obtaining a permit from the National Park Service and adhering to international travel regulations. Visitors are also advised to take necessary safety precautions and stay on designated trails while exploring the canyon.

WHERE IS?
Boquillas Canyon is in the Big Bend National Park in Brewster County, Texas. It is approximately 135 miles southeast of Marfa and about 315 miles southeast of El Paso. To get to Boquillas Canyon, visitors must drive to the park headquarters in Study Butte and then take the park road to the Rio Grande Village. From there, a 2-mile round-trip hike is required to reach the canyon. Visitors can also take a scenic drive along the Ross Maxwell Scenic Drive and take a short walk to the canyon viewpoint.

WHAT'S GOOD/WHAT'S BAD:
I had a great experience hiking into the canyon trail. The hike started as moderate but was easy at the end. If the river water is low, it's possible to hike into the canyon walls at the end. I didn't have cell or WiFi reception, but there was a store with WiFi and amenities about 4 miles away in the campground. There was ample parking at the trailhead and a vault toilet. During the hike, I spotted some wild horses and captured fabulous photos. I'd advise carrying plenty of water and dressing appropriately for the weather. The park had a variety of attractions to explore, and I made sure to take my time and enjoy every bit of it.

DATE(S) VISITED:

WEATHER CONDITIONS:

ACCOMODATIONS:

WHAT WAS THE BEST PART OF TODAY?

SPECIAL MEMORIES:

FORT DAVIS NATIONAL HISTORIC SITE

A breathtaking range of peaks in West Texas, offering scenic vistas, diverse wildlife, and adventure for the nature-lovers and outdoor enthusiasts.

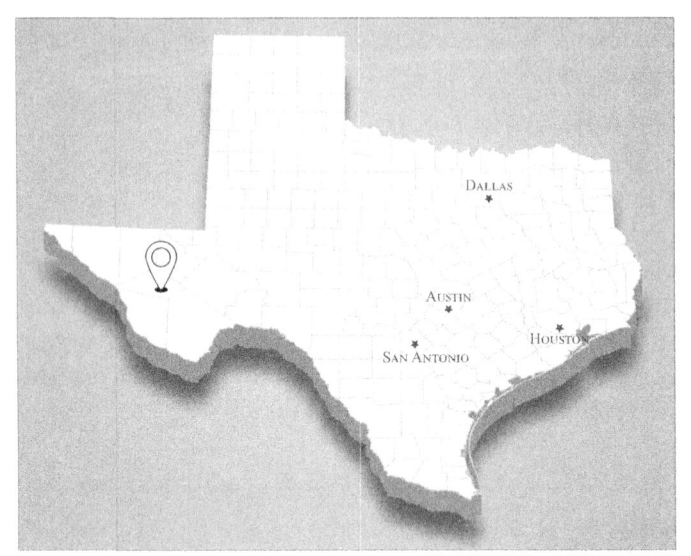

30.598878, -103.886393

WHAT'S ABOUT?:

The Davis Mountains are a range of mountains located in West Texas.
They are part of the larger Chihuahuan Desert region and offer stunning views and diverse landscapes, from desert plains to towering peaks. The mountains are home to the Fort Davis National Historic Site, a former military post of West Texas.
It was established in 1854 and was one of the most important military outposts in the frontier southwest. It protected settlers, mail coaches, and stagecoaches traveling along the San Antonio-El Paso Road. The fort was also home to several African American Buffalo Soldier units. Today, visitors can tour the restored barracks, officers' quarters, and other buildings to learn about the fort's rich history.
The Davis Mountains Scenic Drive is a breathtaking drive through the Davis Mountains. It offers stunning views of the rugged mountains and the surrounding landscape, including rolling hills, forests, and meadows. The drive is approximately 60 miles long and provides access to some of the area's most scenic sites and famous attractions, such as the Fort Davis National Historic Site, the McDonald Observatory, and the Chihuahuan Desert Research Institute.
The road is well-paved and suitable for cars, and it passes by several picnic areas and hiking trails.
The Davis Mountains are also a popular destination for stargazing, as the area has some of the darkest skies in the country, making it ideal for observing the stars and planets.

WHERE IS?
The Davis Mountains are in the west-central part of Texas, in Jeff Davis County. They are approximately 200 miles southwest of Dallas and 175 miles southeast of El Paso. To get there, one can take the I-10 west from either city, then take the TX-17 exit and drive north towards Fort Davis. The scenic drive through the Davis Mountains starts from Fort Davis. It leads you through some of Texas's most beautiful and rugged terrains, offering breathtaking views of the surrounding mountains and valleys.

WHAT'S GOOD/WHAT'S BAD:
This place is a must-visit for history buffs as it provides a fascinating insight into what occurred in the 1800s. The park has done an excellent job of restoring all of the buildings. The Rangers are friendly, and the museum explains everything clearly. It's worth taking the hike above the fort for the fantastic views. The rock cliffs were built to deter native people from invading, a sad part of history, but the museum presents the story well. Visitors can walk around the grounds and into certain buildings, including the medical facility, which is well worth the short walk. Be mindful of fire ants.

DATE(S) VISITED:

WEATHER CONDITIONS:

ACCOMODATIONS:

WHAT WAS THE BEST PART OF TODAY?

SPECIAL MEMORIES:

GUADALUPE MOUNTAINS NATIONAL PARK

Embark on an unforgettable adventure and explore the tallest peak in Texas, where natural beauty and rich history await you.

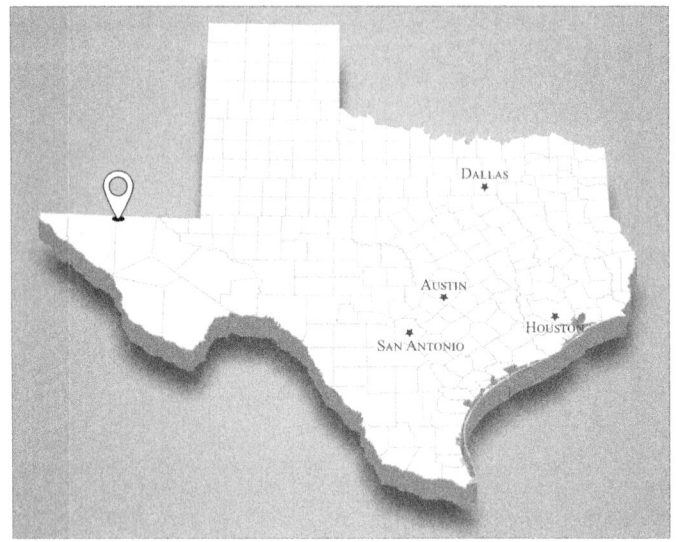

31.892958, -104.820941

WHAT'S ABOUT?:

Guadalupe Mountains National Park is a protected wilderness area in the Chihuahuan Desert in west Texas.

It boasts the highest peak in Texas, Guadalupe Peak, which rises to 8,751 feet.

The park covers over 86,000 acres and is home to diverse flora and fauna, including desert bighorn sheep, mountain lions, and black bears.

Visitors to the park can enjoy various outdoor activities, including hiking, camping, and birdwatching.

One of the most popular trails in the park is the 8.5-mile hike to the top of Guadalupe Peak, which offers breathtaking views of the surrounding desert and mountains.

Another popular attraction is the McKittrick Canyon Nature Trail, which winds through a lush riparian oasis and is especially beautiful in the fall when the leaves of the Bigtooth Maples change color.

Visitors can also take a scenic drive along Guadalupe Ridge Road to admire the stunning panoramic views of the park.

Guadalupe Mountains National Park is a must-visit destination for nature lovers and outdoor enthusiasts with its diverse landscapes, rich wildlife, and many outdoor recreation opportunities.

WHERE IS?
Guadalupe Mountains National Park is located in the Trans-Pecos region of West Texas, in the counties of Culberson and Hudspeth. It is approximately 140 miles southeast of El Paso and about 250 miles west of San Antonio. The nearest cities to the park are Van Horn, Texas, and Carlsbad, New Mexico.
To get to Park, take I-10 to Van Horn and Highway 90 to the park. From Carlsbad, take Highway 62/180 to the park. Visitors can also fly into El Paso International Airport or Midland International Airport, about a 2-hour drive from the park.

WHAT'S GOOD/WHAT'S BAD:
I had an awesome time at this National Park! The scenery is absolutely breathtaking, and there are hikes for all skill levels. The trails have potential fossil finds in the rocks and are home to little critters. The distant mountains are awe-inspiring. Remember to bring plenty of water and sunscreen, as many trails are in unshaded areas. The park has shaded picnic areas to rest and recharge after a hike. The campground near the Pine Springs visitor center is an asphalt parking lot without much shade, but it is well-maintained. If you have a tent, there are some sites on the lot's perimeter, but there isn't much privacy, and it cannot be quiet. Having an RV or trailer can be even worse as you are in the middle of a parking lot.

DATE(S) VISITED:

WEATHER CONDITIONS:

ACCOMODATIONS:

WHAT WAS THE BEST PART OF TODAY?

SPECIAL MEMORIES:

AMISTAD NATIONAL RECREATION AREA

A wonderful area where crystal-clear waters and towering cliffs create a breathtaking landscape for adventure and exploration.

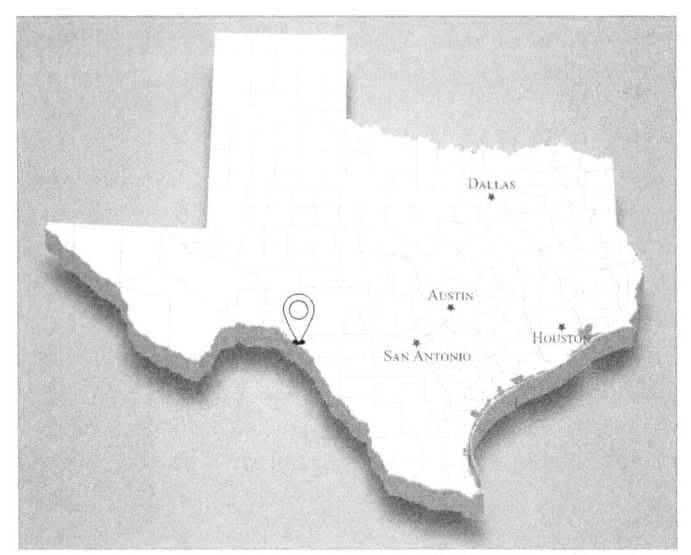

29.465484, -100.988186

WHAT'S ABOUT?:

Amistad National Recreation Area is a beautiful natural area located in Val Verde County. The site is known for its stunning scenery, including the Amistad Reservoir, surrounded by rugged mountains, canyons, and desert landscapes. Visitors to the recreation area can enjoy many activities, from boating, fishing, and swimming in the reservoir to hiking and exploring the rugged wilderness.

The area is also home to a diverse array of wildlife, including a variety of bird species, as well as coyotes, bobcats, and other mammals. The park is also a popular spot for bird watching, with over 400 species of birds known to live in the area.

The Area is home to several cultural sites that offer a glimpse into the rich history and heritage of the area. One of the main cultural attractions is the Seminole Canyon State Park and Historic Site, which is located near Del Rio, Texas. This park is known for its well-preserved pictographs and petroglyphs created by its prehistoric inhabitants. The park offers guided tours and interpretive programs that give visitors a deeper understanding of the area's rich cultural history.

Another cultural site is the Comanche Springs Astronomy Campus, near Fort Stockton, dedicated to studying the night sky. The campus features a state-of-the-art observatory and a variety of educational programs and events that allow visitors to explore the universe and learn about the night sky. Whether you're a history buff, nature lover, or simply looking for a peaceful escape from the city, the Amistad National Recreation Area is a hidden treasure worth discovering.

WHERE IS?
Amistad National Recreation Area is located in southwestern Texas, along the border with Mexico. It is situated in Val Verde County, approximately 120 miles west of San Antonio, 170 miles southwest of Austin, and about 50 miles east of Del Rio. The nearest major city is Del Rio. The easiest way to get to Amistad National Recreation Area is by car. From Del Rio, take US 90 west to Comstock, then turn south on Ranch Road 90 and continue to the park. From San Antonio, take I-35 south to US 90 west, then follow the directions from Del Rio. Several commercial flights serve Del Rio International Airport, just a short drive from the park.

WHAT'S GOOD/WHAT'S BAD:
I enjoyed fishing, swimming, kayaking, and relaxing at Lake Amistad. The contrast between the blue water and the white rock is stunningly beautiful. The lake is a nature lover and fisherman's paradise with its abundance of bass and the expansive recreation area to explore. However, the site can be vast, so it's best to obtain a map before exploring. Fortunately, the rangers are informative and always willing to help.

DATE(S) VISITED:

WEATHER CONDITIONS:

ACCOMODATIONS:

WHAT WAS THE BEST PART OF TODAY?

SPECIAL MEMORIES:

NATURAL BRIDGE CAVERNS

Discover this underground wonder, where nature has carved dramatic, towering formations from solid limestone deep within the earth.

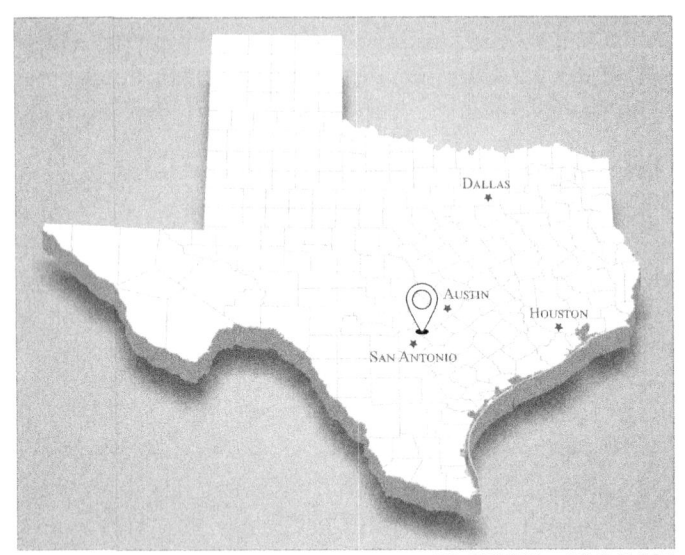

29.693211, -98.341536

WHAT'S ABOUT?:

Natural Bridge Caverns is a fascinating geological wonder in the Texas Hill Country near San Antonio. Natural Bridge Caverns are considered some of the largest known commercial caverns in the state, with a network of underground chambers and passages stretching over 20 acres.

The caverns were formed by an underground river that carved out the limestone rock over thousands of years. The caverns were discovered by four university students in the 1960s. They were exploring the area and stumbled upon the entrance to the cave. The students explored the caverns and eventually convinced a local businessman to invest in the development of the caverns as a tourist attraction.

Visitors can explore the main cavern on a guided tour.

They will see towering stalactites, stalagmites, flowing streams, and sparkling crystal formations.

In addition to the main cavern, Natural Bridge Caverns also offers several outdoor adventures, including a Canopy Challenge Course, a ropes course, and a zip line tour.

The park also features a visitor center with exhibits on the geology and history of the area, a gift shop, and a snack bar.

So whether you are a nature lover, an adventure seeker, or just looking for a fun day out, Natural Bridge Caverns has something for everyone.

WHERE IS?
Natural Bridge Caverns are located in the Texas Hill Country, specifically in New Braunfels, Comal County. The park is about 30 miles north of San Antonio and 65 miles south of Austin. To get there, you can take I-35 to exit 175 and follow the signs to the park. There is a large parking lot available for visitors.

WHAT'S GOOD/WHAT'S BAD:
A fantastic tour with stunning views of stalagmites and stalactites. The cavern was absolutely massive, grand, and impressive. Although there was some up-and-down walking, it wasn't too strenuous for an average person. Our guide was excellent and provided informative commentary about the history and formations in the cavern. The place was immaculate and visually stunning! They had many employees to ensure every guest's safety and satisfaction. The staff was very organized and professional. It's important to wear sturdy walking shoes as some areas can be slippery. Although the gift shops were overpriced, perusing the unique items on display was lovely.

DATE(S) VISITED:

WEATHER CONDITIONS:

ACCOMODATIONS:

WHAT WAS THE BEST PART OF TODAY?

SPECIAL MEMORIES:

SEA RIM STATE PARK

Explore the Unspoiled Coastal Beauty of Sea Rim State Park: A Coastal Adventure Awaits.

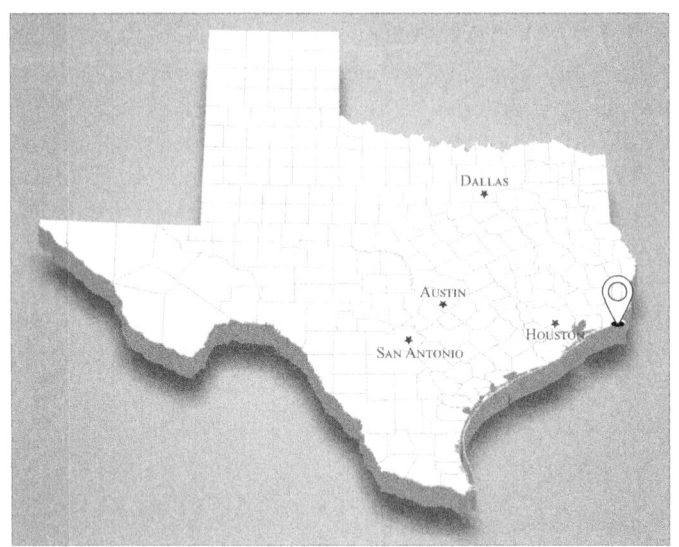

29.676471, -94.044097

WHAT'S ABOUT?:

Sea Rim State Park is near Port Arthur on the Gulf Coast of Texas. It is known for its diverse ecosystem that includes marshes, beaches, and forests, making it a prime destination for nature lovers and outdoor enthusiasts.

The park covers over 4,000 acres of land and provides opportunities for activities such as fishing, boating, camping, and bird-watching.

One of the unique features of Sea Rim State Park is its location on the Gulf of Mexico, which provides visitors with access to a vast array of marine life and ecosystems. The park's extensive marsh areas are home to a wide range of wildlife, including alligators, shorebirds, and various fish species.

In addition, several trails throughout the park allow visitors to explore and admire the area's natural beauty.

Sea Rim State Park offers ample opportunities for those who love fishing to catch red drum, flounder, and other fish species. The park has several boat ramps and fishing piers, making it easy for visitors to get out on the water and catch a big one. Regarding accessibility, several campsites are available for those who want to stay overnight and a day-use area for those who wish to visit for a few hours.

Sea Rim State Park is a unique and beautiful destination that allows visitors to explore the Gulf Coast of Texas and experience its diverse and thriving ecosystem. Whether you're a nature lover, fisherman, or just looking for a peaceful place to relax, Sea Rim State Park is worth visiting.

WHERE IS?
Sea Rim State Park is in Jefferson County, Texas, along the Gulf of Mexico. The park is about 85 miles southeast of Beaumont and about 80 miles southeast of Houston. To get to Sea Rim State Park, take State Highway 87 and follow the signs for the park.

Sea Rim State Park is a paid park with a daily entry fee for visitors. There is a designated parking lot within the park grounds where visitors can park their vehicles. The park also offers camping facilities with additional fees.

WHAT'S GOOD/WHAT'S BAD:
The best beaches along the upper Texas coast were incredibly peaceful and quiet, with more beaches than people. The beaches were beautiful and clean, and the staff was friendly. It's a must-visit if you're in the area, especially for those who enjoy birdwatching. The entrance fee is $5 per person, and there is no shade, so bringing an umbrella or tent is a good idea. Getting food and drink is also essential, as no restaurants are in the park. The campground and park are surrounded by a marsh, which means there are many mosquitoes, but it's not bad on the beach, where there is a breeze.

DATE(S) VISITED:

WEATHER CONDITIONS:

ACCOMODATIONS:

WHAT WAS THE BEST PART OF TODAY?

SPECIAL MEMORIES:

SOUTH LLANO RIVER STATE PARK

Dive into the splendor of the great outdoors, where rolling hills, scenic river views, and diverse wildlife create a nature lover's paradise.

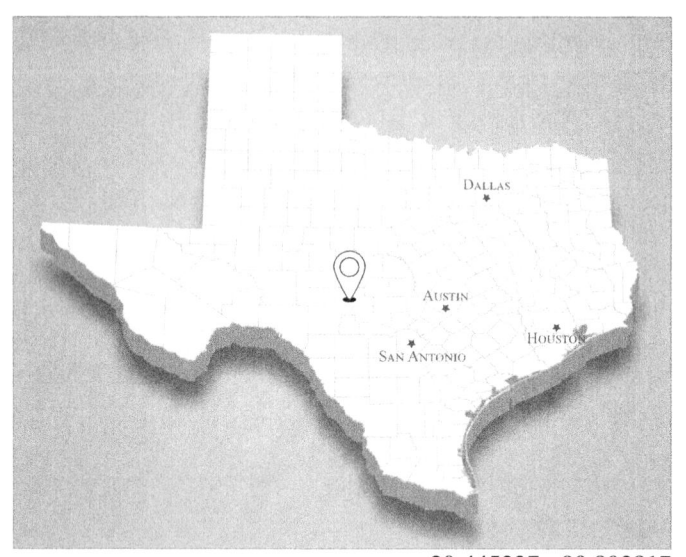

30.445327, -99.803817

WHAT'S ABOUT?:

South Llano River State Park covers over 900 acres in Junction, in Kimble County. It is known for its scenic beauty and outdoor recreation opportunities, with various activities for visitors.

Some popular South Llano River State Park activities include fishing, camping, hiking, and bird watching.

One of the park's highlights is the South Llano River, which runs through the park and provides visitors with opportunities for fishing and swimming.

Tubing and kayaking are popular activities on the South Llano River. The river offers a gentle flow perfect for beginners and experienced paddlers.

Visitors can rent kayaks or bring their own, and spend a day floating down the river, surrounded by the park's beautiful scenery. The river is fed by many springs, providing visitors a consistently cool and clear flow. Several miles of hiking trails also traverse the park, offering visitors scenic views of the river and the surrounding area.

In addition to the recreational opportunities, South Llano River State Park is home to wildlife, including white-tailed deer, squirrels, armadillos, and various bird species. This makes the park an ideal destination for bird watching and wildlife observation.

South Llano River State Park visitors can enjoy these activities and more. There is a park entrance fee and a parking lot for visitors.

WHERE IS?
South Llano River State Park is located in Junction, Texas, in Kimble County. It is approximately 160 miles west of Austin and 165 miles northwest of San Antonio. To get there, you can take I-10 to Junction and then follow the signs to the park, which is located on Park Road 73.

WHAT'S GOOD/WHAT'S BAD:
This state park is a great destination for nature enthusiasts. The top-notch staff and facilities make for a comfortable and enjoyable experience. I particularly enjoyed camping overnight and experiencing the park's Dark Sky site, where I could see the stars in all their glory. One of the highlights of my visit was tubing down the river with my friends and family, taking in the beautiful scenery along the way.
The park is also a bird watcher's paradise, with numerous blinds offering great views of the local birdlife. The River Trail is another must-do, providing a peaceful and scenic walk with plenty of opportunities for bird-watching. The park and campground facilities are well-maintained, including the restrooms. Additionally, a new entry visitor area is currently under construction and will further enhance the park's amenities once completed.

DATE(S) VISITED:

WEATHER CONDITIONS:

ACCOMODATIONS:

WHAT WAS THE BEST PART OF TODAY?

SPECIAL MEMORIES:

BIG THICKET NATIONAL PRESERVE

The home of a diverse ecosystem and rich biodiversity where over 40,000 acres of forest, wetlands, and prairies converge.

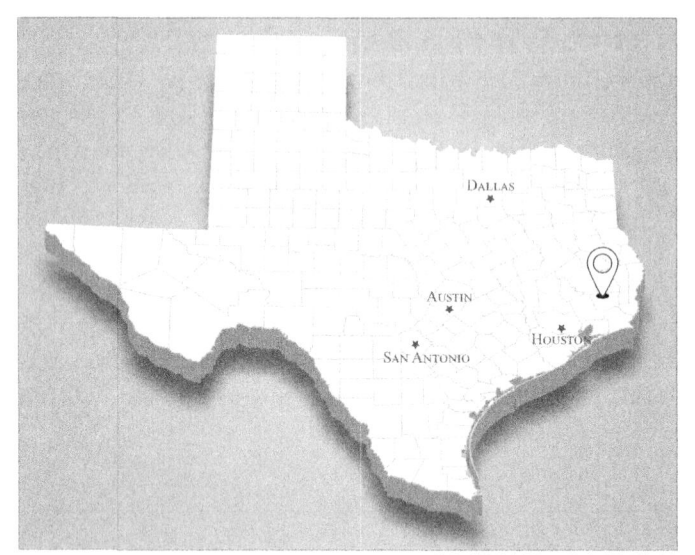

30.458408, -94.386261

WHAT'S ABOUT?:

Big Thicket National Preserve is a protected area in southeastern Texas near Beaumont. This preserve is home to a diverse range of plant and animal species, making it one of North America's most biologically diverse regions. With over 100,000 acres of protected land, Big Thicket National Preserve offers various recreational activities such as hiking, fishing, and wildlife viewing.

One of the unique features of Big Thicket is its mixture of different habitats, including pine forests, swamps, and prairies. This diversity of habitats supports a wide variety of flora and fauna, including over 50 species of mammals and more than 300 species of birds.

Visitors can explore the park's many trails, including the Sandridge Trail, which offers a peaceful hike through the preserve's heart. Or the Kirby Trail, which takes visitors through the dense pine forests of the Big Thicket. Fishing is also popular in the park, with several waterways offering opportunities to catch bass, catfish, and sunfish.In addition to its diverse natural beauty, Big Thicket National Preserve also has a rich cultural history. Native American tribes, such as the Caddo, Karankawa, and Atakapa, have called the area home for thousands of years. The park also played a role in the lumber industry. The abundant timber resources were harvested in the late 19th and early 20th centuries.

Overall, Big Thicket National Preserve is a must-visit destination for anyone looking to experience Texas's natural beauty and rich cultural history.

WHERE IS?
Big Thicket National Preserve is in Southeast Texas, Liberty, Hardin, Jasper, Jefferson, Orange, and Tyler counties. The closest major cities to the preserve are Houston, TX (100 miles), Beaumont, TX (45 miles), and Lake Charles, LA (85 miles). To get to Big Thicket National Preserve, take US Highway 69 or US Highway 287 to Kountze, TX, and follow the signs to the preserve. You can also fly into Houston George Bush Intercontinental Airport or Beaumont Municipal Airport and rent a car to drive to the preserve.

WHAT'S GOOD/WHAT'S BAD:
This national park preserve has so much to offer: from camping and hiking to paddling and hunting, it was perfect for everyone. At the Visitor Center, plenty of displays showcased what the Preserve had to offer, a great gift shop with lots of engaging book titles and clean restrooms. I spent a day and a half hiking through sloughs, creeks, bogs, swamps, pine forests, newly planted forests, overgrown thickets, meadows, and treed corridors. The natural beauty of Southeast Texas was all around, and it was definitely worth exploring. Even just driving through the park was a treat in itself.

DATE(S) VISITED:

WEATHER CONDITIONS:

ACCOMODATIONS:

WHAT WAS THE BEST PART OF TODAY?

SPECIAL MEMORIES:

LAKE MEREDITH NATIONAL RECREATION AREA

A scenic escape for outdoor enthusiasts with its diverse landscapes, recreational activities, and breathtaking views of Lake Meredith.

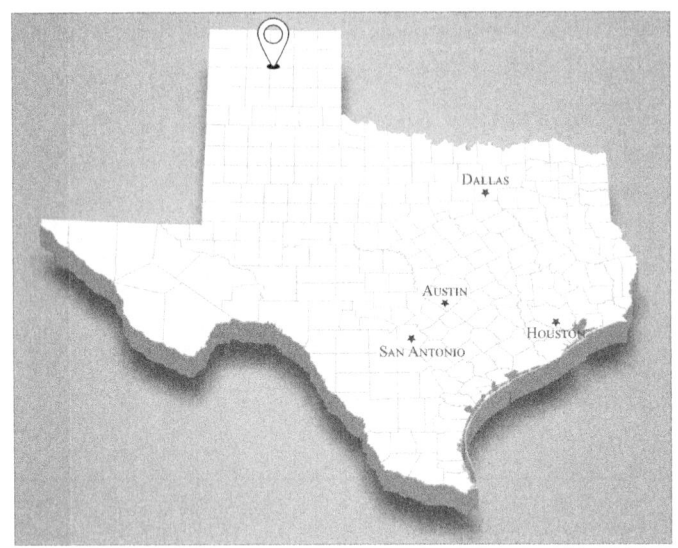

35.643674, -101.586463

WHAT'S ABOUT?:

Lake Meredith National Recreation Area is a scenic recreational destination in the Texas Panhandle near Fritch.

This artificial lake was created by Sanford Dam and offers a variety of recreational activities such as boating, fishing, camping, and hiking. In addition, visitors can enjoy scenic views of the surrounding landscape, including the Canadian River and the famous Alibates Flint Quarries.

The Canadian River is a 710-mile-long river in Texas and Oklahoma that is a tributary of the Arkansas River. The Alibates Flint Quarries, located on the north shore of Lake Meredith in the Texas Panhandle, are a National Monument commemorating the prehistoric use of flint.

The site contains more than 13,000 acres of parkland with hiking trails, picnic areas, campgrounds, and several quarries where visitors can view indigenous peoples' distinctive red and yellow flint for tools and weapons. The quarries also offer a unique opportunity to learn the cultural and geological history of the area. But also the natural beauty of the surrounding landscape.

The lake is home to various fish species, making it a popular destination for anglers, and the surrounding wildlife offers opportunities for wildlife viewing and birdwatching. With its vast recreational opportunities and beautiful natural surroundings, Lake Meredith National Recreation Area is the perfect destination for outdoor enthusiasts and nature lovers.

WHERE IS?
Lake Meredith National Recreation Area is located in the Texas Panhandle, primarily in Hutchinson County, but also extending into Moore and Potter Counties. It is about 35 miles northeast of Amarillo and can be reached by taking exit 80 off of I-40 and following the signs to the park.

WHAT'S GOOD/WHAT'S BAD:
I visited this national recreation area and was impressed by the striking landscape of rocky hills and mountains. Primitive camping is free but is aware that there are no amenities such as water or electricity, so make sure to bring everything you need. The public restrooms are well-maintained and easily accessible. In the Blue West area, the views are simply breathtaking. Although the recreation area offers a range of activities, such as boating, hunting, four-wheeling, and some hiking, I noticed no visitor center or interpretive signs throughout the park. It can be an excellent choice for those who enjoy camping, water sports, and outdoor adventure activities. At the same time, it may not be ideal for those who like to learn about the history and nature of a park.

DATE(S) VISITED:

WEATHER CONDITIONS:

ACCOMODATIONS:

WHAT WAS THE BEST PART OF TODAY?

SPECIAL MEMORIES:

CEDAR HILL STATE PARK AND LAKE JOE POOL

This park offers a variety of outdoor activities, including hiking, mountain biking, and fishing.

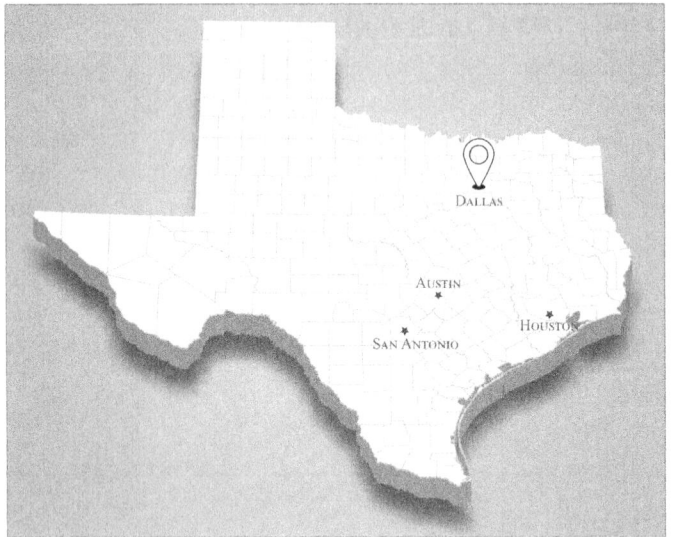

32.621516, -96.978814

WHAT'S ABOUT?:

Cedar Hill State Park and Lake Joe Pool are popular outdoor recreation areas in Texas's Dallas-Fort Worth metropolitan area.

Cedar Hill State Park is a 1,826-acre park located in Cedar Hill. It offers visitors a variety of outdoor activities, such as hiking, mountain biking, fishing, boating, and camping. The park has over 15 miles of hiking and mountain biking trails, a fishing pier, and a boat ramp for fishing and boating on Joe Pool Lake.

Joe Pool Lake is a 7,400-acre reservoir in the heart of the Dallas-Fort Worth metropolitan area. It was created by the US Army Corps of Engineers in the early 1980s and is a popular destination for fishing, boating, and water sports.

The lake has various fish species, including catfish, bass, and crappie. It is known for its good fishing opportunities. There are several boat ramps, marinas around the lake, and picnic areas and parks for visitors to enjoy.

In addition to its outdoor recreational opportunities, Cedar Hill State Park and Joe Pool Lake offer various programs and events throughout the year, including camping trips, birdwatching expeditions, and educational programs for families and children.

With their convenient location and multiple activities, Cedar Hill State Park and Joe Pool Lake are great places for people of all ages to explore and enjoy the great outdoors.

WHERE IS?
Cedar Hill State Park is located in Cedar Hill, in Dallas County. It is approximately 20 miles southwest of downtown Dallas and about 15 miles southeast of Fort Worth. To get to the park, take Highway 67 to Exit 374, then head west on FM 1382. Turn right onto FM 1382 and continue to the park entrance, which will be on the right. The park's address is 1570 FM 1382, Cedar Hill, Texas 75104.

WHAT'S GOOD/WHAT'S BAD:
This is a beautiful spot to enjoy a day with family and friends. There are numerous areas to have a picnic and plenty of opportunities to fish (from the shore or in a boat). For those who love to explore, the site offers various options for hiking or leisurely walking through scenic surroundings. Campsites are available for those who would like to stay the night and come with ample space to accommodate tents or RVs. Bathhouses are conveniently located in the vicinity. Additionally, there are multiple launch sites around the lake for boating enthusiasts. Visitors can also head to one of the two sand beaches for a refreshing swim or engage in water sports like tubing and skiing in the vast expanse of the lake.

DATE(S) VISITED:

WEATHER CONDITIONS:

ACCOMODATIONS:

WHAT WAS THE BEST PART OF TODAY?

SPECIAL MEMORIES:

BALCONES CANYONLANDS NATIONAL WILDLIFE REFUGE

Unlock the secrets of diverse wildlife and pristine wilderness at this National Wildlife Refuge, where adventure and natural beauty await.

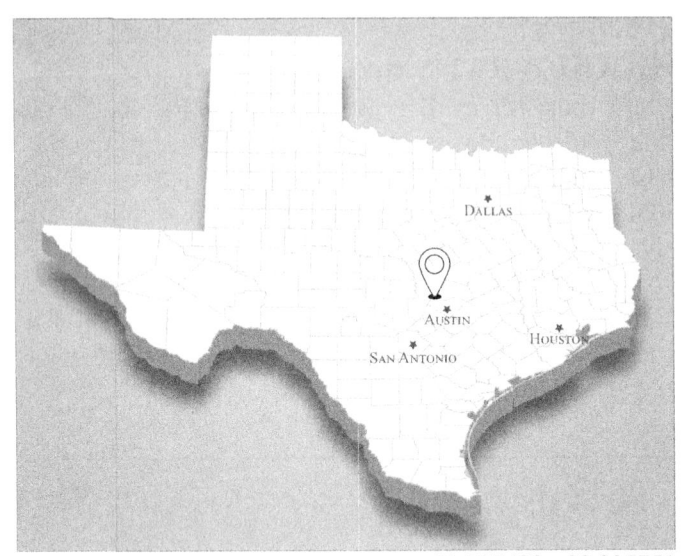

30.505422, -98.025751

WHAT'S ABOUT?:

Balcones Canyonlands National Wildlife Refuge is a protected area established in 1992. It covers over 30,000 acres of land, providing critical habitat for various wildlife species, including many threatened or endangered. The refuge comprises several habitats, including rolling hills, rocky canyons, and wetland areas, all supporting diverse wildlife, from bird species to mammals, reptiles, and amphibians. One of its main features is its system of canyons and caves, providing a unique and beautiful landscape for visitors to explore. Hiking trails meander through the canyons, offering opportunities for bird watching, wildlife viewing, and taking in the breathtaking scenery. The refuge is also home to several historic sites, including the landmark Comanche Lookout Park, which provides panoramic views of the surrounding landscape. Visitors can participate in various recreational activities, including hiking, bird watching, fishing, and wildlife observation. Several ranger-led programs are also offered throughout the year, including nature walks, birding tours, and star-gazing events. Balcones Canyonlands National Wildlife Refuge is the perfect destination for those seeking to disconnect from the daily grind and reconnect with nature. Take a scenic hike, search for signs of wildlife, and breathe in the sweet fragrance of the surrounding flora. Bring binoculars for bird watching, and capture the stunning beauty of the wild through your camera or smartphone. Then, enjoy peaceful moments of reading and journaling at one of the observation decks!

WHERE IS?
Balcones Canyonlands National Wildlife Refuge is in central Texas, in the counties of Burnet and Travis. The closest major city is Austin, which is approximately 30 miles to the east. To get to the refuge, take I-35 to exit 255 and follow FM 1431 west to the refuge entrance. Alternatively, take TX-71 west to the Marble Falls area from Austin and follow FM 1431 west to the refuge. The refuge is located off FM 1431, just west of the intersection with RM 1431. There is a small visitor center and several trails to explore, with ample parking available.

WHAT'S GOOD/WHAT'S BAD:
The hiking area is stunning, with a small creek flowing through the Doeskin Ranch area. It is an excellent location to spot wildlife such as deer, and I heard coyotes during my visit. The trails are ideal for walking, with paths along meadows or into the "balcones." Choosing which access point to visit is essential, as there are at least four different entrances, each a few miles from the other. There are no entrance fees, so one can enjoy the day without worry. Overall, it is a great place to relax and unwind.

DATE(S) VISITED:

WEATHER CONDITIONS:

ACCOMODATIONS:

WHAT WAS THE BEST PART OF TODAY?

SPECIAL MEMORIES:

LADY BIRD LAKE HIKE-AND-BIKE TRAIL

44 TEXAS

A scenic 10-mile trail that offers breathtaking views of the lake and the Austin skyline, perfect for outdoor enthusiasts and nature lovers alike.

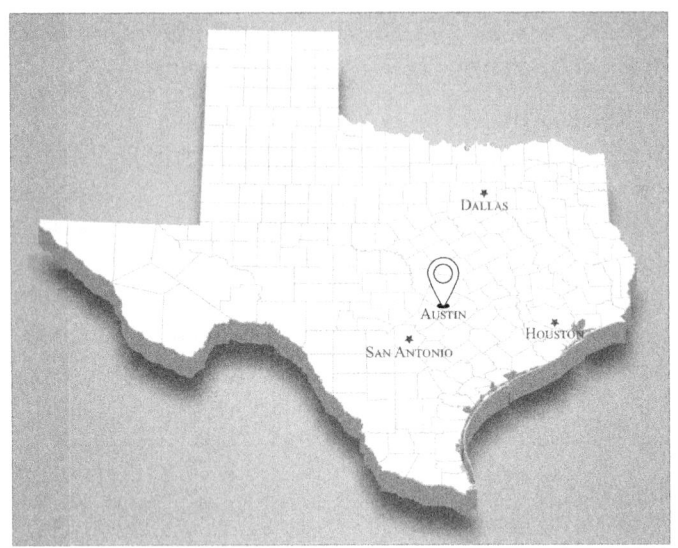

30.248030, -97.724002

WHAT'S ABOUT?:

The Lady Bird Lake Hike-and-Bike Trail is a popular scenic trail in Austin. It is a 10-mile trail that winds around Lady Bird Lake and offers stunning views of the Austin skyline and the opportunity to see wildlife like migratory birds and local fish. The trail is paved and well-maintained, making it suitable for biking, jogging, walking, and rollerblading activities.

One of the most appealing features of the Lady Bird Lake Hike-and-Bike Trail is its serene and peaceful environment. As you make your way around the lake, you'll be surrounded by lush greenery and beautiful flora, which provides a refreshing escape from the hustle and bustle of city life. In the evenings, the trail is lit, allowing visitors to enjoy a peaceful evening walk or bike ride with a stunning view of the city skyline.

The trail is also surrounded by various parks and picnic areas, making it a great place to spend a day with family and friends. You can picnic, go fishing or relax and enjoy the beautiful scenery. Additionally, several restaurants, cafes, and shops along the trail make it easy to grab a snack or a drink as you make your way around the lake.Overall, the Lady Bird Lake Hike-and-Bike Trail is a must-visit for anyone who loves the outdoors and wants to experience the beauty of Austin. Whether you're a fitness enthusiast, a nature lover, or just looking for a relaxing escape from the city, this trail offers something for everyone. You're guaranteed to leave feeling refreshed, inspired, and reinvigorated.

WHERE IS?
A scenic 10-mile trail that offers breathtaking views of the lake and the Austin skyline, perfect for outdoor enthusiasts and nature lovers alike.

WHAT'S GOOD/WHAT'S BAD:
I love walking on endless, peaceful trails along the lake and riverfront in July or February. It is a must for me whenever I visit. It allows me to enjoy the serenity and wildlife before anything else. The hike-and-bike trail along Lady Bird Lake is well-maintained and spotless. It is perfect for walkers and bikers, and I always feel secure walking alone. Moreover, there are numerous spots along the trail where free parking is available.

DATE(S) VISITED:

WEATHER CONDITIONS:

ACCOMODATIONS:

WHAT WAS THE BEST PART OF TODAY?

SPECIAL MEMORIES:

BARTON SPRINGS POOL

A natural spring-fed pool offering crystal clear waters, a perfect place to immerse yourself in nature and rejuvenate your senses.

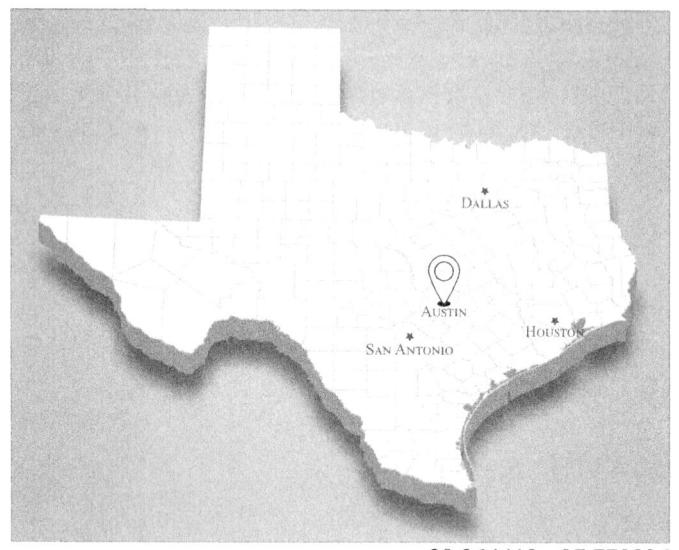

30.264413, -97.770826

WHAT'S ABOUT?:

The Barton Springs Pool in Austin is a natural pool that offers visitors a unique blend of natural beauty and recreational fun.

Located in the heart of Zilker Park, this iconic destination features crystal-clear water at 68-70 degrees Fahrenheit year-round. The water in Barton Springs Pool is at a constant temperature due to the underground spring that feeds it. This water source is constantly at that temperature and replenishes the pool, keeping the water temperature constant.

In addition, the large volume of water in the pool and the surrounding earth's insulating effect help maintain the water temperature, making it the perfect place to escape the heat during the hot Texas summers.

Visitors can enjoy swimming, lounging, and soaking up the sun on the spacious lawn surrounding the pool while enjoying the park's lush greenery.

The natural setting and refreshing water create a peaceful, serene atmosphere that visitors can experience as they dive into the pool, swim and enjoy the scenic surroundings.

So whether you're a local resident looking for a refreshing escape, or a visitor, the Barton Springs Pool offers a unique and unforgettable experience that leaves you feeling relaxed, refreshed, and rejuvenated.

WHERE IS?

The Barton Springs Pool is located in Austin and can be found within Zilker Metropolitan Park at 2201 William Barton Dr, Austin, TX 78746. It is easily accessible by car, with parking near the pool, and is close to public transportation options such as buses and trains.

WHAT'S GOOD/WHAT'S BAD:

This natural spring pool is in the city and has beautiful clean water. Swimming is possible most of the year, and the pool area is great for sunbathing. There are lockers and clean restrooms with a few steps up, and lifeguards are always present. It's a great place to relax and take some photos. A park for jogging and picnicking is a bit farther away, and there are safe parking lots. The spring is stroller-friendly, with plenty of ramps for accessibility. The spring is long and ranges from 3-5 feet, with a deeper section closer to the center with a diving board. I also saw various water vegetation, tadpoles, fish, salamanders, and birds enjoying the spring.

DATE(S) VISITED:

WEATHER CONDITIONS:

ACCOMODATIONS:

WHAT WAS THE BEST PART OF TODAY?

SPECIAL MEMORIES:

LONGHORN CAVERN STATE PARK

Embark on an awe-inspiring adventure into an underground realm, where you can explore the magnificent beauty of the limestone caves.

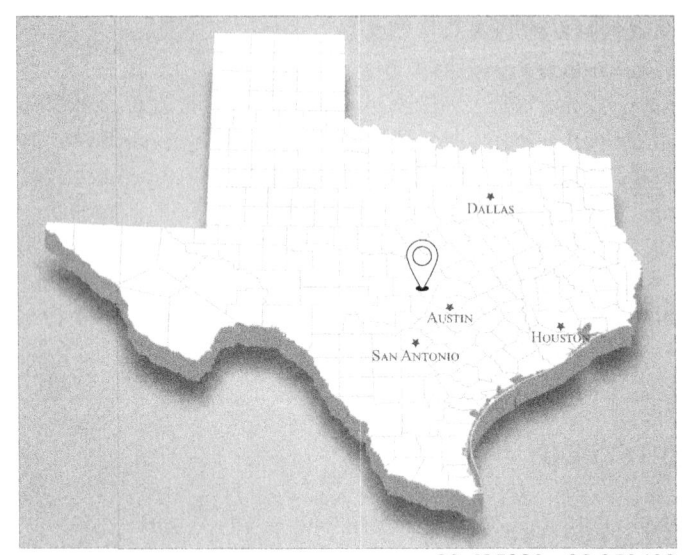

30.685280, -98.350429

WHAT'S ABOUT?:

Longhorn Cavern State Park, located in Burnet, is a unique and fascinating destination that offers visitors a chance to explore the natural beauty and wonder of the Hill Country region. The park is home to a vast and intricate network of caves, formed over millions of years by the slow movement of water through the limestone rock.

Visitors can take guided tours of the caves, which provide an up-close look at the unique geologic formations and diverse ecosystems that inhabit the underground world. Visitors can see many features along the way, including stunning rock formations, underground lakes, and even the remnants of an old Confederate gunpowder factory.

In addition to the cave tours, Longhorn Cavern State Park offers a range of outdoor activities. These include hiking, fishing, and picnicking, making it an excellent destination for anyone looking to enjoy the natural beauty of the Texas Hill Country.

A visit to Longhorn Cavern State Park evokes a sense of awe and wonder. Visitors can explore the incredible natural formations slowly carved out over millions of years. The experience can be both educational and thrilling, as visitors learn about the geology and ecology of the region and gain a deeper appreciation for the wonders of the natural world.

WHERE IS?
The Longhorn Cavern State Park is in Burnet County, specifically at 6211 Park Road 4 S, Burnet, TX 78611, USA.
The park is in the heart of the Texas Hill Country and is easily accessible by car. Visitors can reach the park by taking State Highway 29 or State Highway 281, which connect to major highways in the area.
Longhorn Cavern State Park is approximately an hour's drive from Austin and San Antonio, making it an excellent destination for day trips or weekend getaways. The park provides ample parking for visitors, and several campsites and cabins are available for those who wish to stay overnight.

WHAT'S GOOD/WHAT'S BAD:
This is a must-visit place for anyone who loves caves. Thanks to our guide, I highly recommend the 90-minute cave tour, which was informative and fun. Making reservations in advance is best, especially during the busy season. They also offer gem mining which was a total blast; we found some beautiful gems. I would love to come back one day and do the wild cave tour. The experience was definitely worth the price, so it's not a cheap outing but totally worth it for anyone interested in caves.

DATE(S) VISITED:

WEATHER CONDITIONS:

ACCOMODATIONS:

WHAT WAS THE BEST PART OF TODAY?

SPECIAL MEMORIES:

FOSSIL RIM WILDLIFE CENTER

Embark on a wild and unforgettable journey, explore the habitats of exotic species, and witness some of the world's most fascinating animals up close.

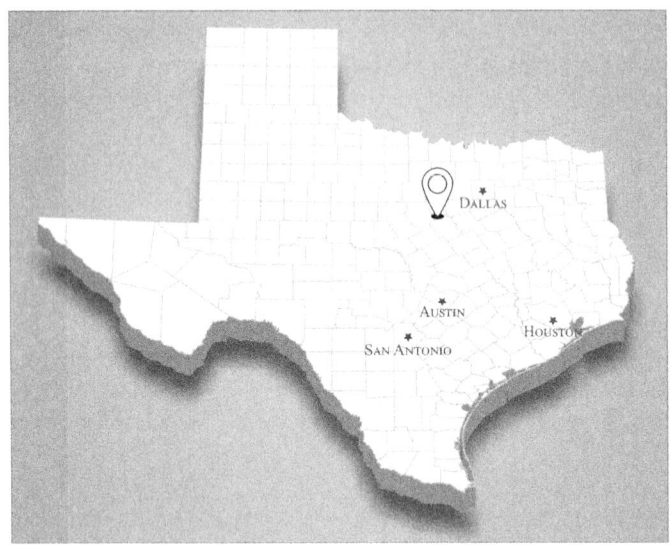

32.180562, -97.796556

WHAT'S ABOUT?:

The Fossil Rim Wildlife Center in Glen Rose is a unique and exciting destination. It offers visitors a chance to get up close and personal with some of the world's most fascinating animals. The park is home to many exotic and endangered species, including cheetahs, giraffes, rhinoceroses, and many others.

Visitors can take guided tours of the park, which provide an up-close look at the animals and their natural habitats. Along the way, visitors can see a wide range of wildlife, including some of the rarest and most fascinating species on the planet.

In addition to the guided tours, Fossil Rim Wildlife Center offers a range of outdoor activities, including hiking, biking, and fishing, making it an excellent destination for anyone looking to explore the natural beauty of the Texas countryside.

A visit to Fossil Rim Wildlife Center can evoke a sense of wonder and amazement as visitors come face-to-face with some of the world's most magnificent creatures. The experience can be both educational and inspiring, as visitors learn about the importance of conservation and gain a deeper appreciation for the diversity and complexity of the natural world.

Overall, a visit to Fossil Rim Wildlife Center is an opportunity to connect with the animal kingdom's beauty and majesty and explore one of Texas's most unique and fascinating destinations.

WHERE IS?
The Fossil Rim Wildlife Center is in Glen Rose, specifically at 2155 County Road 2008, Glen Rose, TX 76043, USA. The park is about an hour's drive southwest of Fort Worth, making it a great destination for day trips or weekend getaways. Visitors can reach the park by taking U.S. Highway 67 or State Highway 144, which connect to major highways in the area. Fossil Rim Wildlife Center is located in a remote part of the Texas countryside, with no public transportation available. Visitors must have their own vehicles to explore the park. However, the park offers a scenic drive-through and several other guided tours, which visitors can take to view the wildlife up close.

WHAT'S GOOD/WHAT'S BAD:
I had an unforgettable experience at Fossil Rim, which was entirely different from my African photo safaris, but in a great way. As the animals are not threatened by humans, they are much more visible, and many will come right up to the vehicle to eat the food provided. Watching two blackbucks headbutting each other for 5 minutes and feeding the giraffes and ostrich were some of my favorite moments. This is an excellent place for families and those curious about animals. Fossil Rim is doing a great job helping endangered species; they take excellent care of the animals and allow them to roam in a familiar habitat.

DATE(S) VISITED:

WEATHER CONDITIONS:

ACCOMODATIONS:

WHAT WAS THE BEST PART OF TODAY?

SPECIAL MEMORIES:

SANTA ELENA CANYON

Discover a breathtaking natural wonder and experience the raw beauty of the Texas landscape in all its glory.

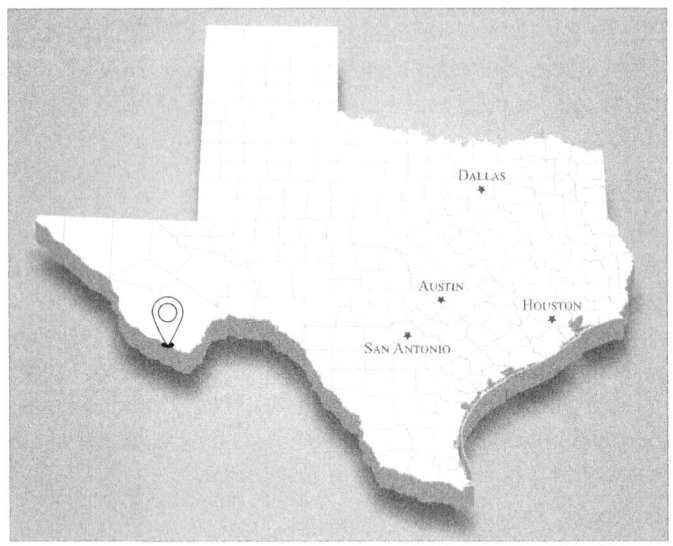

29.167408, -103.610219

WHAT'S ABOUT?:

The Santa Elena Canyon is a stunning natural wonder that attracts visitors from all over the world.

The canyon is part of the Rio Grande, which forms the border between Texas and Mexico. It is known for its towering limestone cliffs and dramatic vistas.

Visitors to the Santa Elena Canyon can hike along the canyon floor or ride a raft down the river, providing a unique and exhilarating perspective on this awe-inspiring landscape. The views from the canyon floor are remarkably breathtaking, with towering cliffs rising up on either side and the river flowing gently below.

In addition to hiking and rafting, the Santa Elena Canyon is also a popular spot for birdwatching, with a wide variety of species found in the area.

Visitors can also explore the nearby hot springs and other natural attractions, which provide a unique and refreshing way to experience the beauty of the Texas wilderness.

Exploring the Santa Elena Canyon is a breathtaking experience that can leave visitors feeling awestruck and peaceful as they are transported to a serene natural wonderland.

The rugged beauty of the Texas landscape is on full display here, with visitors feeling both invigorated and relaxed in the presence of this majestic genuine masterpiece.

WHERE IS?
The Santa Elena Canyon is located in Big Bend National Park in southwest Texas, specifically along the Rio Grande River, which forms the border between the United States and Mexico. The canyon can be reached by car via several routes, including the Ross Maxwell Scenic Drive. The park is about 300 miles southeast of El Paso and about 500 miles west of Houston. Visitors can also reach the park by air. Several nearby airports, including the Midland International Air and Space Port, are about a 3-hour drive from the park. Once inside the park, visitors can access the Santa Elena Canyon by hiking the Santa Elena Canyon Trail, a moderate 1.7-mile round-trip hike providing stunning views of the canyon and the Rio Grande River. Visitors can also access the canyon by rafting down the river, with several local outfitters offering guided rafting trips.

WHAT'S GOOD/WHAT'S BAD:
The view of the Rio Grande cutting through the mountain is absolutely stunning. I made my way down to the river to get a closer look at the canyon, and there's even a hiking trail that takes you higher up for an even better view. However, the trail may not be suitable for those with limited mobility or young children. Also, keep in mind that the heat can be intense during the summer months, so it's essential to bring plenty of water and wear appropriate footwear, such as water shoes or sandals. Otherwise, your feet might get muddy if you wade through the water barefoot and have to put your socks and shoes back on.

DATE(S) VISITED:

WEATHER CONDITIONS:

ACCOMODATIONS:

WHAT WAS THE BEST PART OF TODAY?

SPECIAL MEMORIES:

ROCKPORT BEACH

Escape to a serene beach with soft, powdery sand and crystal-clear, inviting waters perfect for swimming and a range of water activities.

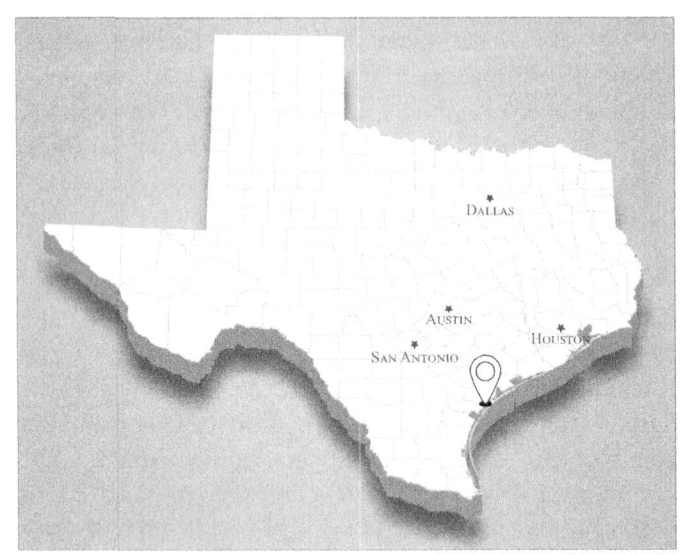

28.026677, -97.046265

WHAT'S ABOUT?:

Rockport Beach in Texas is a picturesque coastal destination located in the charming town of Rockport. Its soft white sand, crystal clear waters, and gentle waves make it a popular spot for swimming, sunbathing, and many water activities.

The beach is approximately 1,250 feet long and 200 feet wide, providing ample space for visitors to relax and enjoy the area's natural beauty. Several covered pavilions, picnic areas, and grills are also available. It is a great spot for a family outing or a day trip with friends.

For those interested in water activities, the beach offers a range of options, including fishing, boating, kayaking, and windsurfing. The calm and gentle waters of the beach make it an ideal spot for beginners. In contrast, more experienced water enthusiasts can use the area's natural beauty to explore and discover the local marine life.

In addition to its natural beauty and recreational opportunities, Rockport Beach has various amenities, including a playground, restrooms, and showers. A beachfront pavilion offers a range of snacks and refreshments, making it easy to spend an entire day at the beach without leaving.

Rockport Beach in Texas is a beautiful and inviting coastal destination that offers visitors a chance to relax, unwind, and enjoy the area's natural beauty. Whether you want to swim, sunbathe, or explore the local marine life, this beach is a great place to do it all.

WHERE IS?
Rockport Beach is located in Rockport, specifically at 320 Navigation Circle, Rockport, TX 78382, USA. It is a small coastal town located on the eastern shore of Aransas Bay in southern Texas. The beach is easily accessible by car, and ample parking is available on-site. The closest major airport for visitors flying into the area is Corpus Christi International Airport, approximately 35 miles south of Rockport. Visitors can rent a car or take a taxi to the beach from the airport.

WHAT'S GOOD/WHAT'S BAD:
I really enjoyed this beach. It's definitely one of my favorites. The water is spotless and shallow, perfect for families with young kids. I arrived early in the morning, so it wasn't too crowded, and I spent most of the day there, having a great time. Parking was close enough that hauling all my beach gear wasn't too tricky. The beach has shaded grassed areas perfect for resting and relaxing from the sun. The water has a gentle wave that won't knock you down, which makes it all the more enjoyable. I think this beach is an excellent value for the price, at just $10 per carload.

DATE(S) VISITED:

WEATHER CONDITIONS:

ACCOMODATIONS:

WHAT WAS THE BEST PART OF TODAY?

SPECIAL MEMORIES:

WHITE ROCK LAKE PARK

An urban oasis boasting crystal-clear waters, scenic trails, and a wide array of recreational activities, a perfect escape for nature lovers and outdoor enthusiasts.

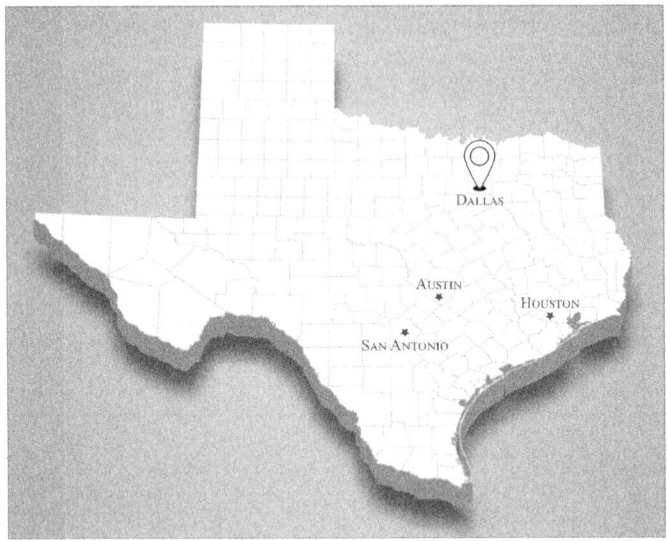

32.840951, -96.715162

WHAT'S ABOUT?:

White Rock Lake Park is a stunning urban oasis in Dallas, providing a peaceful retreat for visitors seeking to escape the hustle and bustle of city life.

The park spans 1,015 acres and features natural landscapes, including sparkling blue waters, rolling hills, and scenic forests.

The park is home to several miles of picturesque walking and biking trails that wind through the woods, offering visitors a chance to explore the park's natural beauty.

White Rock Lake provides ample opportunities for fishing, kayaking, and paddle-boarding, making it a popular destination for water sports enthusiasts.

In addition to its natural splendor, the park is home to several historic landmarks, including the charming Bath House Cultural Center and the White Rock Lake Museum.

The park also hosts various events throughout the year, such as art shows, concerts, and festivals, making it a hub of community activity.

Whether looking for a peaceful place to enjoy a picnic, a serene spot to meditate and reflect, or an exciting outdoor destination, White Rock Lake Park has something to offer everyone.

WHERE IS?
White Rock Lake Park is located in Dallas. It is five miles northeast of downtown Dallas, just off the Northwest Highway. To reach White Rock Lake Park, visitors can take the Northwest Highway and turn onto one of the several roads leading to the park. The park has several parking lots throughout its grounds, with the largest near the Bath House Cultural Center. Alternatively, visitors can take public transportation to White Rock Lake Park. The Dallas Area Rapid Transit (DART) bus service has several stops near the park's entrance, making it easily accessible to those without a car.

WHAT'S GOOD/WHAT'S BAD:
This is an excellent spot for a peaceful time with nature, Southwestern style! It's a safe, pleasant, and relaxing place to spend a few hours walking, picnicking, jogging, or birdwatching while taking in the city skyline in the background. The biking and walking trails are great; worrying about constant oncoming traffic is unnecessary. Keep an eye out for the beautiful white pelicans and the waterfall over the spillway.

DATE(S) VISITED:

WEATHER CONDITIONS:

ACCOMODATIONS:

WHAT WAS THE BEST PART OF TODAY?

SPECIAL MEMORIES:

CASCADE CAVERNS

51 TEXAS

Explore a fascinating underground world filled with rock formations, intricate cave systems, and a rich history of human habitation that spans centuries.

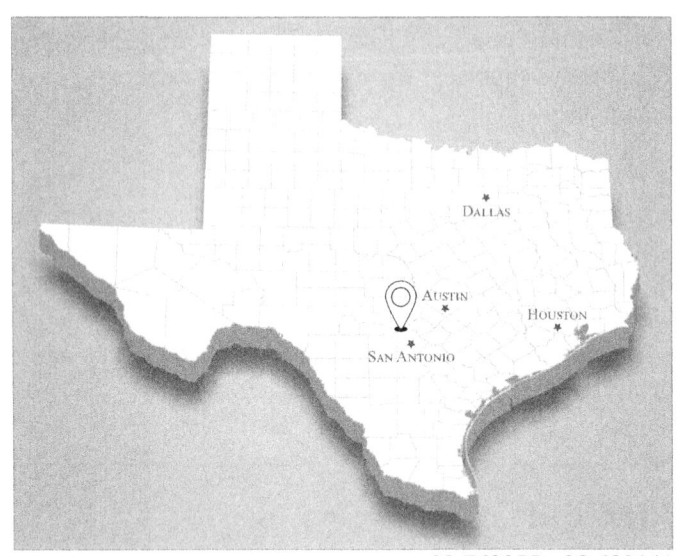

29.763355, -98.680141

WHAT'S ABOUT?:

Cascade Caverns is a remarkable natural wonder in the beautiful Texas Hill Country. This stunning limestone cave system boasts various geological formations, including stalactites, stalagmites, and flowstones, formed over millions of years.

Visitors can embark on a guided tour of the cave system, which winds through a maze of underground chambers and tunnels. The tour provides a chance to explore the intricate formations, learn about the history of the caverns, and discover the unique ecosystem that thrives in this underground world.

The caverns are also home to several wildlife species, including bats, salamanders, and spiders. Visitors can observe them in their natural habitat. Additionally, the cave's underground river system provides a unique setting for visitors to experience a true sense of wonder and awe.

Outside the caverns, the park offers several hiking trails, picnic areas, a gift shop, and a café serving refreshments. The park also hosts annual special events, including concerts, nature walks, and educational programs.

Located just a short drive from San Antonio and Austin, Cascade Caverns is easily accessible. It offers visitors a unique opportunity to experience the natural beauty of the Texas Hill Country. Whether you're a nature lover, an adventure seeker, or simply looking for a peaceful escape, Cascade Caverns is a must-see destination in Texas.

WHERE IS?
Cascade Caverns is located at 226 Cascade Caverns Rd, Boerne, TX 78015, in the Texas Hill Country. It can be reached by car via Interstate 10, and the park offers ample parking for visitors.

Cascade Caverns is about 10 miles west of Boerne and approximately 25 miles northwest of San Antonio. Other nearby cities include Comfort and Kerrville, within a 30-minute drive of the caverns.

WHAT'S GOOD/WHAT'S BAD:
I had a great time visiting this cavern just a few minutes north of San Antonio. The cavern is unique, and it was definitely worth the visit. The admission price was very reasonable, at around $20 per adult. The cave has a fascinating history, interesting formations, and animals. It's an active wet cave, and it was cool to see all the different formations and learn about the different flooding. The tour was only 45 minutes long, and I liked that it was a smaller group. I recommend wearing sneakers or some sole rubber shoes because they can be slippery. The tour guide was informative, and the facilities were well-maintained and clean. It's a quiet park with trails to explore, so it's a perfect spot for a relaxing day out.

DATE(S) VISITED:

WEATHER CONDITIONS:

ACCOMODATIONS:

WHAT WAS THE BEST PART OF TODAY?

SPECIAL MEMORIES:

PEDERNALES FALLS STATE PARK

Discover the natural beauty of cascading waterfalls, sprawling hills, and diverse wildlife that awaits at this picturesque state park.

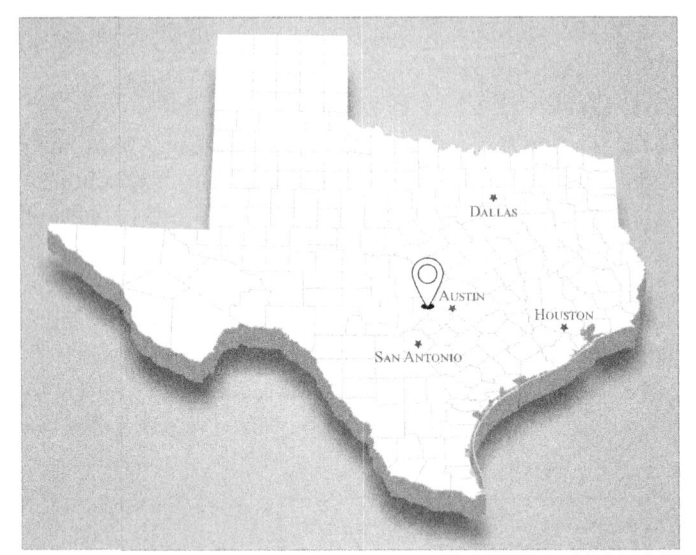

30.307976, -98.257545

WHAT'S ABOUT?:

Pedernales Falls State Park is a natural wonderland waiting to be explored in the heart of the Texas Hill Country.

The park is a popular destination for outdoor enthusiasts, families, and anyone who wants to experience the natural beauty of Texas: it has crystal clear waters, breathtaking scenery, and abundant wildlife,

The park's main attraction is the Pedernales River, which winds through the park and allows visitors to swim, kayak, and fish. The river also flows over cascading waterfalls and rapids, creating a stunning, dramatic landscape perfect for exploring.

Hiking and biking are also popular activities in the park, with miles of trails that wind through the rugged terrain and offer stunning views of the surrounding hills and valleys.

In addition, the park offers picnic areas, nature trails, and bird-watching opportunities for those looking for a more leisurely activity.

With its peaceful and serene surroundings, Pedernales Falls State Park is also a great place to spend a romantic day as a couple. Whether you're taking a stroll along the riverbank, having a picnic under the shade of a tree, or watching the sunset over the hills, the park offers a variety of experiences that are sure to create lasting memories.

WHERE IS?
Pedernales Falls State Park is located in the Texas Hill Country, approximately 30 miles west of Austin. To reach the park from Austin, take US-290 west to Dripping Springs, then turn left onto Ranch Road 12 and follow the signs to the park. The park has a large parking lot with ample space for visitors.

WHAT'S GOOD/WHAT'S BAD:
I absolutely adore this park! It's not only gorgeous but also simple to locate and enter. The trails were clean and clearly marked. I wandered to explore and then sat down to enjoy the scenic view. This park has various natural vegetation areas, waterfalls, and other picturesque natural landscapes. I took many photographs and explored the guided nature trails as well. There is also a bird blind/preserve in the park for bird-watching enthusiasts. I also made the Twin Waterfalls trail, but I wish I had spent more time at the pools. The pools are an absolute wonder to behold! Booking a reservation to visit this State Park online is a breeze. The cost is only $12 per vehicle.

DATE(S) VISITED:

WEATHER CONDITIONS:

ACCOMODATIONS:

WHAT WAS THE BEST PART OF TODAY?

SPECIAL MEMORIES:

SAN FERNANDO CATHEDRAL

The oldest cathedral in Texas, where history, beauty, and spirituality collide in the heart of San Antonio.

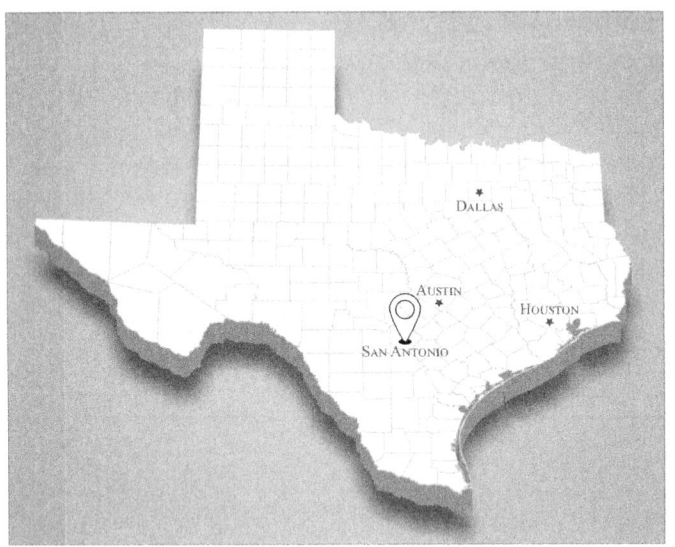

29.424532, -98.493851

WHAT'S ABOUT?:

San Fernando Cathedral, located in the heart of San Antonio, is a historic and beautiful place of worship that has been a part of the city's history for over 250 years. The cathedral was initially built in 1731, making it one of the oldest cathedrals in the United States. Despite several renovations over the centuries, the cathedral has maintained its original Spanish colonial architecture and charm.

The cathedral's most notable feature is its twin bell towers, adorned with intricate carvings and sculptures. The cathedral's interior is just as impressive, featuring beautiful stained glass windows, elaborate wooden altars, and stunning frescoes. One of the most unique features of the cathedral is its open-air atrium, which allows natural light to filter into the building, creating a peaceful and serene atmosphere.

In addition to its architectural and aesthetic beauty, San Fernando Cathedral also holds significant historical and cultural value. It was the site of several key events during the Texas Revolution, including the Battle of the Alamo. It has been an important religious center for the city's Catholic community for centuries. The cathedral is also home to several important artifacts and relics, including the remains of several of San Antonio's early Catholic bishops.

Visitors to San Fernando Cathedral can take guided tours of the building, attend Mass, or admire this important landmark's beautiful architecture and rich history.

WHERE IS?

San Fernando Cathedral is located in the heart of downtown San Antonio, Texas. It is easily accessible by car, bus, or foot from many of the city's popular attractions. To reach the cathedral by car, take I-37 South or I-10 West to downtown San Antonio and look for parking in the surrounding area. Public transportation is also available, with bus stops near the cathedral on several major routes. To reach the cathedral on foot, explore the charming streets of downtown San Antonio and look for the towering spires of the cathedral, which are visible from many locations throughout the city.

WHAT'S GOOD/WHAT'S BAD:

This is a magnificent piece of history. Despite the facade undergoing renovation, the church is open to visitors. The church has a beautiful and simple design. However, unlike the more ornate style on the East Coast, the main altar and statues have a very elaborate Spanish look. The architecture is similar to the churches in Spain, France, and Prague. The craftsmanship is impressive, with stunning ceilings and arches. The interior is well-kept and beautiful, providing a quiet place to connect with one's soul. The gift shop is also lovely and includes a section on the history of the Cathedral. The Cathedral has a stunning statue of the Assumption, among other notable features. They offer confession seven days a week for almost two hours each day. If Father Carlos presides over your mass, you'll be overjoyed to listen to him sing. The square in front of the Cathedral is also very friendly, and overall it's a fantastic experience.

DATE(S) VISITED:

WEATHER CONDITIONS:

ACCOMODATIONS:

WHAT WAS THE BEST PART OF TODAY?

SPECIAL MEMORIES:

SAN ANTONIO MISSIONS NATIONAL HISTORICAL PARK

54 TEXAS

Discover the rich history of Spanish colonial missions, and learn about the indigenous culture in these UNESCO World Heritage sites.

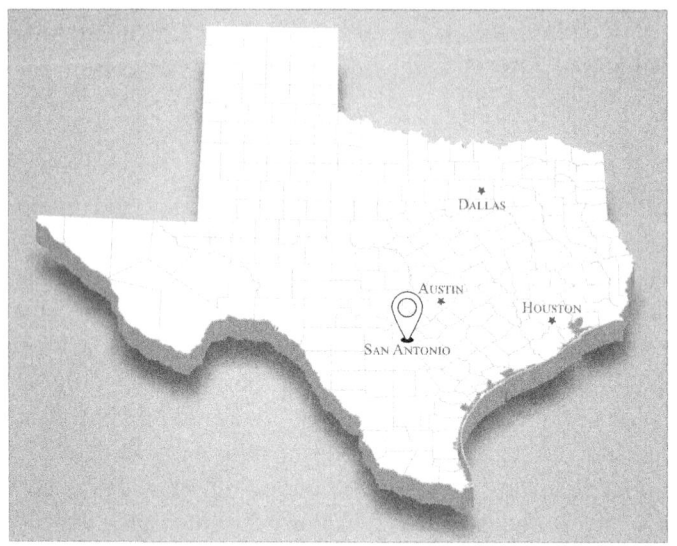

29.360183, -98.480125

WHAT'S ABOUT?:

San Antonio Missions National Historical Park is a unique park in San Antonio that provides a glimpse into the Spanish colonial era.

The park is comprised of four of the five Spanish missions built in the area between the late 1700s and early 1800s. The missions were made to spread Christianity to the native populations and used as military outposts and agricultural centers.

The four missions that make up the park are Mission Concepción, Mission San Juan Capistrano, Mission San José, and Mission Espada. Alamo, the fifth and best-known of the missions, is not part of the park. Each mission has its own distinct history, architecture, and cultural significance, providing visitors with an opportunity to learn about the Spanish colonial period in Texas.

Visitors can take self-guided tours of the missions and learn about their history through exhibits, audio tours, and ranger-led programs.

The park is also home to the famous River Walk, a network of walkways along the San Antonio River, which provides a scenic and leisurely way to explore the city.

The park is famous for tourists, school groups, and history buffs. It offers a unique cultural experience that is not found anywhere else.

WHERE IS?
San Antonio Missions National Historical Park is located in south central Texas and can be reached by car or public transportation. The park is a few miles south of downtown San Antonio and is easily accessible from I-37. Visitors can park in the designated areas and take a short walk to the missions.

WHAT'S GOOD/WHAT'S BAD:
When I was in San Antonio, I visited all 5 missions, which was a must-see experience. The Alamo is located downtown, and the others are just a short drive away. Additionally, a cycling trail leads to them by the river. I was able to visit all the missions for free, with one of them having a visitor center and a theatre that provides more information. Each mission had restrooms and drinking water, and plenty of car parking. I was fascinated by their unique history and how each mission focused on something different. My favorite was Mission Espada, where I found the handmade mats super cool, and the ranger was fantastic! While it may not be the ideal destination for families with young children, the missions offer a great educational opportunity for those interested in history and cultural heritage.

DATE(S) VISITED:

WEATHER CONDITIONS:

ACCOMODATIONS:

WHAT WAS THE BEST PART OF TODAY?

SPECIAL MEMORIES:

GOLIAD STATE PARK & HISTORIC SITE

Experience history and nature intertwined, where stunning landscapes and rich historical landmarks await your discovery in the heart of Texas.

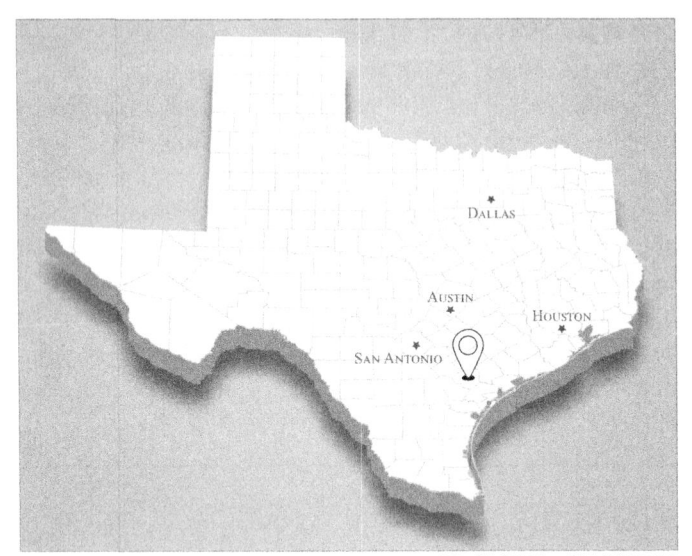

28.656559, -97.385239

WHAT'S ABOUT?:

Goliad State Park & Historic Site is in the small town of Goliad. It is a historic park that offers visitors a chance to explore the rich history of Texas.

Goliad was the site of a critical battle in the Texas Revolution, known as the Battle of Coleto Creek, which took place in 1836. The Goliad Massacre, in which 342 Texas prisoners of war were executed by Mexican troops, also occurred in 1836.

The site includes two missions, Mission Espiritu Santo and Presidio La Bahia, established in the early 1700s.

The Presidio La Bahía, a Spanish fort that was built in 1749 and played a significant role in the Texas Revolution.

The reconstructed mission church at Mission Espiritu Santo serves as a museum, showcasing artifacts and exhibits related to the history of the mission and the surrounding area.

Visitors can also explore the beautifully landscaped grounds, picnic areas, and nature trails. The park provides an excellent opportunity for visitors to learn about Texas history and culture and enjoy outdoor activities such as hiking, bird watching, and picnicking. The park also offers ranger-led tours, educational programs, and annual special events.

The site is also home to a large pecan grove, one of the largest in Texas. It provides a habitat for a variety of wildlife, including many species of birds.

WHERE IS?
Goliad State Park & Historic Site is located in Goliad County. It is approximately 121 miles southeast of San Antonio and 87 miles northeast of Corpus Christi. To reach the park, take US 183 to Goliad and follow the signs to the park located at 108 Park Road 6, Goliad, TX 77963.

WHAT'S GOOD/WHAT'S BAD:
During my visit to this park, I was drawn to its rich history. It costs $4 for adult admission, while children aged 12 and under get in for free. Mission Espiritu Santo was the highlight of my visit, with its intriguing exhibits that depict the life of the Spanish missions. I especially appreciated the mural displayed in the museum, which provided insight into the various communities that inhabited the area. The park boasts numerous trails that are ideal for hiking, a well-maintained campground, and canoe trails. It's worth checking out the gift shop in the ranger headquarters, where I found reasonably-priced items. Additionally, the park rangers were approachable and helpful in answering my questions.

DATE(S) VISITED:

WEATHER CONDITIONS:

ACCOMODATIONS:

WHAT WAS THE BEST PART OF TODAY?

SPECIAL MEMORIES:

SAN JACINTO MONUMENT

A Monument symbol of Texas independence and home to the iconic "Star of Texas" observation deck offering breathtaking views of the surrounding area.

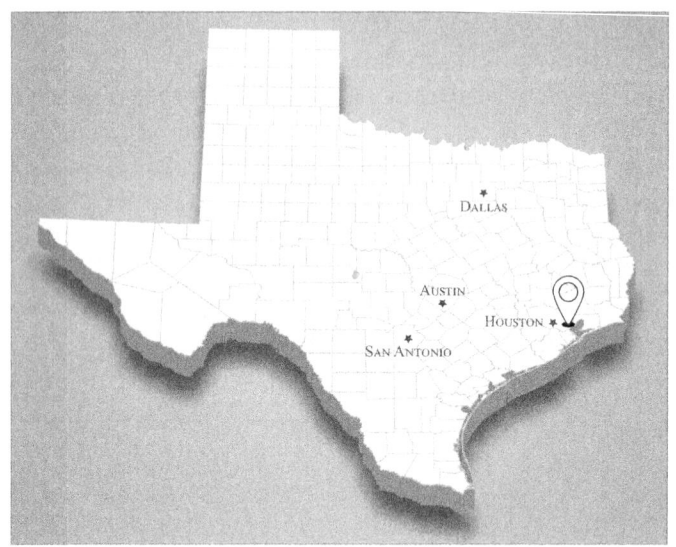

29.750655, -95.080136

WHAT'S ABOUT?:

The San Jacinto Monument is a 570-foot tall obelisk that serves as a memorial to the Battle of San Jacinto, fought on April 21, 1836. The battle was the decisive engagement of the Texas Revolution. It resulted in the independence of the Republic of Texas from Mexico.

The monument, dedicated in 1939, is located on the grounds of the San Jacinto Battleground State Historic Site in La Porte, Texas, and is the tallest stone column monument in the world. Visitors can take an elevator to the top of the memorial for panoramic views of the surrounding area. The site also features exhibits and interactive displays about the history of the battle and the Texas Revolution. Additionally, the site includes the San Jacinto Museum of History, which features a variety of artifacts, paintings, and maps related to the battle and the broader history of Texas.

The monument also houses a Texans' Hall of Fame, recognizing essential figures in the state's history.

In 1984, the San Jacinto Battleground State Historic Site was designated a National Historic Landmark.

Visitors to the monument can learn about the history of Texas, and its fight for independence and view exhibits about the battle, its participants, and the state's early history.

WHERE IS?
The San Jacinto Monument is located in La Porte, near Houston. It can be reached by taking I-10 east from Houston to the exit for Battleground Road. Turn right onto Battleground Road and continue straight until you reach the entrance to the San Jacinto Battleground State Historic Site, where the monument is located. Visitors can park in the lot, take a shuttle to the monument, or walk up the 589 steps to the observation deck.

WHAT'S GOOD/WHAT'S BAD:
I stumbled upon a hidden historical gem I didn't know existed until I saw the exit sign. The monument is taller and more impressive than the Washington Memorial, and its engineering project and design elements are of a far more complex nature. The monument has a small museum at its base that is not a world-class collection, but it is good enough. The 200-ton limestone star at the top of the monument is most impressive and displays a five-sided star that can be viewed cleanly from every angle. The site is beautiful; it has many Oak Trees and a beautiful reflection pool. The history of the 20-minute battle that created Texas is fascinating. A short film is available to fill in some of the historical details.

DATE(S) VISITED:

WEATHER CONDITIONS:

ACCOMODATIONS:

WHAT WAS THE BEST PART OF TODAY?

SPECIAL MEMORIES:

USS LEXINGTON IN CORPUS CHRISTI

★ 57 TEXAS

A floating piece of history that offers visitors an unforgettable experience as they explore the decks of one of America's longest-serving aircraft carriers.

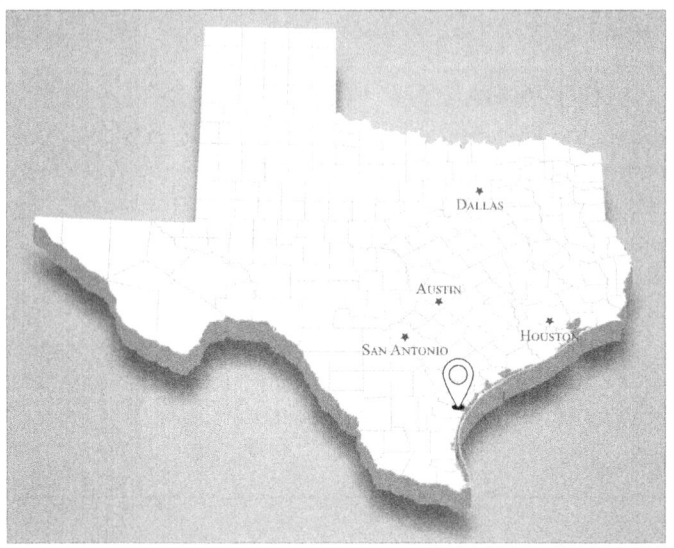

27.816333, -97.390410

WHAT'S ABOUT?:

The USS Lexington is a museum ship and former aircraft carrier. Commissioned in 1943, the USS Lexington served in World War II, the Korean War, and the Vietnam War. It was decommissioned in 1991 and became a museum ship in 1992. The USS Lexington Museum on the Bay is a floating museum showcasing the ship's history and its role in American military history. Visitors can tour the ship and see exhibits that display the history of naval aviation and the life of sailors on board. In addition, the ship features several restored aircraft and a flight simulator that allows visitors to experience what it was like to be a pilot on the USS Lexington. The museum also features educational programs, interactive exhibits, and annual special events. The USS Lexington is said to be haunted by the spirits of former crew members due to many stories of strange and unexplained events that have taken place onboard. Some people believe that the ghosts of the fallen crew members remain on the ship because they cannot complete their mission. Or because they died suddenly and unexpectedly. There have been reports of ghostly sightings and eerie sounds (such as footsteps and unexplained noises) which are said to be the ghosts of the crew members. Whether the ghosts really haunt the USS Lexington is a matter of personal belief. Still, the stories and legends surrounding the ship have added to its fascination.Whether you're a history buff, a military enthusiast, or simply looking for a unique experience, visiting the USS Lexington Museum on the Bay is a must-see attraction in Corpus Christi.

WHERE IS?
The USS Lexington Museum on the Bay is in Corpus Christi at 2914 N Shoreline Blvd. It is easily accessible by car and off US Highway 181, near downtown Corpus Christi. The Corpus Christi International Airport also serves the museum, with various transportation options available to reach the museum from the airport.

WHAT'S GOOD/WHAT'S BAD:
I had an incredible time visiting the USS Lexington, a World War II aircraft carrier with a vast collection of vintage airplanes on display on the flight deck. The information signs by each plane were very informative. In addition, they provided details about aerial combat missions that each type of plane accomplished, making it an educational experience. I was also impressed that the site was handicap accessible, and I enjoyed seeing older veterans able to visit and appreciate the museum. Overall, it's a one-of-a-kind attraction that I highly recommend visiting.

DATE(S) VISITED:

WEATHER CONDITIONS:

ACCOMODATIONS:

WHAT WAS THE BEST PART OF TODAY?

SPECIAL MEMORIES:

MCNAY ART MUSEUM

Experience an exquisite collection of art in a stunning Spanish colonial revival mansion with lush gardens in Texas.

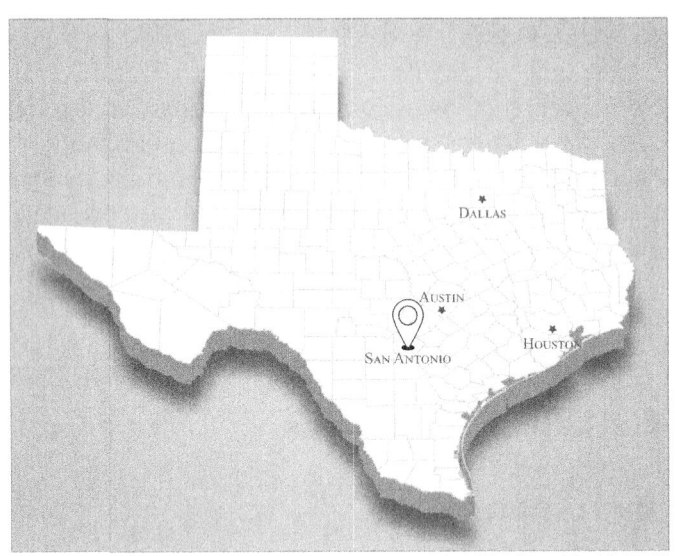

29.485365, -98.456251

WHAT'S ABOUT?:

The McNay Art Museum in San Antonio is a must-visit for art lovers. It is interesting from a historical point of view because it was founded in 1954 by Marion Koogler McNay. She was an artist and art teacher who bequeathed her Spanish Colonial Revival-style mansion and collection of 700 art objects to create the museum. The mansion itself, called the Spanish Colonial Revival-style mansion, was built in 1926 and is considered a historical landmark. The museum has since expanded to include additional galleries and buildings.

This Museum has an extensive collection of over 24.000 art objects that span over 5.000 years - from ancient Egypt to medieval Europe and contemporary art. It also has a significant collection of Latin American art, which includes paintings, sculptures, and folk art. It is renowned for its impressive 19th and 20th-century European and American art collection, featuring works by influential artists such as Picasso, Matisse, and O'Keeffe. In addition to the permanent collection, the museum hosts several temporary exhibitions each year, showcasing the works of contemporary artists worldwide. Visitors can enjoy the outdoor sculpture garden, featuring modern and contemporary sculptures nestled among native Texas landscaping. The museum also offers a range of educational programs, including lectures, gallery talks, and workshops, making it an excellent destination for art enthusiasts of all levels. With its diverse collection, stunning architecture, and tranquil setting, the museum offers visitors a unique and unforgettable experience.

WHERE IS?
The McNay Art Museum is in San Antonio at 6000 North New Braunfels Avenue. It is situated in the heart of Alamo Heights and can be easily reached by car or public transportation. If you are driving, ample parking is available at the museum, with both surface lots and parking garages. Additionally, the museum is accessible by bus, with several routes stopping nearby. Visitors can also take a taxi or ride-sharing service to the museum.

WHAT'S GOOD/WHAT'S BAD:
The art museum is a wonderful place to visit in San Antonio, as it boasts a beautiful space filled with rich artwork from celebrated artists. I believe it's one of the most impressive art museums in the Southwest, with a collection mostly from 1800 onwards that is worth exploring. If you're planning a trip to San Antonio, I highly recommend adding this museum to your list if you're an art lover. The admission fee of $20 is reasonable, the staff is friendly, and parking is easy. You're guaranteed an enjoyable couple of hours exploring the art collection as an adult. However, I should mention that this isn't a recommended activity for children. However, the museum does offer some kid-friendly activities, which I would suggest calling in advance to check availability.

DATE(S) VISITED:

WEATHER CONDITIONS:

ACCOMODATIONS:

WHAT WAS THE BEST PART OF TODAY?

SPECIAL MEMORIES:

LYNDON B. JOHNSON NATIONAL HISTORICAL PARK

A unique glimpse into the life and legacy of the 36th President of the United States.

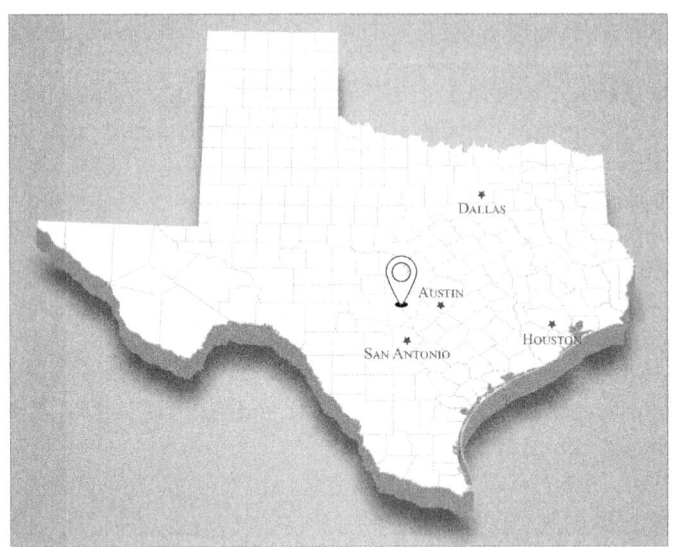

30.243315, -98.606121

WHAT'S ABOUT?:

The Lyndon B. Johnson National Historical Park is near Johnson City in the Texas Hill Country. The park preserves the birthplace, boyhood home, and ranch of the 36th President of the United States, Lyndon B. Johnson.

Visitors can explore the various structures on the site, including the historic Texas White House, where President Johnson conducted much of his presidency. They can also see exhibits and artifacts that glimpse his life and presidency.

He is remembered for passing sweeping civil rights legislation, including the Civil Rights Act of 1964 and the Voting Rights Act of 1965, which helped to end racial segregation in the United States.

Johnson was known for his larger-than-life personality, love of the outdoors and Texas, and passion for politics. He was nicknamed "LBJ" and "The Master of the Senate" and is remembered as one of the most influential American Presidents of the 20th century.

The park also features nature walks and wildlife viewing opportunities, and a visitors center with a museum that provides a comprehensive look at Johnson's life and legacy. So, whether you're a history buff, a fan of the 36th President, or interested in the beauty of the Texas Hill Country, the Lyndon B. Johnson National Historical Park is a must-visit destination.

WHERE IS?
The Lyndon B. Johnson National Historical Park is in Stonewall near Johnson City. The park can be reached by driving from Austin or San Antonio, located about 50 miles west of Austin and about 70 miles north of San Antonio. The park is open from 9:00 a.m. to 5:00 p.m. except for Christmas Day. Visitors can take a self-guided tour of the park, which includes the birthplace, boyhood home, and ranch of Lyndon B. Johnson, as well as the Johnson family cemetery. The park also features exhibits, a film, and a bookstore; ranger-led tours are available.

WHAT'S GOOD/WHAT'S BAD:
I had the chance to visit the LBJ Ranch near Johnson City, Texas, and it was quite an experience. I found a gift shop and restrooms in the parking lot when I arrived. The park is extensive, and visitors can take their own cars on a self-guided tour. One of the park's highlights is the museum near the primary residence. The museum showcases a film about the president and the Air Force 1 1/2 jet he used to travel from the nearest major airports to the ranch. It was evident that LBJ had a special affection for the Hill Country, and this park provides an insight into his life. The only regret is that visitors are not allowed to tour the house.

DATE(S) VISITED:

WEATHER CONDITIONS:

ACCOMODATIONS:

WHAT WAS THE BEST PART OF TODAY?

SPECIAL MEMORIES:

BOB BULLOCK TEXAS HISTORY MUSEUM

A must-visit destination for history buffs and curious visitors, offering a comprehensive look at the rich cultural heritage of the Lone Star State.

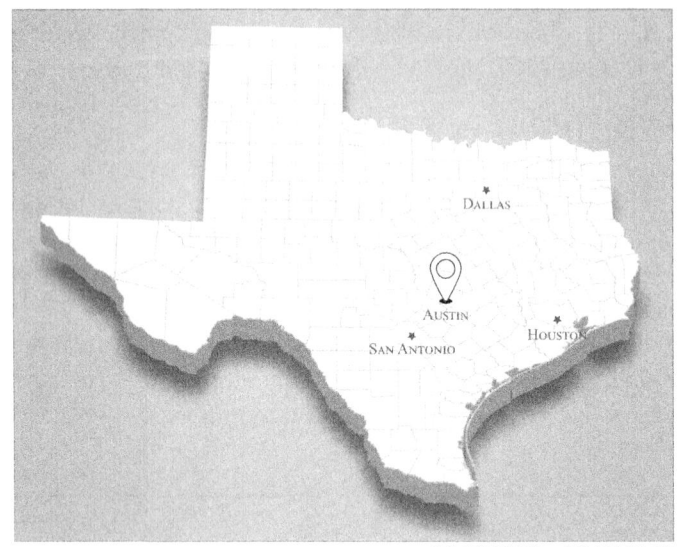

30.280209, -97.738353

WHAT'S ABOUT?:

The Bob Bullock Texas History Museum is located in Austin, showcasing Texas's rich and diverse history. This museum is dedicated to providing visitors with an interactive and educational experience about Lone Star State.

It was opened in 2001 and is named after the late Lieutenant Governor Bob Bullock, who played a significant role in Texas politics and was passionate about preserving the state's history.

The museum features three floors of exhibits that span from the indigenous people of Texas to the present day.

Visitors learn about the state's early days as a Spanish colony, its fight for independence from Mexico, and its journey to becoming one of the largest and most economically prosperous states in the United States. The museum also explores Texas' unique culture and contributions to the nation, including its music, food, and oil industry.

Visitors can explore interactive exhibits, view historical artifacts and documents, watch films, and participate in educational programs and events.

The museum also boasts a large theater that screens films that explore different aspects of Texas history and culture.

The Bob Bullock Texas History Museum is a must-visit destination for those interested in learning about Texas history and culture.

WHERE IS?
The Bob Bullock Texas State History Museum is at 1800 North Congress Avenue in Austin. It is easily reachable by car, with ample parking available, and is also accessible by public transportation, with several bus routes stopping near the museum.

WHAT'S GOOD/WHAT'S BAD:
I found the Texas history museum an exceptional place to gain a quick and thorough understanding of the state's history. I was fascinated by the artifacts on display, such as the ship. Several informative videos and an IMAX theater were available. In addition, the volunteers there were very welcoming and knowledgeable. One can learn about the state's past, values, and importance to various industries in just two hours. Of course, one could also spend an entire day exploring all the details. Overall, the museum is a fantastic representation of Texas's past and present. Moreover, it is located conveniently with a parking garage under the building.

DATE(S) VISITED:

WEATHER CONDITIONS:

ACCOMODATIONS:

WHAT WAS THE BEST PART OF TODAY?

SPECIAL MEMORIES:

⭐ PRESIDENT GEORGE H. W. BUSH MUSEUM IN COLLEGE STATION

A fascinating destination that showcases the life and legacy of the 41st President of the United States.

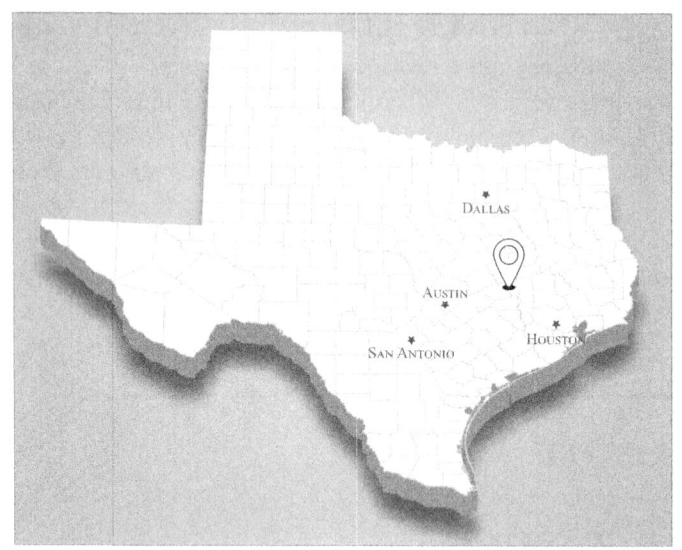

30.595975, -96.354354

WHAT'S ABOUT?:

The George H.W. Bush Presidential Library and Museum, also known as the President George H. W. Bush Museum, is located in College Station and serves as a testament to the legacy of the 41st President of the United States, George H. W. Bush.

The museum traces President Bush's life and career, from his time as a naval aviator to his service in Congress and then his presidency from 1989 to 1993.

George H. W. Bush was a World War II veteran and the youngest aviator in the US Navy at 18. He served as the Central Intelligence Agency (CIA) director before being elected Vice President under Ronald Reagan.

During his presidency, he signed the Americans with Disabilities Act into law, which provided protection for people with disabilities.

After leaving office, President Bush continued to be active in public life, including leading relief efforts following the 2004 Indian Ocean tsunami.

The museum features interactive exhibits, archives, and a replica of the Oval Office. Visitors can also view artifacts and personal items belonging to President Bush and learn about his policies and initiatives. The museum is operated by the National Archives and Records Administration.

It is a must-visit destination for history buffs, political enthusiasts, and anyone interested in learning more about the life and legacy of President George H. W. Bush.

WHERE IS?
The George H.W. Bush Presidential Library and Museum is located on the campus of Texas A&M University in College Station, Texas. It can be reached by car via TX-6 and is also accessible by the Brazos Valley Transit Authority bus system.

WHAT'S GOOD/WHAT'S BAD:
I had a great time visiting the presidential museum and learned a lot of things about the president that I didn't know. The exhibit on presidential humor was fantastic, and I appreciated President Bush's stance on the importance of humor in leadership. The displays were easy to follow and provided a lot of information. I was impressed with how well-done the whole museum was, especially the sections on 9/11. The prices were reasonable, but keep in mind that you need to pay for parking on campus. The staff was all very informative and willing to answer questions, and there were some great interactive rooms. I'd say this museum is easily a three-hour visit!

DATE(S) VISITED:

WEATHER CONDITIONS:

ACCOMODATIONS:

WHAT WAS THE BEST PART OF TODAY?

SPECIAL MEMORIES:

NATIONAL MUSEUM OF THE PACIFIC WAR

A fascinating glimpse into the history of the Pacific War, with engaging exhibits and displays that explore the complexities of this pivotal conflict.

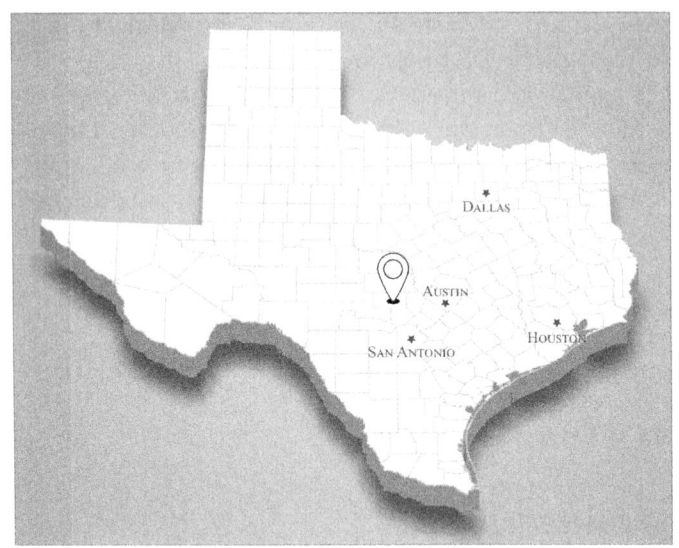

30.273530, -98.867877

WHAT'S ABOUT?:

The National Museum of the Pacific War in Fredericksburg is a world-class museum dedicated to preserving and sharing the history of the Pacific Theater during World War II. The museum features an extensive collection of artifacts, photographs, and interactive exhibits that tell the stories of the men and women who fought and served during this pivotal time in world history. The museum is housed in a stunning, multi-building complex that spans six acres in the heart of historic Fredericksburg. Visitors can explore indoor and outdoor exhibits that bring to life the battles, strategies, and technologies of the Pacific War. The complex includes the George H.W. Bush Gallery, which features interactive exhibits on the causes and consequences of the war, as well as exhibits on the battles of Pearl Harbor, Guadalcanal, and Okinawa. The gallery also includes an authentic Japanese mini-submarine and a U.S. Navy PT boat that was used in combat. Other exhibits at the museum include a re-creation of a Pacific island battlefield, complete with bunkers, pillboxes, and a landing craft. There is also a vast collection of military aircraft, tanks, and artillery, including a fully restored F4U Corsair fighter plane and a replica of the atomic bomb dropped on Nagasaki. The museum also hosts special events and educational programs throughout the year, including lectures, workshops, and guided tours. Whether you're a history buff or simply interested in learning more about the sacrifices and bravery of the men and women who fought in World War II, this is a must-visit destination in Texas.

WHERE IS?
The National Museum of the Pacific War is at 305 East Austin Street, Fredericksburg, TX 78624. The museum can be reached by car, located on the main road through town. The nearest major airport is San Antonio International Airport, about an hour and a half drive from Fredericksburg. Visitors can also take a shuttle or rent a car from the airport to the museum.

WHAT'S GOOD/WHAT'S BAD:
In my opinion, this is one of the most excellent museums I have ever visited. It's meticulously organized, and there's so much information that you could spend days exploring it. The staff was amiable and informative as well. I particularly enjoyed the submarine and airplane exhibits featuring illuminating light and audio. I've visited the museum three times, and each time has been an excellent experience. It's impossible to fully appreciate everything the museum offers in a single day, so I was happy to discover that tickets are valid for two days. The museum covers 33,000 square feet and presents exciting, informative, inspiring stories, artifacts, pictures, and movies about this historic event in American history. The admission price was more than reasonable, and discounts were available for teachers, seniors, and veterans, which is lovely.

DATE(S) VISITED:

WEATHER CONDITIONS:

ACCOMODATIONS:

WHAT WAS THE BEST PART OF TODAY?

SPECIAL MEMORIES:

LBJ PRESIDENTIAL LIBRARY

A fascinating place that offers a unique window into the life and legacy of President L. B. Johnson, showcasing his impact on American history and politics.

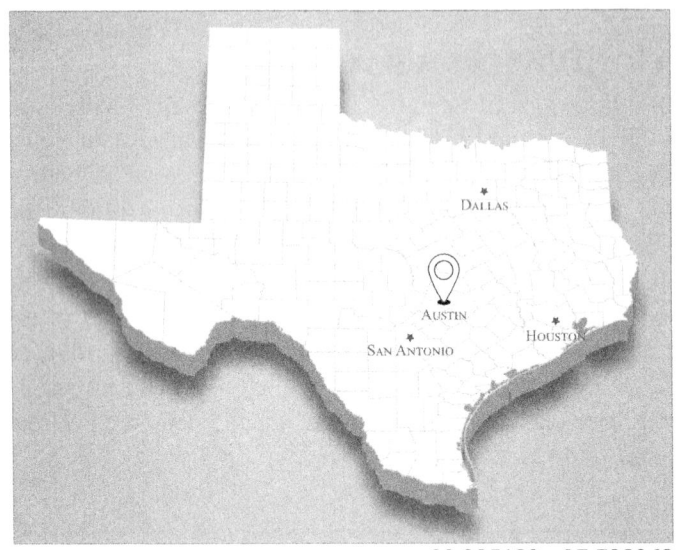

30.285182, -97.728368

WHAT'S ABOUT?:

The LBJ Presidential Library, located in Austin, is a museum dedicated to the presidency and life of 36th U.S. President Lyndon B. Johnson.

Visitors can explore the library's extensive archives and exhibits, including a replica of the Oval Office, artifacts from Johnson's time in office, and multimedia displays that bring the history of the 1960s to life.

In addition, through interactive exhibits, visitors can learn about Johnson's domestic and foreign policies, including the Civil Rights Act, the War on Poverty, and the Vietnam War.

The library also features exhibits on Johnson's wife, Lady Bird Johnson, and their family.

Also, it has a beautiful outdoor area, including a peaceful pond and a reflecting pool, which provides a relaxing place to reflect and learn more about the history of the United States.

Emotional experiences to be had at the LBJ Presidential Library include a sense of patriotism, as well as empathy for the challenges faced by President Johnson during his time in office.

The LBJ Presidential Library is a fascinating educational destination offering a unique perspective on a pivotal moment in American history.

WHERE IS?
The LBJ Presidential Library is at 2313 Red River St, Austin, TX 78705. It is located on the University of Texas at Austin campus, in the heart of Austin. The Library is accessible by car and public transportation. A paid parking lot is on-site, and the building is also served by several Austin public transportation routes. The nearest Capital MetroRail station is UT Station, approximately a 10-minute walk from the Library.

WHAT'S GOOD/WHAT'S BAD:
This museum was an excellent experience for me. I learned much about President LBJ and his life from the various exhibits, photos, and videos on display. The three floors of exhibits included a replica of his Oval Office and many artifacts from his presidency. I also enjoyed watching short films that further enriched my understanding of his presidency. The entrance fee was nominal, and the museum was worth a visit. You can only pay with credit cards for admission; free parking is available. Don't miss this museum if you're in the area. It provides a beautiful experience and a new perspective on President Johnson's life.

DATE(S) VISITED:

WEATHER CONDITIONS:

ACCOMODATIONS:

WHAT WAS THE BEST PART OF TODAY?

SPECIAL MEMORIES:

DEALEY PLAZA NATIONAL HISTORIC LANDMARK DISTRICT

Experience a powerful journey, step into American history, and explore the legacy of President Kennedy at this thought-provoking historical site.

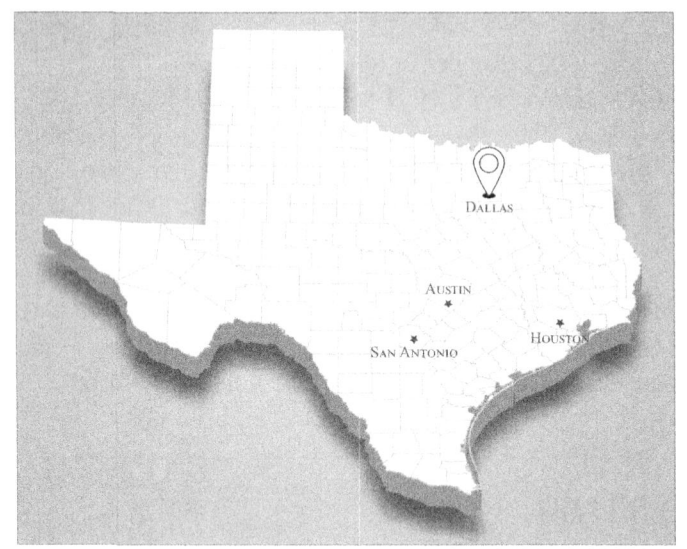

32.778705, -96.808016

WHAT'S ABOUT?:

The Dealey Plaza National Historic Landmark District, located in downtown Dallas, is a historic site that holds an important place in American history. The area was the site of the assassination of President John F. Kennedy on November 22, 1963, and is now a memorial to his life and legacy.

Visitors can explore the site's many historic buildings and monuments, including the Texas School Book Depository building, the Sixth Floor Museum, and the John F. Kennedy Memorial Plaza. The Sixth Floor Museum provides an in-depth look at the assassination, including a comprehensive exhibit that covers the events leading up to the assassination, the investigation, and the legacy of President Kennedy.

In addition to the museum, visitors can explore the surrounding area, including the grassy knoll and the nearby memorial plaza, which features a large white monument dedicated to President Kennedy.

A visit to the Dealey Plaza National Historic Landmark District can evoke emotions, from contemplation and sadness to awe and admiration. The site serves as a reminder of the fragility of life and the importance of preserving the memory of those who have had a significant impact on our world.

A visit to the Dealey Plaza National Historic Landmark District is an opportunity to explore a significant moment in American history. Also, to pay tribute to President Kennedy and to reflect on the events that have shaped our country.

WHERE IS?
The Dealey Plaza National Historic Landmark District is in downtown Dallas, specifically at 500 Main St, Dallas, TX 75202, USA. The site is easily accessible by car, bus, or train and is located near several major highways, including I-35E and I-30. Paid parking is available nearby, and visitors can also use public transportation, with several bus routes and light rail stations serving the area. The Dealey Plaza National Historic Landmark District is near several other historical and cultural attractions, including the Dallas Museum of Art, the Perot Museum of Nature and Science, and the Nasher Sculpture Center. It is a great destination for anyone interested in exploring the city's rich cultural offerings.

WHAT'S GOOD/WHAT'S BAD:
I was not disappointed by the experience of visiting Dealey Plaza. As soon as I arrived, I recognized the area from the historical photos, which was a strange and eerie feeling. Surprisingly, the plaza looks the same as on that fateful November 1963. I saw the Texas book depository, the plinth from where Zapruder filmed the motorcade, the slow turn from Houston onto Elm Street, the grassy knoll, the picket fence, the rail yards, and the triple underpass. All frozen in time. Ironically, although there isn't much to see, there's much to contemplate, study, evaluate, and consider. Dealey Plaza is a unique location, and its infamy is due to an incident that lasted only a few seconds. Yet, its consequences have reverberated to this day.

DATE(S) VISITED:

WEATHER CONDITIONS:

ACCOMODATIONS:

WHAT WAS THE BEST PART OF TODAY?

SPECIAL MEMORIES:

TOP O'HILL TERRACE

Step back in time and explore the mystery and intrigue of a once-secret Prohibition-era casino in the heart of Texas.

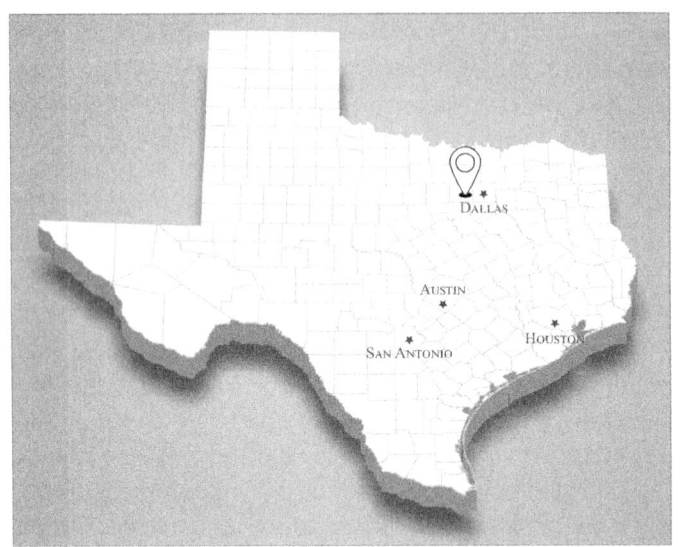

32.736101, -97.156507

WHAT'S ABOUT?:

The Top O'Hill Terrace in Arlington is a historic and fascinating destination that offers visitors a glimpse into the glamour and intrigue of the 1920s and 30s.

The area was once a famous casino and nightclub, frequented by Hollywood stars and other notable figures of the time, and has since been transformed into a beautiful and unique cultural attraction.

Visitors to Top O'Hill Terrace can take guided tours of the historic buildings and grounds, which provide an up-close look at the art and architecture of the time and the colorful history of the area. Along the way, visitors can see many features, including beautiful gardens, fountains, and other unique features.

In addition to the guided tours, Top O'Hill Terrace offers a range of outdoor activities, including hiking and picnicking, making it a great destination for anyone looking to explore the natural beauty of the Texas countryside.

A visit to Top O'Hill Terrace can evoke a sense of nostalgia and wonder as visitors are transported back in time to an era of elegance and sophistication. The experience can be educational and entertaining as visitors learn about the area's history and gain a deeper appreciation for the art and architecture of the time.

A visit to Top O'Hill Terrace is an opportunity to explore a unique and fascinating part of Texas history and connect with the past's beauty and elegance.

WHERE IS?
The Top O'Hill Terrace is in Arlington, specifically at 3001 W Division St, Arlington, TX 76012, USA. The area is easily accessible by car, with several major highways and roads in the vicinity, including I-30, State Highway 360, and Division Street. In addition, the Top O'Hill Terrace is just a short drive from Dallas and Fort Worth, making it an excellent destination for day trips or weekend getaways. The area is also served by public transportation, with several bus routes that stop nearby. Visitors can also use ride-sharing services like Uber or Lyft to get to and from the Top O'Hill Terrace.

WHAT'S GOOD/WHAT'S BAD:
As a history enthusiast, I highly recommend visiting this place as it is truly unique. It offers a unique historical perspective on the conflict between sin and salvation during the Prohibition era. Vickie Bryant, the curator, provided expert commentary on the exhibits; her presentation was captivating. The memorabilia, music, and slides are all wonderful, but what makes the experience unforgettable is the passion and knowledge demonstrated by the docent. She narrated the story as if having a personal conversation. As a result, I felt free to ask questions and share anecdotes. You don't want to miss this highly entertaining and enlightening attraction!

DATE(S) VISITED:

WEATHER CONDITIONS:

ACCOMODATIONS:

WHAT WAS THE BEST PART OF TODAY?

SPECIAL MEMORIES:

MAJESTIC THEATRE IN SAN ANTONIO

Step back in time and immerse yourself in the glamour and sophistication of a bygone era at this stunning Art Deco theater.

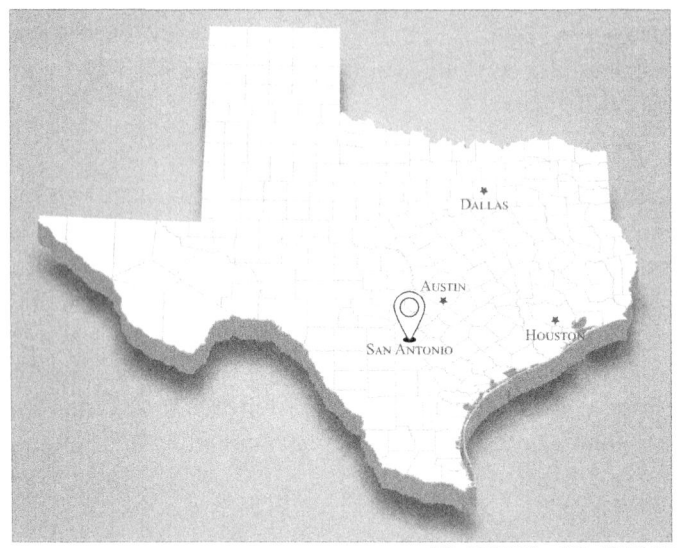

29.426502, -98.490667

WHAT'S ABOUT?:

The Majestic Theatre in San Antonio was built in 1929. It is a stunning example of Art Deco architecture and an iconic city landmark.

The theater was designed to be a grand and opulent venue for live entertainment, which has certainly lived up to that expectation.

The Majestic Theatre's lavish and ornate interior features intricate detailing, glittering chandeliers, and gold leaf finishes, all creating an atmosphere of glamour and sophistication. The theater is known for its exceptional acoustics, carefully maintained over the years, making it an ideal venue for live performances.

Over the years, the Majestic Theatre has hosted various shows and performances, including Broadway productions, concerts, and film screenings. Notable performers who have graced the stage include Elvis Presley, Bob Dylan, and the Rolling Stones, among many others.

In addition to its impressive interior and rich history, the theatre is known for its commitment to the community. It offers educational programs and outreach initiatives that promote the arts and engage young people.

The Majestic Theatre is a true cultural gem of San Antonio, offering visitors a chance to experience the grandeur and elegance of a bygone era. Whether you love theater, music, or film, visiting this magnificent venue will be an unforgettable and inspiring experience.

WHERE IS?
The Majestic Theatre is in downtown San Antonio, specifically at 224 E. Houston St., San Antonio, TX 78205, USA. The theater is easily accessible by car, with parking available in several nearby garages and surface lots. Public transportation is also available, with several bus routes serving the area and a nearby light rail station. Visitors can reach the theater via the San Antonio International Airport, about 9 miles north of downtown. Visitors can take a taxi or rental car from the airport to the theater or use a rideshare service like Uber or Lyft.

WHAT'S GOOD/WHAT'S BAD:
I was blown away by the Majestic Theater's grandeur and history. The architecture, from the walls to the ceilings, was original and well-maintained, and the acoustics were top-notch. It's a beautiful building that hearkens back to a time long gone. Unfortunately, the seating can be a bit cramped. Some people around us were confused by the numbering system, which numbered with only even numbers. Also, I was surprised at the high price of a single draft wine served in a plastic cup, which cost $25.

DATE(S) VISITED:

WEATHER CONDITIONS:

ACCOMODATIONS:

WHAT WAS THE BEST PART OF TODAY?

SPECIAL MEMORIES:

KING RANCH VISITOR CENTER

Experience the traditions and legacy of the iconic Texas ranching culture, an engaging glimpse into the region's rich history and unique way of life.

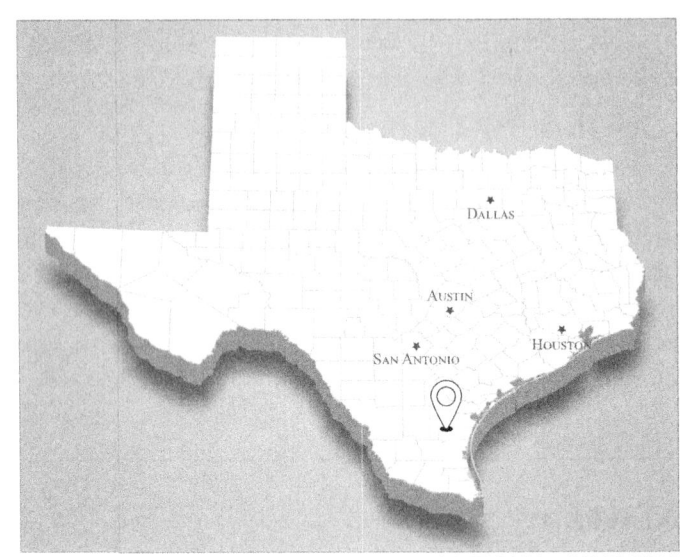

27.522381, -97.895898

WHAT'S ABOUT?:

The King Ranch Visitor Center in Kingsville offers visitors a chance to experience the history, culture, and natural beauty of one of the most iconic ranches in the world.

Established in 1853, the King Ranch covers over 800,000 acres and has played a pivotal role in the history and development of Texas.

The visitor center offers a range of exhibits, displays, and interactive experiences that showcase the ranch's heritage and legacy, including the history of ranching, the importance of conservation, and the traditions of the vaquero culture.

Visitors can take a guided tour of the ranch, exploring its scenic landscapes, diverse ecosystems, and abundant wildlife. The tour offers a unique and intimate view of the ranch, providing an up-close look at the working ranch operations, including cattle drives, horse training, and ranching techniques.

In addition to the tours and exhibits, the visitor center offers various educational programs, workshops, and events throughout the year. They allow visitors to learn about ranching, conservation, and the natural environment.

The King Ranch Visitor Center is a must-see destination for anyone interested in Texas's history, culture, and natural beauty.

Its engaging exhibits, scenic tours, and range of educational programs offer a unique and unforgettable glimpse into the region's rich heritage and unique way of life.

WHERE IS?
The King Ranch Visitor Center is in Kingsville, specifically at 501 E. Escondido Rd, Kingsville, TX 78363, USA. Kingsville is located in southern Texas, about 140 miles southwest of Corpus Christi. The visitor center is easily accessible by car via Highway 77, which runs through the town. The closest major airport for visitors flying into the area is the Corpus Christi International Airport, approximately 40 miles northeast of Kingsville. From there, visitors can rent a car or take a taxi to the visitor center.

WHAT'S GOOD/WHAT'S BAD:
I had a wonderful time at this ranch. The tour was informative, and I learned a lot about the history of the place. The tour's driver was knowledgeable and could answer all of our questions. I was lucky to see the mares and cows giving birth during my visit, which was a fantastic experience. The horses were stunning, especially the male quarter horses. I was also impressed by the Longhorns kept on the ranch as pets to help preserve the breed. The King Ranch is a place of great historical significance, and I would highly recommend it to anyone. In addition to the tour, the museum and saddle shop was worth a visit and made for a full day of activities. Don't miss out on this experience!

DATE(S) VISITED:

WEATHER CONDITIONS:

ACCOMODATIONS:

WHAT WAS THE BEST PART OF TODAY?

SPECIAL MEMORIES:

KING WILLIAM HISTORIC DISTRICT

Explore the beauty and charm of a lively neighborhood filled with historic buildings, where you can enjoy cultural events, shops, and inviting restaurants.

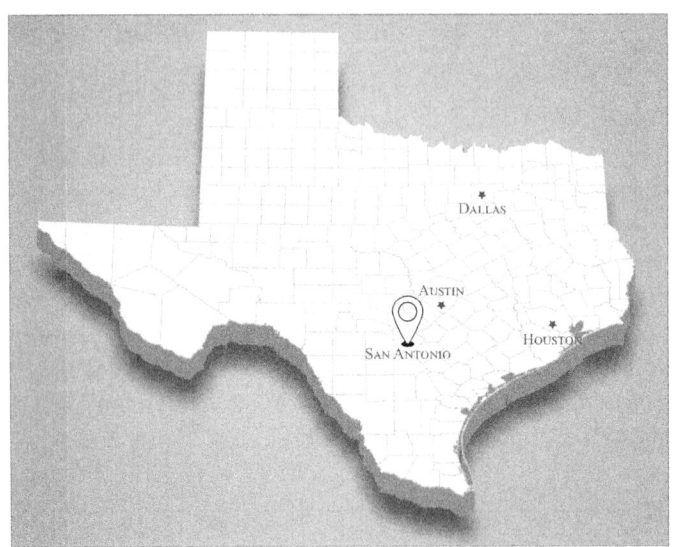

29.415980, -98.490331

WHAT'S ABOUT?:

The King William Historic District in Texas is a charming neighborhood in downtown San Antonio's southern part. The district is known for its beautiful homes and historic architecture. It is a popular destination for those looking to explore the rich history and culture of the area.

The district is named after King Wilhelm I of Prussia and was established in the late 1800s as a residential area for affluent German immigrants. Today, the neighborhood is home to diverse residents and is considered a vibrant and welcoming community.

Visitors to the King William Historic District can stroll along the tree-lined streets, taking in the stunning architecture of the homes and buildings. Many homes have been beautifully restored, offering a glimpse into the area's history.

In addition to its beautiful homes, the district has a range of local businesses, including art galleries, cafes, and boutiques. Visitors can stop in at one of the many shops or restaurants or participate in one of the district's many cultural events, including art shows, concerts, and festivals.

Overall, the King William Historic District is a beautiful and welcoming neighborhood that offers visitors a chance to step back in time and explore the rich history and culture of the area. Whether you are a history buff, an art lover, or simply looking for a charming and picturesque neighborhood, the King William Historic District is a must-visit destination in Texas.

WHERE IS?
The King William Historic District is located in the southern part of downtown San Antonio. The district is easily accessible by car, with several major highways running nearby, including I-35 and I-10. There is also ample parking available throughout the neighborhood. The district can be reached by bus or streetcar for visitors who prefer public transportation. In addition, the VIA Metropolitan Transit system operates several routes that stop near the district, including Route 11 and the VIVA Culture line. The neighborhood is also easily accessible by bike, with several bike rental stations.

WHAT'S GOOD/WHAT'S BAD:
This is a fantastic location to park and explore the beautiful houses, offering a tranquil and safe atmosphere. Walking around the neighborhood is a great way to take in the history and architecture of the homes. I even had the opportunity to talk to a local, who provided some interesting facts about the area. The houses in this neighborhood are unique. Many have historical significance, usually explained by an inscription that can be easily read from the sidewalk. Some of the houses even offer tours, which I recommend checking out. It's a great way to experience a different side of San Antonio, away from the touristy part of the Riverwalk.

DATE(S) VISITED:

WEATHER CONDITIONS:

ACCOMODATIONS:

WHAT WAS THE BEST PART OF TODAY?

SPECIAL MEMORIES:

TEXAS RANGER HALL OF FAME AND MUSEUM

Explore the fascinating history and culture of one of the world's most legendary law enforcement agencies at a world-class museum in Texas.

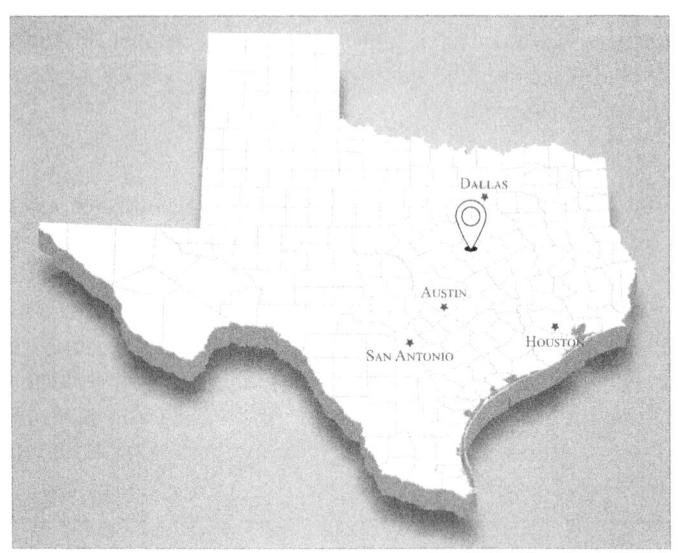

31.554759, -97.120002

WHAT'S ABOUT?:

The Texas Ranger Hall of Fame and Museum in Waco is a fascinating and unique destination that offers visitors an opportunity to explore the history and legacy of the Texas Rangers. The museum is dedicated to preserving the rich history and tradition of this legendary law enforcement agency, which has played a vital role in the past and culture of Texas.

Visitors can take a self-guided tour of the museum's exhibits, which include a wide range of artifacts, memorabilia, and interactive displays. The presentations cover a broad range of topics, from the early days of the Texas Rangers to their modern-day operations. It provides visitors with a comprehensive look at the history and impact of this iconic law enforcement agency.

In addition to the exhibits, the Texas Ranger Hall of Fame and Museum also offers a range of educational programs and events, including lectures, demonstrations, and special exhibitions.

Visiting the Museum can evoke a sense of admiration and respect because visitors learn about the bravery and dedication of the men and women who have served as Texas Rangers over the years. Overall, it is an opportunity to connect with the rich history and tradition of one of the world's most iconic law enforcement agencies and to gain a deeper appreciation for Texas's unique culture and heritage.

WHERE IS?
The Texas Ranger Hall of Fame and Museum is in Waco, specifically at 100 Texas Ranger Trail, Waco, TX 76706, USA.
The museum is situated just off I-35, making it easily accessible by car. Visitors can take exit 335B if heading southbound on I-35 or exit 335 if running northbound and follow signs to the museum. The museum is also accessible by public transportation, with several bus routes serving the area. Visitors can take the Waco Transit System's Route 9 or Route 10, which stop near the museum.

WHAT'S GOOD/WHAT'S BAD:
This place is incredibly fascinating but can be overwhelming as an enormous amount of information is presented. For those who, like me, might get lost in the text, a movie is available that covers many of the same topics. In addition, many exhibits are on display, featuring intricate sculptures and various educational sections. The museum is a fantastic journey through time, covering everything from the beginning of civilization to the present day. I recommend taking around two hours to explore it. This place is unforgettable if you want personal accounts, weapons, and artifacts. The photos are also really wonderful.

DATE(S) VISITED:

WEATHER CONDITIONS:

ACCOMODATIONS:

WHAT WAS THE BEST PART OF TODAY?

SPECIAL MEMORIES:

LOST MAPLES STATE NATURAL AREA

70 TEXAS

A breathtaking scenic wonder that showcases the awe-inspiring beauty of fall foliage.

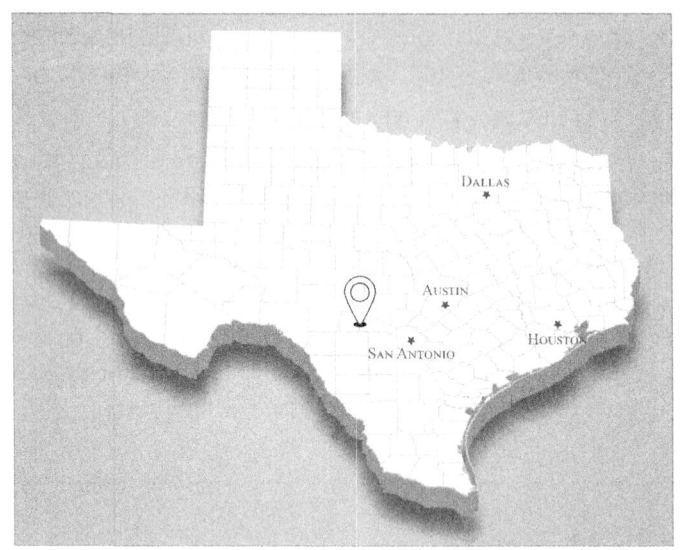

29.807594, -99.570397

WHAT'S ABOUT?:

Lost Maples State Natural Area in Texas is a breathtaking park showcasing nature's stunning beauty. The park is known for its vibrant autumn colors, as the bigtooth maple trees turn from green to brilliant shades of red, orange, and yellow. When visiting Lost Maples, one can't help but feel a sense of awe and wonder as one gazes upon the vibrant hues that seem to light up the entire park. The contrast between the bright, radiant leaves and the evergreen trees provides an incredible visual experience that will leave a lasting impression.

Wildlife in the park includes white-tailed deer, gray fox, raccoon, squirrel, armadillo, and many species of birds, such as turkey vultures, golden-cheeked warblers, and scissor-tailed flycatchers.

The park offers a variety of recreational activities such as hiking, bird watching, fishing, picnicking, and camping. Several miles of trails wind through the park, including the East Trail and West Trail, which offer stunning views of the surrounding hills and canyons.

Lost Maples State Natural Area is also known for its unique geology. Its exposed rock formations, caves, and sinkholes provide a unique landscape for visitors to explore.

Whether it's a leisurely stroll or a hike through the park, visitors will feel a sense of peace and tranquility surrounded by the natural beauty of the Texas Hill Country. The memories and emotions that are created here are truly unforgettable.

WHERE IS?
The Lost Maples State Natural Area is near Vanderpool in the Texas Hill Country. It can be reached by driving west from San Antonio on US Highway 90 to Hondo, then turning north onto State Highway 173. The park is approximately 38 miles north of Hondo. Another option is to drive east from Kerrville on State Highway 39 to Vanderpool and then turn south onto State Highway 187 to reach the park.

WHAT'S GOOD/WHAT'S BAD:
I visited this beautiful park with great hiking trails and scenery, especially during late fall and early winter when the trees are brilliantly colored. The hiking trails were well-maintained and marked, and while some trails were steep and challenging, they were clearly labeled on the map and with signs. I recommend the East Trail to East-West Trail counterclockwise for a three-hour hike. It's essential to bring plenty of water, wear a hat and sunscreen, and pack some snacks to enjoy at the scenic overlook about halfway. The park also offers nice picnic tables and clean restrooms in the parking lot area. I suggest going on a weekday to avoid crowds. It is a great ride and a beautiful location that is worth visiting.

DATE(S) VISITED:

WEATHER CONDITIONS:

ACCOMODATIONS:

WHAT WAS THE BEST PART OF TODAY?

SPECIAL MEMORIES:

CAVERNS OF SONORA

A cave network that offers a captivating adventure with its unique and stunning mineral formations and eerie underground beauty.

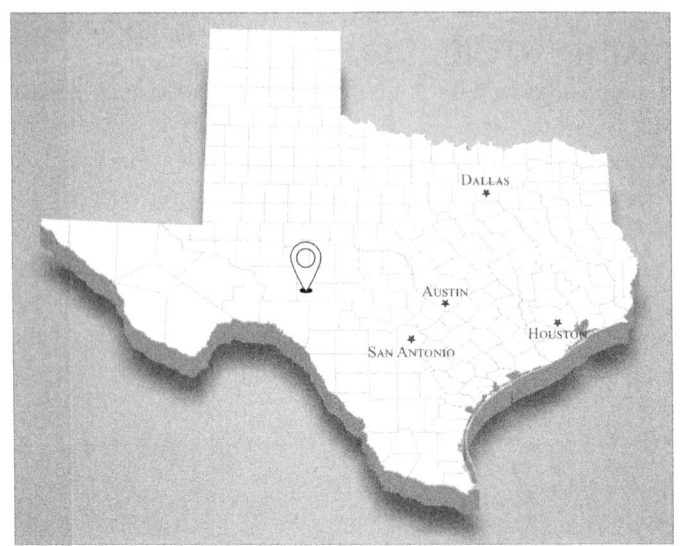

30.555143, -100.811827

WHAT'S ABOUT?:

The Caverns of Sonora, located in the central region of Texas, are a natural wonder that provides visitors a unique and captivating experience.

The caves are home to a stunning array of mineral formations, including delicate helictites, shimmering soda straws, and massive flowstones.

The guided tours offered provide the opportunity to explore and admire the intricate beauty of the caves, as well as learn about their geology and history.

As you descend into the depths of the caves, you are surrounded by the eerie stillness and beauty of the underground world. The colorful mineral formations are illuminated, casting a warm glow that accentuates their beauty. The silence of the caves is only broken by the gentle drips of water echoing throughout the chamber. The sense of awe and wonder is palpable as you navigate through the narrow passages and admire the intricate shapes and colors of the formations.

Visitors to the Caverns of Sonora can enjoy various activities, including guided tours, camping, and wildlife viewing.

In addition to admiring the magnificent mineral formations, visitors can learn about the history of the caves and the wildlife that inhabits them.

The Caverns of Sonora offer a unique and unforgettable experience that combines natural beauty, geological significance, and educational opportunities.

WHERE IS?
The Caverns of Sonora is located in Sonora and can be reached by car. From San Antonio, it is approximately a 2-hour drive west on I-10. It is roughly a 2-hour drive southwest of Austin on I-35 and Hwy. 277. From Dallas, it is approximately a 4-hour drive south on I-35. Once you reach Sonora, follow the signs to the Caverns of Sonora, located at 1711 PR 4468, Sonora, TX 76950.

WHAT'S GOOD/WHAT'S BAD:
In my opinion, this cave is the best I have ever visited. Even though Carlsbad Caverns is larger in scale, Sonora's cave is more impressive regarding the small details. Every square inch of the room is covered in sparkling crystals that are just incredible. The cave's formations are unique; they look like something out of a winter wonderland or fairyland, with pine tree-like stalagmites and snowball and icicle-shaped formations. As an active cave, it is well-protected from human contact, which adds to the feeling of walking in a glass house. This hidden gem is on a working ranch with RV and camping areas. The $20 per person fee for the tour is definitely worth it.

DATE(S) VISITED:

WEATHER CONDITIONS:

ACCOMODATIONS:

WHAT WAS THE BEST PART OF TODAY?

SPECIAL MEMORIES:

EIGHT WONDERS OF PORT ARANSAS

A vibrant coastal town in Texas known for its stunning beaches, wildlife, and fishing villages that attract adventure-seekers and beach-lovers alike.

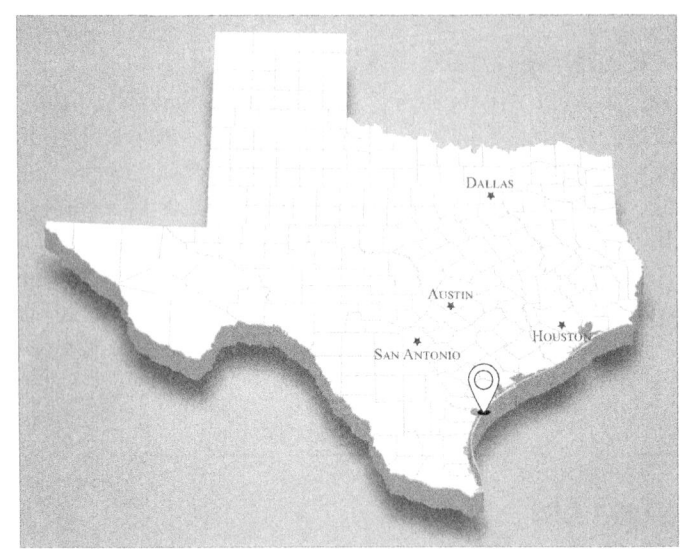

27.835415, -97.061276

WHAT'S ABOUT?:

Port Aransas is a charming coastal town, a popular vacation destination for families, nature lovers, and water sports enthusiasts. It is known for its stunning beaches, fishing opportunities, and laid-back atmosphere, In the early 2000s, a group of knowledgeable Port Aransas historians created a list of the island's most valuable treasures. They designated the "Eight Wonders of Port Aransas" as the most distinctive and must-see sights for residents and tourists alike.

Lydia Ann Lighthouse: This historic lighthouse, built in 1857, was the first lighthouse on the Texas Gulf Coast and is now a museum open for tours.

North and South Jetties: These two jetties, located at the entrance to Corpus Christi Bay, offer great opportunities for fishing, bird watching, and nature walks.

The Tarpon Inn: Established in 1886, it is the oldest building on Mustang Island. It was a hub for tarpon fishermen, including President Franklin D. Roosevelt. Its lobby walls are adorned with tarpon scales caught by these sportsmen.

The University of Texas Marine Science Institute: This world-renowned research facility offers visitors the chance to learn about marine life and ecosystems in the Gulf of Mexico.

Port Aransas Museum: This museum showcases the history and culture of Port Aransas, including its early days as a thriving port town.

Farley Boat Works: This historic boatyard, established in the early 1900s, is now a museum and park showcasing the history of the local fishing industry.

Chapel on the Dunes: This beautiful chapel, nestled on the dunes of St. Joseph's Island, offers a peaceful and serene setting for reflection and contemplation.

Farley Boat Hull: This historic fishing boat, dating back to the 1930s, serves as a reminder of Port Aransas' maritime heritage and is now a popular spot for photo opportunities.

WHERE IS?

Port Aransas is located on Mustang Island in the Gulf of Mexico. It is in Nueces County, approximately 18 miles northeast of Corpus Christi, and can be reached by car. The quickest route is via the Texas State Highway 361, which connects the city with Corpus Christi. There are also options to fly into Corpus Christi International Airport, drive to Port Aransas, or take a ferry from the nearby town of Aransas Pass.

WHAT'S GOOD/WHAT'S BAD:

Port A is one of my favorite places! The beach is always clean, and the maintenance is impressive. I've never seen any seaweed or jellyfish, which is excellent. The water is crystal clear, and I always enjoy relaxing here. The people are friendly, and many restaurants with varying price points can meet anyone's budget. In addition to hotels, vacation rentals cater to every budget. Getting a beach parking permit and parking right on the beach is also possible, making your beach gear easily accessible. For me, Port Aransas and Mustang Island are the best beaches in Texas.

DATE(S) VISITED:

WEATHER CONDITIONS:

ACCOMODATIONS:

WHAT WAS THE BEST PART OF TODAY?

SPECIAL MEMORIES:

GRAPEVINE HISTORIC MAIN STREET DISTRICT

A lively and charming collection of historic buildings and streets that take visitors back in time and offer a unique shopping and dining experience.

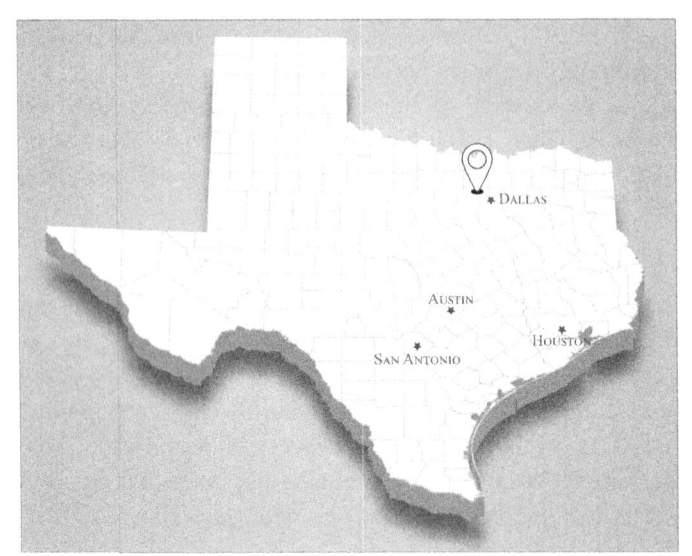

32.933685, -97.078413

WHAT'S ABOUT?:

The Grapevine Historic Main Street District is a bustling hub of activity that offers a truly unique experience. The area blends history and modernity with a vibrant energy that can be felt when you step onto its streets. The district has a collection of well-preserved, historic buildings dating back to the late 1800s, each with its own story.

As you wander through the district streets, you will be transported back in time, surrounded by the charming architecture and the authentic feel of a bygone era. You will experience a sense of nostalgia and appreciation for the area's rich history while feeling excitement and vitality as you take in the sights and sounds of the present-day hustle and bustle.

The area is filled with unique shops, galleries, and restaurants housed in beautifully restored buildings, allowing you to immerse yourself in the culture and history of the town. In addition, you can browse the shelves of antique shops and visit local art galleries, where you can admire the work of local artists. The street is also home to various festivals and events throughout the year, including live music, street performances, and food and wine tastings.

The Grapevine Historic Main Street District is where you can escape the fast-paced modern world and immerse yourself in the charm and character of a bygone era while still experiencing a vibrant and lively atmosphere.

WHERE IS?

The Grapevine Historic Main Street District is located in the city of Grapevine. Grapevine is situated within the Dallas-Fort Worth metropolitan area, approximately 20 miles northeast of downtown Fort Worth and 25 miles northwest of downtown Dallas. The easiest way to reach the Grapevine Historic Main Street District is by car. The district is located along Main Street in Grapevine. It is easily accessible from several major highways, including State Highway 114 and State Highway 121. A nearby regional airport, Dallas-Fort Worth International Airport, is just a short drive from the district.

WHAT'S GOOD/WHAT'S BAD:

I had a fabulous time in this town as it has excellent restaurants and shops. There are many exciting things to see, and the town has a friendly atmosphere for families and all others. It feels like a movie set for any period piece! I recommend visiting during off-seasons, like early March or early October, since the crowds can get heavy during big community events. The wineries in the area are perfect for families, with some even offering juice tastings for kids. Additionally, there's a great variety of shopping and dining options to suit everyone's taste. In the evenings, live music can be found everywhere. I would definitely recommend making this area a stop when passing through!

DATE(S) VISITED:

WEATHER CONDITIONS:

ACCOMODATIONS:

WHAT WAS THE BEST PART OF TODAY?

SPECIAL MEMORIES:

BLUE HOLE IN WIMBERLEY

A breathtaking natural swimming hole surrounded by lush greenery, offering a refreshing escape for nature enthusiasts and adventure seekers alike.

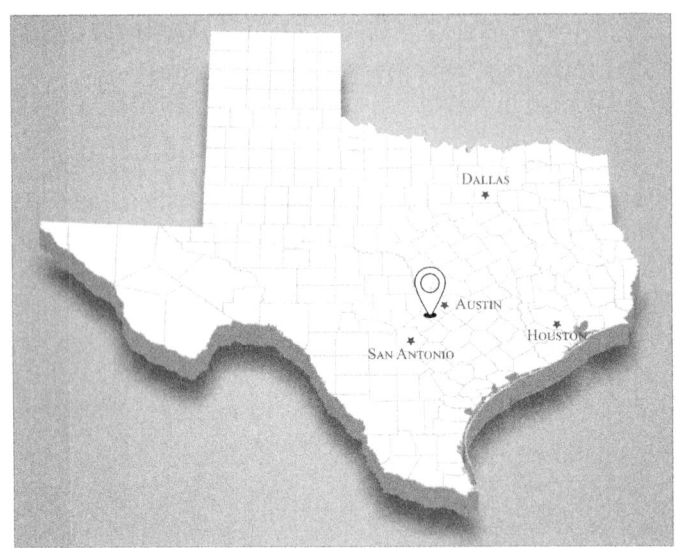

30.002369, -98.090840

WHAT'S ABOUT?:

The Blue Hole in Wimberley is a stunning swimming hole surrounded by lush vegetation and crystal-clear water. Visitors to the Blue Hole feel a sense of peace and serenity as they soak in the tranquility of the area.

The area's natural beauty is breathtaking, with towering trees and vibrant greenery surrounding the crystal blue water. The water is so clear that visitors can see all the way to the bottom, adding to the serene atmosphere.

The Blue Hole is a popular swimming, fishing, and picnicking destination. It is perfect for those looking to escape the hustle and bustle of city life and connect with nature.

The sound of waterfalls and the gentle trickle of the river create a peaceful background noise, adding to the sense of serenity.

The Blue Hole is located in the Blue Hole Regional Park, a part of the parks system of Hays County that offers a variety of recreational opportunities for visitors. The park features hiking trails, picnic areas, fishing spots, and wildlife viewing areas, making it an excellent destination for nature enthusiasts. It also allows visitors to learn about the area's history and geology. Visitors can enjoy scenic views from various lookout points and participate in educational programs. Guided tours to gain a deeper understanding of the park's natural beauty.

Whether you're looking for a place to swim, fish, or relax, the Blue Hole in Wimberley is a must-visit destination for anyone seeking a peaceful escape in Texas.

WHERE IS?
The Blue Hole is located in Wimberley, in Hays County. You can take Ranch Road 12 from Austin to Wimberley to reach it. From there, take FM 3237 to Blue Hole Road and follow the signs to the park.

WHAT'S GOOD/WHAT'S BAD:
This place is a must-visit when in Wimberley. The park is a hidden gem and a cool place to relax and swim. The water in the park is fed by a fresh spring, which is quite cold sometimes, so I recommend bringing some warm clothes. The rocks can be slippery, so wearing water shoes is a good idea. We had a great time on the rope swing. I suggest bringing goggles or snorkels as there are fish to see in the deeper areas. Note that you must make reservations to enter the Blue Hole, and the parking spots can fill up quickly, so it's best to arrive early. There are also bathrooms and changing rooms available.

DATE(S) VISITED:

WEATHER CONDITIONS:

ACCOMODATIONS:

WHAT WAS THE BEST PART OF TODAY?

SPECIAL MEMORIES:

DEVIL'S SINKHOLE STATE NATURAL AREA

A mysterious and intriguing location featuring a massive vertical sinkhole that drops 400 feet into the Earth and is home to a unique colony of bats.

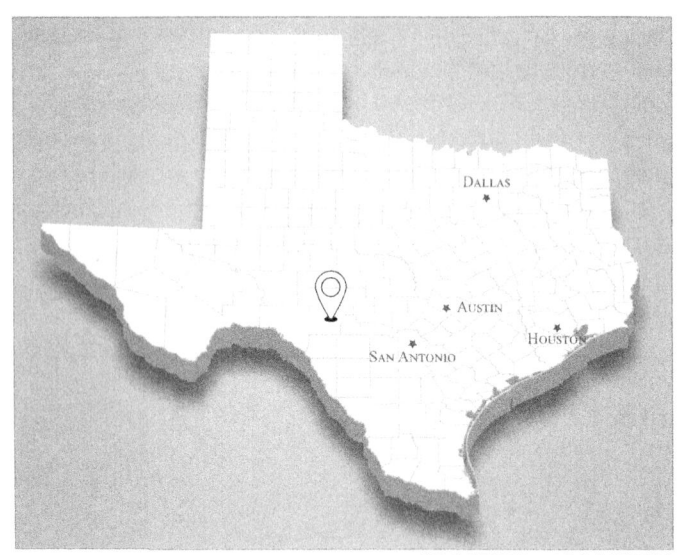

30.015873, -100.208503

WHAT'S ABOUT?:

The Devil's Sinkhole State Natural Area is located in Rocksprings and is a unique and breathtaking natural attraction. This natural area is home to a sizeable vertical sinkhole that descends more than 400 feet and is surrounded by scenic landscapes and diverse wildlife. The main species of bats seen in the sinkhole are the Mexican Free-tailed bats. During the summer months, hundreds of thousands of Mexican Free-tailed bats emerge from the sinkhole at dusk in search of food. Visitors can witness this impressive sight from the viewing platform provided. However, it is essential to note that bats are a protected species, and visitors should not disturb them or their habitat. Visitors can go on scenic hikes and nature walks to enjoy the diverse flora and fauna of the park. The area is also famous for birdwatching. It is home to various bird species, including the endangered golden-cheeked warbler. Additionally, the park offers guided tours of the sinkhole, where visitors can learn about the unique geological formations and the park's history.

The park allows visitors to escape the daily life's hustle and bustle and connect with nature. The serene surroundings and stunning views provide a peaceful and relaxing atmosphere, allowing visitors to slow down and appreciate the beauty of the natural world.

Access to the sinkhole is limited to guided tours, and the park can be challenging to reach due to its remote location. Before visiting, it's a good idea to check the park's website or contact them for tour times and availability information.

WHERE IS?

The Devil's Sinkhole State Natural Area is in Rocksprings, about 65 miles west of Uvalde. The park can be reached by taking U.S. Route 377 and then turning onto Ranch Road 335. The park is at the end of Ranch Road 335 and is clearly marked with signs.

WHAT'S GOOD/WHAT'S BAD:

I had a fun experience seeing the bat emerge at the Devil's Sinkhole near Rocksprings. The tour guides were enthusiastic and informative, taking us about ten miles outside town to see the bats at dusk. The bats swirl out of a deep hole in the ground in huge clouds. It's incredible to see! It's important to note that you must have a guide to visit the Devil's Sinkhole. To sign up, go to the Rocksprings visitor office in the county courthouse on the square. Tours are available at 10am and 1pm Wednesday through Saturday. Even though they are bats, this is a must-see in the area. Also, on your way back, stop the car and turn off the lights to enjoy the beautiful Texas stars.

DATE(S) VISITED:

WEATHER CONDITIONS:

ACCOMODATIONS:

WHAT WAS THE BEST PART OF TODAY?

SPECIAL MEMORIES:

GORMAN FALLS

76 TEXAS

A hidden gem featuring a mesmerizing 60-foot waterfall surrounded by lush greenery, inviting visitors to immerse themselves in the beauty of nature.

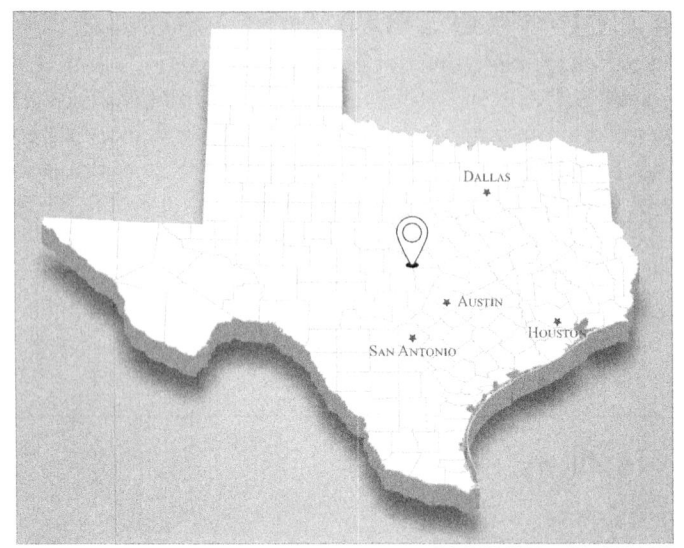

31.058127, -98.482059

WHAT'S ABOUT?:

Gorman Falls is a popular hiking destination located within the Colorado Bend State Park in Central Texas. The park covers over 5,000 acres of rolling hills, meadows, and scenic canyons. It is home to a diverse array of wildlife and plant species. The highlight of the park is the breathtaking Gorman Falls. This stunning waterfall cascades over 60 feet into a crystal-clear pool below. The falls are surrounded by lush vegetation and towering cliffs, creating a serene and peaceful atmosphere. Visitors can hike through the park to reach the waterfall, and the journey is just as awe-inspiring as the destination.

The trail leading to Gorman Falls winds through the park's dense vegetation, and the waterfall's sound grows louder with each step. When visitors finally reach the waterfall, they are greeted by a stunning sight of crystal clear water cascading into a crystal clear pool. The surrounding cliffs are covered in vegetation, and the falling water sounds music to the ears.

One unique aspect of Gorman Falls is its delicate ecosystem, which is sustained by the delicate balance of the water flow, the surrounding vegetation, and the local wildlife. This ecosystem is so unique that it is designated as a state natural area, which ensures its protection and preservation for future generations.

Visitors can spend hours exploring the area, swimming in the clear pool, and enjoying the serene atmosphere. The feeling of being surrounded by natural beauty is truly unparalleled, and the experience is one that visitors will never forget.

WHERE IS?
The Gorman Falls is located in the Colorado Bend State Park. The park is located in Bend and can be reached from Austin, Texas, about 2 hours drive. Visitors must hike the 2.9 miles of Gorman Falls Trail to reach the falls. The trail is considered an easy hike and takes visitors through a scenic landscape of the Texas Hill Country and offers views of the Colorado River before reaching the falls.

WHAT'S GOOD/WHAT'S BAD:
The trail to the falls covers 3 miles in and out. It is relatively flat but rocky, so watching your footing is essential. I recommend wearing comfortable hiking shoes for this hike. The highlight of the trail was the stunning Gorman Falls. It's a moderately challenging hike that most healthy and active individuals can do. The sun and heat could be the most difficult part of the hike, but carrying enough water and wearing a good hat can help you overcome it. The last leg of the trail is a steep and slick descent to the falls, but you can hold onto wires for support. The scenery is breathtaking, serene, and worth the effort. This is an under-appreciated treasure in the Texas State Park system.

DATE(S) VISITED:

WEATHER CONDITIONS:

ACCOMODATIONS:

WHAT WAS THE BEST PART OF TODAY?

SPECIAL MEMORIES:

WESTCAVE PRESERVE

A well-kept secret where crystal-clear waters, lush greenery, and unique cave formations offer stunning and awe-inspiring scenery.

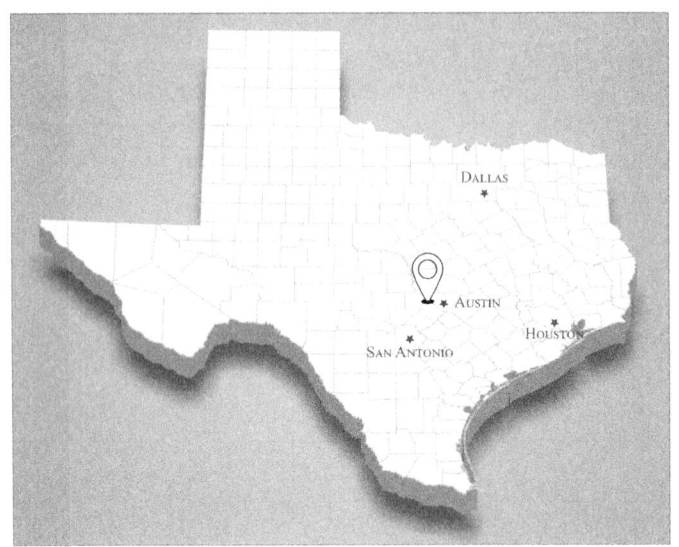

30.337163, -98.140849

WHAT'S ABOUT?:

The Westcave Preserve is a hidden gem in the Texas Hill Country, surrounded by lush greenery and breathtaking natural beauty. As one of the most serene places in the state, visitors can experience peace and relaxation while exploring the many trails and caves within the preserve.

One of the main attractions of Westcave is the stunning 30-foot waterfall, which cascades into a lush grotto and provides a perfect backdrop for photos and picnics. The trail to the waterfall takes visitors through a forest of oak, cedar, and cypress trees and past several limestone cliffs. It provides an opportunity to see the diverse and abundant wildlife that calls the preserve home.

In addition to the waterfall, visitors can explore several limestone caves and sinkholes and hike the trails that wind through the preserve. The guided tours offered by Westcave staff are a great way to learn about the area's unique geology and history and gain a deeper appreciation for the beauty and diversity of Texas Hill Country.

Whether you're a nature lover, a photographer, or simply looking for a peaceful escape from the city, Westcave Preserve is the perfect place to visit. So why not pack a picnic, grab your hiking shoes, and experience the magic of this magnificent hidden gem in Texas.

WHERE IS?
The Westcave Preserve is in Round Mountain, about 30 miles west of Austin. It is accessible by car and is located at 24814 Hamilton Pool Road, Round Mountain, TX 78663. Visitors can park in the designated lot and take a guided tour or hike the trails to explore the preserve. Admission to the Westcave Preserve in Texas is not free and requires a fee to be paid to enter. The fee structure and charges may vary, so checking the official website or contacting the preserve directly for the latest information on admission fees and ticket prices is advisable.

WHAT'S GOOD/WHAT'S BAD:
I went on a nice hike that was relatively easy and led to "The Grotto," with fantastic scenery and great photo opportunities, including a small cave. Our guide provided insightful information about geology, local wildlife, and plants. She gave us enough time to take photos when we arrived at the most beautiful spots on the trail. The grotto is stunning. Some steep stairs are in one area, but they are not too bad. It's a nice change of pace for outdoor activities if you're willing to drive a bit outside of Austin. Reservations are limited to protect the preserve's flora and fauna, so plan ahead if you want to visit. Overall, it was an excellent tour!

DATE(S) VISITED:

WEATHER CONDITIONS:

ACCOMODATIONS:

WHAT WAS THE BEST PART OF TODAY?

SPECIAL MEMORIES:

MALAQUITE BEACH

Imagine a serene and secluded beach with crystal-clear emerald waters and soft white sand where you can lounge or play beach games with friends and family.

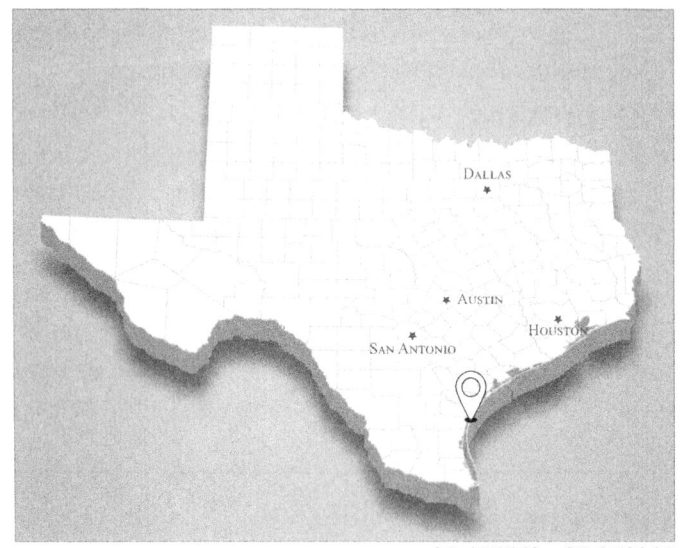

27.477560, -97.273910

WHAT'S ABOUT?:

Malaquite Beach is a hidden gem in the heart of Texas, located on the Gulf of Mexico.

Its pristine waters and white sand make it the perfect spot for a day trip or weekend getaway.

The beach is nestled in a protected cove, offering calm waters and great swimming. The gentle waves are perfect for bodyboarding, kayaking, or paddleboarding.

If you prefer to stay on shore, you can enjoy a leisurely stroll along the beach, sunbathe, or relax in the shade of an umbrella.

Plenty of picnic areas and barbecues allow you to enjoy a meal while taking in the stunning view.

The beach is also home to diverse wildlife, from pelicans to dolphins.

The clear water allows for excellent visibility, making it a prime spot for snorkeling and scuba diving. Whether an experienced diver or a beginner, you'll find plenty to explore in the rich underwater environment. And if you're looking for adventure, you can take a fishing trip and try catching redfish, trout, and other Gulf species.

With its stunning natural beauty and endless activities, Malaquite Beach is a must-visit destination for anyone looking for a fun and relaxing beach experience.

WHERE IS?
Malaquite Beach is located in southern Texas on the Gulf of Mexico on the northern end of Padre Island. To reach the beach, one can drive down Padre Island National Seashore, which is about 50 miles long, and the beach is located at the end of the drive. Parking is available on the beach; visitors can park their vehicles on the sand. The entrance fee to Padre Island National Seashore is $10 per person for 7 days or $35 for an annual pass. Visitors can purchase the pass at the entrance station, and it grants access to both Malaquite Beach and the entire Padre Island National Seashore. The park is open year-round, and the hours of operation vary depending on the season.

WHAT'S GOOD/WHAT'S BAD:
I really enjoy this beach because it's very peaceful and serene. Unlike other beaches, there are no cars to worry about, and I can easily park my car on the pavement. The bathroom and shower facilities are excellent, and the beach is clean and less crowded. I love taking long walks on the beach, gazing at the waves, and just unwinding. The water is crystal clear, making swimming even more enjoyable. However, even though the entrance fee is only $10, it doesn't stop some inconsiderate people from littering or ignoring the litter. To keep the beach pristine and clean, I suggest raising the entrance fee to discourage those who don't care about the environment from visiting this beautiful beach.

DATE(S) VISITED:

WEATHER CONDITIONS:

ACCOMODATIONS:

WHAT WAS THE BEST PART OF TODAY?

SPECIAL MEMORIES:

JACOB'S WELL IN WIMBERLEY

A hidden gem, enticing visitors with its natural beauty and mysterious depths that lead to an underground spring.

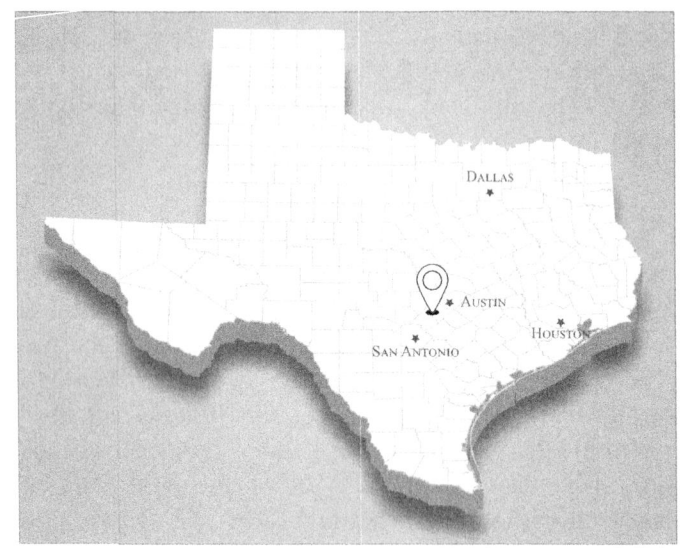

30.039171, -98.126341

WHAT'S ABOUT?:

Jacob's Well in Wimberley is a stunning natural swimming hole that provides visitors with a unique and refreshing experience. Jacob's Well is known for its crystal clear waters, towering cliffs, and depth of over 30 meters.

The well offers a breathtaking escape from the city and is a popular destination for swimming, snorkeling, and exploring.

The well is a unique geological formation; it is considered one of the most significant underwater caves in Texas and is a popular destination for experienced divers. It is fed by a spring that provides a steady flow of fresh, cool water. Its unique geology creates a tranquil environment.

Visitors to Jacob's Well are surrounded by towering trees and greenery, providing a peaceful and serene atmosphere for picnics, hiking, or simply lounging by the water.

The well is also a popular spot for photography and birdwatching, with various bird species often seen in the area.

Admission to the park is not free, but visitors can purchase a daily pass.

The park may reach capacity on busy days, and reservations are recommended. Visitors can also make a reservation for guided snorkeling or diving tours to explore the well.

Jacob's Well is a must-visit destination for anyone in the Wimberley area.

WHERE IS?
Jacob's Well Natural Area is located in Wimberley, Texas, approximately 35 miles southwest of Austin. The well can be reached by driving to the park, which is located at 1699 Mount Sharp Rd, Wimberley, TX 78676. From Austin, take Ranch Road 12 towards Wimberley and turn right on Mount Sharp Road. The park is a short distance from the road on the right-hand side. There is a parking lot for visitors to park and access the well.

WHAT'S GOOD/WHAT'S BAD:
The well is relatively easy to reach by foot and an unusual and remarkable sight! The ranger we met was extremely friendly and shared fantastic stories about the well. These include deep diving events and a free diver who retrieves items that end up on the first shelf. The actual view is even more impressive than the pictures. It's hard to secure reservations, but finally getting there made it all worth it. The water is chilly but crystal clear and rejuvenating! If you are visiting the Hill Country, then it's a definite must-see!

DATE(S) VISITED:

WEATHER CONDITIONS:

ACCOMODATIONS:

WHAT WAS THE BEST PART OF TODAY?

SPECIAL MEMORIES:

JAPANESE TEA GARDEN IN SAN ANTONIO

A tranquil oasis that combines stunning landscaping with a cultural heritage for an escape from the bustling city.

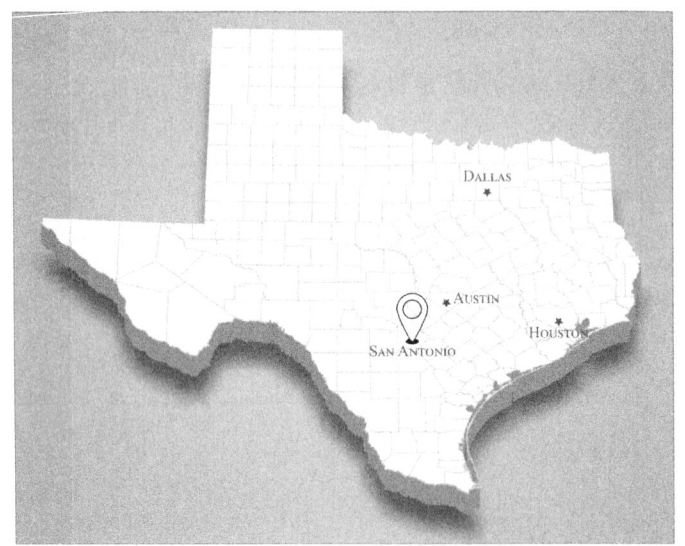

29.460517, -98.477370

WHAT'S ABOUT?:

The Japanese Tea Garden is a peaceful and serene oasis in the city's heart.

The garden features traditional Japanese elements such as koi ponds, bridges, and lanterns, as well as a variety of plants, flowers, and trees that create a lush and verdant landscape.

Visitors can wander along the winding paths, admire the carefully tended gardens, and stop to rest on one of the many benches.

In addition, the tea house offers a chance to experience traditional Japanese tea ceremonies and sample delicious green tea.

The Japanese Tea Garden in San Antonio was founded in the late 19th century. It was initially created as part of a Japanese exhibit for the San Antonio World's Fair in the 1880s.

The tea garden was later incorporated into the city's public park system and continues to be a popular attraction. It offers visitors a chance to learn about Japanese culture and traditions and has become a beloved landmark in the city.

With its beautiful setting, the Japanese Tea Garden is the perfect place to spend a peaceful afternoon, meditate, or appreciate nature's beauty.

WHERE IS?
The Japanese Tea Garden is located in Brackenridge Park, 3853 N St. Mary's St, San Antonio, Texas 78212. It can be reached by car, and a parking lot is available. Additionally, the park can be reached by VIA bus route number 4.

WHAT'S GOOD/WHAT'S BAD:
I found the atmosphere at this place to be very calm and peaceful, and the grounds were well-maintained. It was a wonderful place to relax and enjoy nature. The lagoon was enormous, and the waterfall was stunning. There were so many beautiful koi fish swimming in the shallow lagoon. I was amazed by the beauty and detail of the gardens. The stonework and trails were beautiful as well. If you love nature and gardens, this is the perfect place to find tranquility and appreciate the earth's beauty. It is a peaceful sanctuary that allows you to escape the crowds and feel at ease. The best part is that it is free, and although the parking is limited, it is manageable.

DATE(S) VISITED:

WEATHER CONDITIONS:

ACCOMODATIONS:

WHAT WAS THE BEST PART OF TODAY?

SPECIAL MEMORIES:

MARFA PRADA STORE IN VALENTINE

An unexpected art installation that challenges conventional ideas about luxury and consumerism.

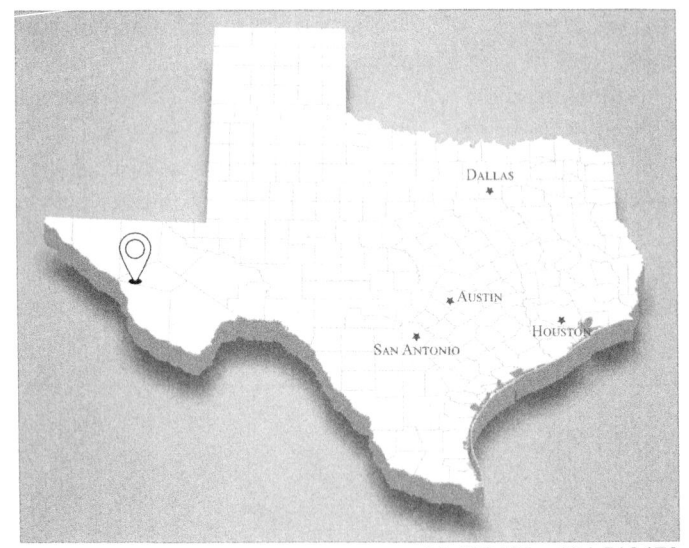

30.603483, -104.518473

WHAT'S ABOUT?:

The Marfa Prada Store is a contemporary art installation that will leave a lasting impression on visitors.

This quirky and unique structure, often called the "Marfa Prada Museum," was created by artist and architect Elmgreen and Dragset. It is a full-scale replica of a Prada store with merchandise and mannequins. The goal of the installation is to challenge visitors' perceptions of luxury, value, and the role of art in commerce. As visitors approach the Marfa Prada Store, they will be struck by its stark desert surroundings and unexpected appearance.

The installation prompts visitors to consider the commercialization of art and the power of branding. The artists chose to let the installation degrade over time as a commentary on the commodification of culture and the rapid obsolescence of luxury goods. By allowing the elements to take their toll on the once-pristine store, they sought to highlight the ephemeral nature of consumer culture and the emptiness of luxury brands. Vandalism at the installation was in line with the artists' intentions, as it added to the deterioration and deconstruction of the store.

By leaving the damages unrepaired, Elmgreen & Dragset encouraged visitors to question consumer culture's values and think about the consequences of our constant desire for newness and perfection.

WHERE IS?
The Marfa Prada Store is located in Valentine. It is situated near Marfa and can be easily reached by car. To get there, one can take the US-67 highway from Marfa and turn onto Ranch Road 2810. The drive from Marfa to the Marfa Prada Store takes about 30 minutes and offers scenic views of the surrounding landscape. A small parking lot near the store makes it easy for visitors to park and explore the site.

WHAT'S GOOD/WHAT'S BAD:
If you want to add an interesting spot to your travels, you should check out this unique art installation in the middle of nowhere. Although there are no services or souvenirs and you can't go inside, it's still worth the stop. I found it to be a very unusual yet intriguing work of art. I was surprised to learn that it was stocked with Prada bags and shoes from the 2005 collection when it was built, which must have been a considerable expense. It's definitely an original and quirky piece of art that's good for a picture. Plenty of room to park and turn around makes it an easy stop on your trip.

DATE(S) VISITED:

WEATHER CONDITIONS:

ACCOMODATIONS:

WHAT WAS THE BEST PART OF TODAY?

SPECIAL MEMORIES:

MARFA LIGHTS VIEWING CENTER

A unique opportunity to witness the mysterious lights of the Marfa desert and explore the legends surrounding them in a breathtaking setting.

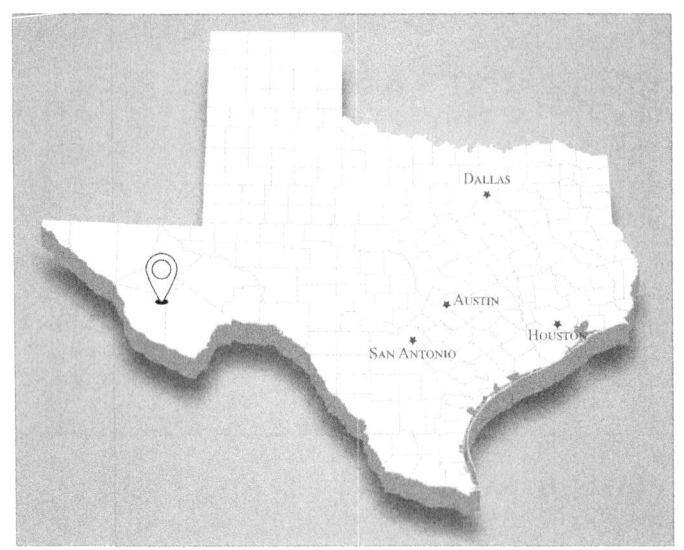

30.275217, -103.882738

WHAT'S ABOUT?:

The Marfa Lights Viewing Center in Marfa is a unique and mystical destination that offers visitors the chance to experience one of the state's most intriguing phenomena.

This viewing center provides the ideal location for observing the mysterious lights reported in the area for over a century. Visitors can enjoy stunning views of the surrounding landscape while they wait for the lights to appear. The experience can be both awe-inspiring and humbling, as the lights remain one of the world's most mysterious and unexplained natural events.

People have reported seeing strange lights in the sky, hovering and moving in different directions, and changing colors. Some believe the lights are supernatural, while others think they are caused by natural causes such as atmospheric conditions, vehicle headlights, or swamp gas. Despite numerous studies and investigations, the true cause of the Marfa Lights remains unknown. The Marfa Lights Viewing Center allows visitors to observe and try to understand the phenomenon for themselves.

The center is open year-round and offers views of the wide open skies, providing the perfect backdrop for a quest to witness the mysterious Marfa Lights.

Whether you are a local or a traveler, visiting the Marfa Lights Viewing Center will leave a lasting impression and a sense of wonder.

WHERE IS?
The Marfa Lights Viewing Center is located in Marfa and can be reached by driving on US-67. Take the 90 West towards Presidio from Marfa, and the center will be found on the left side of the road, approximately 9 miles from Marfa. The Marfa Lights Viewing Center is open 24 hours a day, and there is no admission fee to visit the center. The Marfa Lights Viewing Center and the Marfa Prada Store in Valentine are approximately 17 miles apart. They are both located in the general area of Marfa, a remote and beautiful region of West Texas, near the border with Mexico, which can be reached by driving on highway 90.

WHAT'S GOOD/WHAT'S BAD:
I found the mystery lights to be a fascinating and entertaining sight. During my visit, I saw as many as seven lights of different colors - white, yellow, and red - appearing and disappearing randomly. The experience was even more spectacular because of the thunderhead rolling in from the southeast. We had a great time watching the lightning and the colors in the sky. We brought night vision equipment to better view the lights, which I recommend you do. These lights are not car headlights or campfires - they jump up, split and merge. I enjoyed the complete darkness and how people were mindful of keeping it that way, speaking in hushed tones, adding to the unique and special experience. The new building was a great addition to the area, with fantastic tables to sit, chat, and take pictures of the lights. I recommend this place to anyone looking for a unique and exciting experience.

DATE(S) VISITED:

WEATHER CONDITIONS:

ACCOMODATIONS:

WHAT WAS THE BEST PART OF TODAY?

SPECIAL MEMORIES:

CADILLAC RANCH IN AMARILLO

Experience a unique blend of art and Americana where 10 vintage Cadillacs half-buried in the Texas soil make for an unusual roadside attraction.

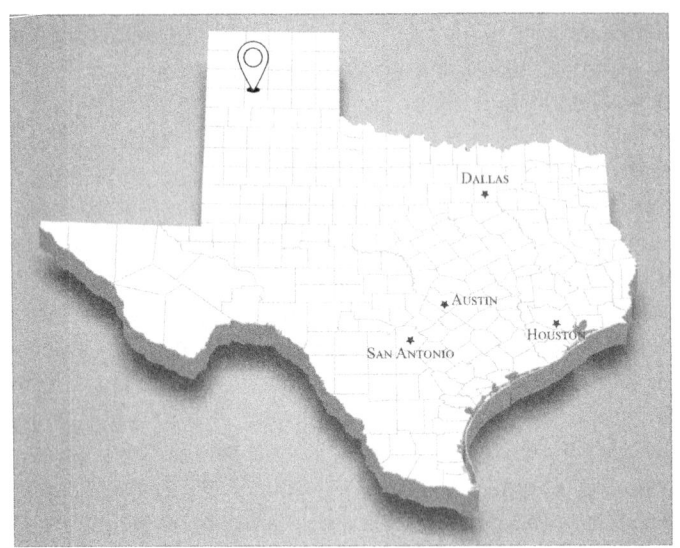

35.189100, -101.987360

WHAT'S ABOUT?:

Cadillac Ranch in Amarillo was created by artists known as the Ant Farm in 1974. It is a public art installation comprising ten vintage Cadillac cars buried nose-first in the ground.

The cars were placed as a testimony to the evolution of the iconic American automobile and its impact on American culture.

The vehicles are painted with colorful graffiti, and visitors are encouraged to add their artistic touches, making Cadillac Ranch a constantly evolving canvas.

The installation has become a popular attraction and a symbol of American pop culture, attracting visitors worldwide.

This iconic landmark is a must-visit destination for art lovers, car enthusiasts, and anyone looking for a unique and memorable experience. When visiting the Cadillac Ranch, visitors are encouraged to explore the site, take pictures, and even leave their mark by spray-painting the cars with vibrant colors.

The Cadillac Ranch represents a fusion of art, technology, and Americana. It offers a glimpse into the car culture of the 1950s and 1960s.

The emotions that visitors can experience at the Cadillac Ranch range from awe and inspiration to humor and nostalgia.

With its unique blend of history, art, and fun, the Cadillac Ranch is a truly one-of-a-kind attraction that should not be missed.

WHERE IS?
The Cadillac Ranch is located in Amarillo, on the west side of Route 66, near the intersection of I-40 and Route 66. To reach the Cadillac Ranch, take I-40 west from Amarillo, exit 60, and follow the frontage road west for about 1/4 of a mile until you see the Cadillac Ranch.

WHAT'S GOOD/WHAT'S BAD:
I highly recommend stopping at Cadillac Ranch, located right on Route 66. It is a fascinating art installation of ten Cadillacs half-buried in a cattle field. What makes it even more unique is that the cars are constantly repainted by a steady stream of artists, hippies, and curious visitors who purchase a couple of spray paint cans to leave their mark. It's a fun and interactive experience that allows you to be part of the art. You can bring your own spray paint or purchase some there. And don't forget to check out the gift shop/RV park about a mile east of the cars, where you can find all kinds of souvenirs with themes such as Route 66, Cadillac Ranch, Jesus, and the Second Amendment.

DATE(S) VISITED:

WEATHER CONDITIONS:

ACCOMODATIONS:

WHAT WAS THE BEST PART OF TODAY?

SPECIAL MEMORIES:

THE GHOST TOWN OF TERLINGUA

A captivating blend of history and natural beauty, with a mix of a desert landscape and abandoned buildings that evoke a sense of mystery and wonder.

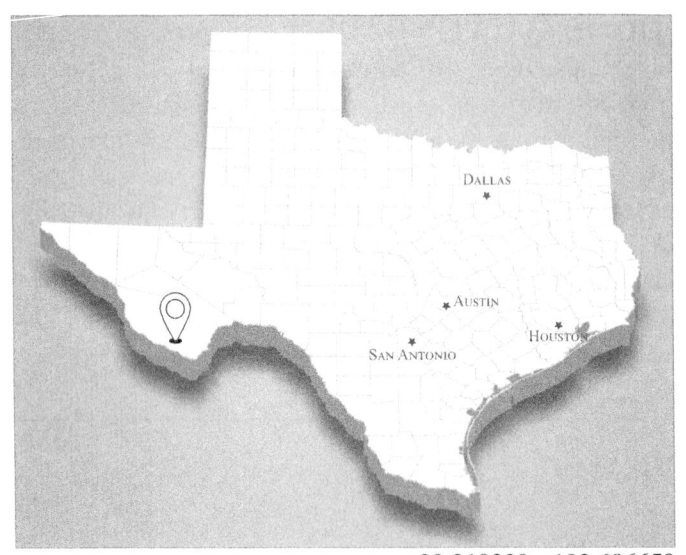

29.319339, -103.606659

WHAT'S ABOUT?:

The Ghost Town of Terlingua, located in West Texas, is a fascinating and unique destination that offers a glimpse into the state's rich history. This abandoned mining town is a site of beauty and mystery, as its history is intertwined with the story of the Chisos Mining Company, which once operated in the area. The town was once a thriving mercury-mining community in the late 1800s and early 1900s. The remnants of that era can still be seen today as abandoned buildings, equipment, and structures.

Today, the town is known for its vibrant arts scene, with many local artists and musicians calling Terlingua home and a thriving tourism industry. Visitors can tour the town's historic ruins, including the old Chisos Mining Company office and the Terlingua Mercantile Company, and explore the surrounding desert landscape on foot or by ATV. The town is also home to several restaurants, bars, and shops, making it an ideal place to relax and enjoy the beauty of the West Texas wilderness.

Another curiosity is the town's annual chili cook-off, which draws thousands of visitors each year and is one of the largest chili cook-offs in the world.

Whether you're a history buff, an outdoor enthusiast, or looking for a unique and memorable experience, the Ghost Town of Terlingua is a must-visit destination. You'll live an off-the-beaten-path adventure in Texas that will leave you with a lasting impression.

WHERE IS?
The Ghost Town of Terlingua is located in the southwestern part of Texas, in the Big Bend region near the border of Mexico. It can be reached by taking Highway 170 from Study Butte or driving through the scenic Terlingua Ranch. The ghost town is about an hour's drive from the town of Alpine and two hours from the city of Marfa. Some visitors also like to camp or stay in an RV to fully immerse themselves in the unique desert atmosphere of Terlingua.

WHAT'S GOOD/WHAT'S BAD:
I stayed in a beautiful casita in Terlingua, which was an amazing experience. Our stay in a ghost town provided us with many memories. As we sat outside, admiring the picturesque views and waiting for the sunset with a cold beer, we were even graced with a visit from a Road Runner. It was indeed one of my finest memories. The people in Terlingua were super friendly, and we were amazed at how they could survive in the summer heat. The area's history was fascinating, and we enjoyed seeing many birds and rabbits near the Starlight restaurant. If you plan to travel to Big Bend, I highly recommend this small town as it has everything you need.

DATE(S) VISITED:

WEATHER CONDITIONS:

ACCOMODATIONS:

WHAT WAS THE BEST PART OF TODAY?

SPECIAL MEMORIES:

SPARKY POCKET PARK IN AUSTIN

A quirky space filled with brightly colored murals, playful sculptures, and whimsical seating areas to immerse themselves in an artistic environment.

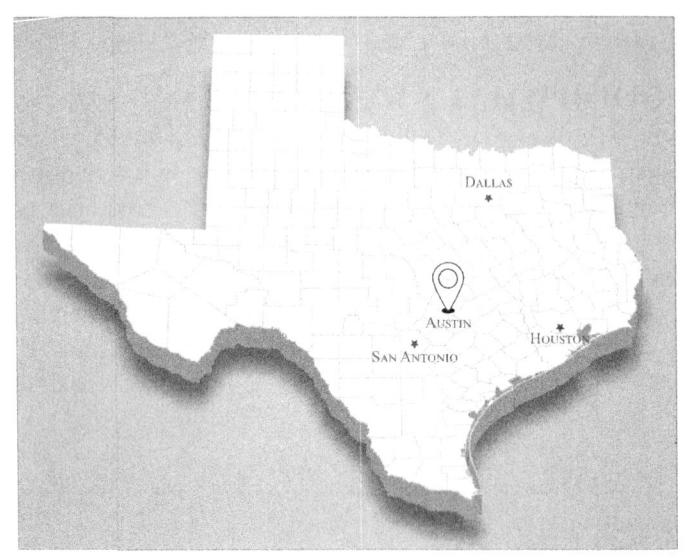

30.299283, -97.732240

WHAT'S ABOUT?:

Sparky Pocket Park is a small neighborhood park in Austin.

The park features a children's playground, a picnic area, and a small open green space. It is a quiet and peaceful place, perfect for families and individuals looking for a quick escape from the hustle and bustle of the city.

Visitors can bring a picnic lunch and enjoy the tranquility of the surrounding trees and grass.

The Sparky Pocket Park in Austin is known for its vibrant mural art and small, intimate size. Visitors can take a leisurely stroll through the park, admiring the colorful and whimsical murals that adorn its walls.

The park provides a quiet oasis in the city's heart, where visitors can relax or sit and appreciate the art. With its lively and eye-catching murals, Sparky Pocket Park is a popular spot for photography. It provides a unique and captivating backdrop for memories.

Sparky Park, previously an electrical substation, now showcases a unique collection of artistic expressions. The masterpieces in the park are created using the former substation's parts, offering a fun and eccentric experience for families, kids, and grandparents.

So take a magical walk through the park's artistic junkyard to experience something unusual.

WHERE IS?
The Sparky Pocket Park is located in Austin, at the intersection of Sparky Lane and Hargrave Street in the Rosedale neighborhood. The exact address of the park is 2400 Harris St, Austin, TX, 78703. You can drive or take public transportation, such as a bus or taxi, to reach the park and get off at the Harris St. stop. The park is easily accessible and located in a convenient area in Austin.

WHAT'S GOOD/WHAT'S BAD:
I came across a fun and unique place to take pictures. The impressive artistic display comprised stones, gems, and other materials. It was interesting to see the little trinkets past visitors had left in the pockets of the rocks. The location was in the middle of a neighborhood and was next to an electrical substation. Although it wasn't an actual park, it was a beautiful spot to stop and enjoy the contributions of those who had visited before. It's pretty minor and won't take long to explore, but I recommend planning to spend at least 15-20 minutes.

DATE(S) VISITED:

WEATHER CONDITIONS:

ACCOMODATIONS:

WHAT WAS THE BEST PART OF TODAY?

SPECIAL MEMORIES:

CATHEDRAL OF JUNK IN AUSTIN

A one-of-a-kind structure of 60 tons of discarded items invites visitors to explore a whimsical, towering assemblage of treasures and eclectic curiosities.

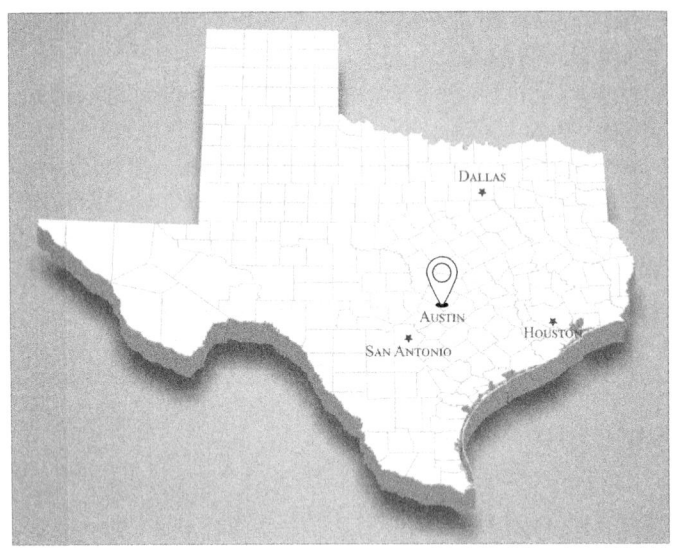

30.218673, -97.771411

WHAT'S ABOUT?:

The Cathedral of Junk in Austin is a unique and quirky attraction that offers visitors an unforgettable experience. It's a towering structure made from 60 tons of discarded items, collected and arranged by Vince Hannemann since 1989. The structure is made entirely of recycled materials, including everything from bicycles to appliances to old toys and household items. Visitors can climb, explore, and get lost in the maze-like creation of an entire suburban backyard. The structure is ever-changing, as the owner continues to add and remove items to keep the result fresh and exciting for visitors. Visitors to the Cathedral of Junk are sure to be captivated by the sheer size and scale of the structure and the intricate details and unusual arrangements of the items used to create it. The recycled materials' colors, textures, and shapes combine to create a sensory overload. Visitors will be amazed at the creativity and resourcefulness that has gone into building this one-of-a-kind creation. At the Cathedral of Junk, visitors can experience wonder and awe as they explore the endless twists and turns of the labyrinthine structure. They can also experience a sense of delight and playfulness as they interact with the different elements of the structure and appreciate the creativity and resourcefulness of the artist who created it. Visitors can explore the structure for free just by calling ahead, and it's also available for rent for special events like parties and weddings. Whether visitors are young or old, art lovers, or simply seeking an unconventional experience, the Cathedral of Junk is a must-visit attraction in Austin.

WHERE IS?
The Cathedral of Junk is located in the backyard of Vince Hannemann at 4422 Lareina Drive, Austin, Texas, 78745. One can use GPS navigation to input the address or take the MoPac Expressway/TX-1 Loop and exit at Lareina Drive to reach it. From there, it is a short drive to the property. It's recommended to call ahead to check if the structure is open to visitors or if it has been rented for an event.

WHAT'S GOOD/WHAT'S BAD:
The most helpful tip for visiting this place is to call first. Call the owner until he picks it up because it's on private property. It's a truly unique, engaging, and bizarre collection of junk that creates a towering structure you can walk through. The cathedral of junk contains colorful rooms like the yellow and pink room, several tunnels you can walk through, and a slide in the back. Despite its unusual appearance, the structure has been approved as safe to visit. Be sure to sign the wall inside. Remember that it's in the backyard of a man's house in a suburban neighborhood. Try to respect the neighbors by parking up the street. It's an essential place to visit and experience the weirdness that Austin has to offer.

DATE(S) VISITED:

WEATHER CONDITIONS:

ACCOMODATIONS:

WHAT WAS THE BEST PART OF TODAY?

SPECIAL MEMORIES:

BARNEY SMITH'S TOILET SEAT ART MUSEUM

Discover the unique collection of over 1,000 toilet seat art pieces, a quirky and memorable destination for those seeking a truly one-of-a-kind experience.

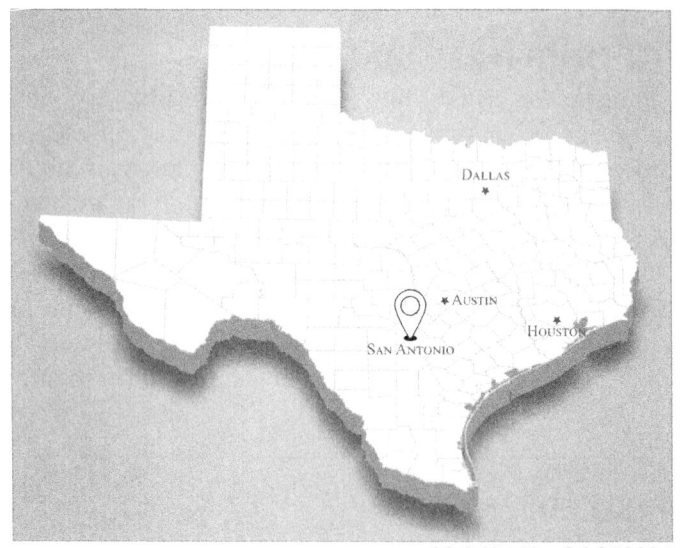

33.069462, -96.858034

WHAT'S ABOUT?:

The Barney Smith's Toilet Seat Art Museum in San Antonio is a one-of-a-kind museum featuring an extensive collection of toilet seat art created by retired master plumber Barney Smith.

He has found a unique way to display his passion for art by creating works on toilet lids. Starting with collected, used toilet seats, he transformed them into colorful and eclectic pieces by painting and adding various objects.

The museum boasts over 1,200 unique toilet seat art pieces, including a toilet seat decorated with coins from around the world, another adorned with matchsticks, and many others made from various materials such as golf tees, bottle caps, and even horseshoes.

Visitors to the museum can expect to be amazed by the creative and often humorous works on display. They may even leave with a newfound appreciation for toilet seat art.

Initially housed in his garage, his collection grew too large, leading him to open his folk museum.

The museum is open by appointment only.

Visitors are welcome to bring their own toilet seats or lids to be engraved with their name by Barney, leaving a lasting mark in the museum's history.

Visiting Barney Smith's Toilet Seat Art Museum is a quirky and lighthearted experience that will surely bring a smile to anyone's face.

WHERE IS?
The Barney Smith's Toilet Seat Art Museum is located in San Antonio. The museum is at 239 Abiso Ave, San Antonio, TX 78212. It can be reached by taking a car or using public transportation. If you're driving, you can use a GPS device or map to navigate to the museum. If you're taking public transport, you can use the bus or train system to reach the nearest stop and then walk to the museum.

WHAT'S GOOD/WHAT'S BAD:
This place is unique, and you must see it to believe it. It's incredible to see thousands of toilet seats decorated in various ways and hung on almost every surface. It's worth visiting and a great opportunity for a good laugh.

DATE(S) VISITED:

WEATHER CONDITIONS:

ACCOMODATIONS:

WHAT WAS THE BEST PART OF TODAY?

SPECIAL MEMORIES:

HUECO TANKS IN EL PASO

A geological formation with ancient Native American rock art, offering visitors a chance to explore the history and natural beauty in one intriguing location.

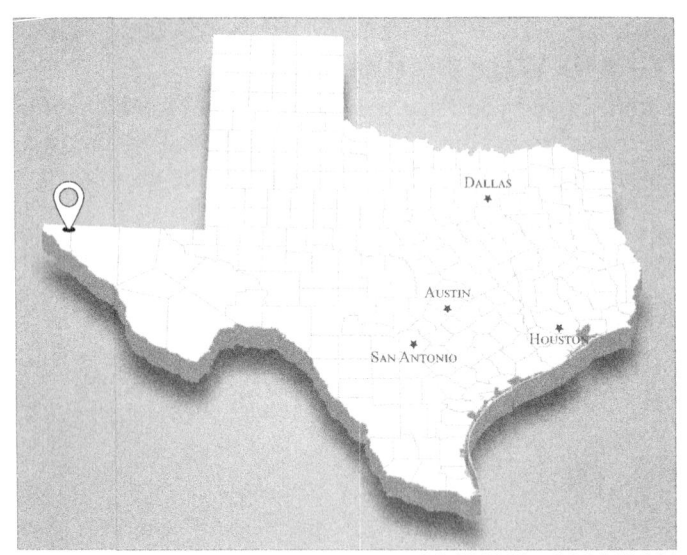

31.926819, -106.042664

WHAT'S ABOUT?:

Hueco Tanks is a historic site in El Paso, at the border of the Chihuahuan Desert, that offers a unique blend of natural beauty and cultural significance.

This natural park features several large, hollowed-out rock formations known as "huecos," which feature drawings dating back thousands of years. And used as water sources by Native Americans and early settlers.

Visitors can hike through the park to see these natural wonders and learn about the history and cultural significance of the area.

Additionally, the park offers stunning views of the surrounding desert landscape and rock climbing, bird watching, and picnicking opportunities. The park also has several picnic areas and camping sites, making it a great place to spend a day or even an overnight trip.

The mysteries surrounding these rock formations and the native cultures that used them make Hueco Tanks an intriguing place to visit. If you would like to explore the site and learn more about the history and cultural significance of the huecos, it is recommended to make a reservation in advance because the park is limited in the number of visitors.

Whether interested in history or nature or just looking for a quiet escape from the city, Hueco Tanks will captivate and intrigue you with its beauty and serenity.

WHERE IS?
Hueco Tanks State Park is at 6900 Hueco Tanks Road No. 1, El Paso, Texas, 79938. The park can be reached by taking the Trans Mountain Road exit from I-10 and heading east. The park is located about 30 minutes from downtown El Paso.

WHAT'S GOOD/WHAT'S BAD:
If you're in the area, make sure to visit this site. It's essential to have a guide to show you the best-preserved pictographs in the crevices and caves. Without one, you'll just see piles of rocks. Carry water, as it can get hot, and if you have mobility issues, take walking sticks, as there are little scrambles to get closer to the pictoglyphs. Hueco Tanks is like an oasis in the desert, with plenty of trails and hiking and few people around. Remember to wear a hat and sunscreen and be alert for snakes and scorpions. Also, remember that you must have a reservation as they only allow 70 people daily.

DATE(S) VISITED:

WEATHER CONDITIONS:

ACCOMODATIONS:

WHAT WAS THE BEST PART OF TODAY?

SPECIAL MEMORIES:

NATIONAL MUSEUM OF FUNERAL HISTORY

A unique and fascinating museum dedicated to the history and cultural significance of funerals and mourning traditions.

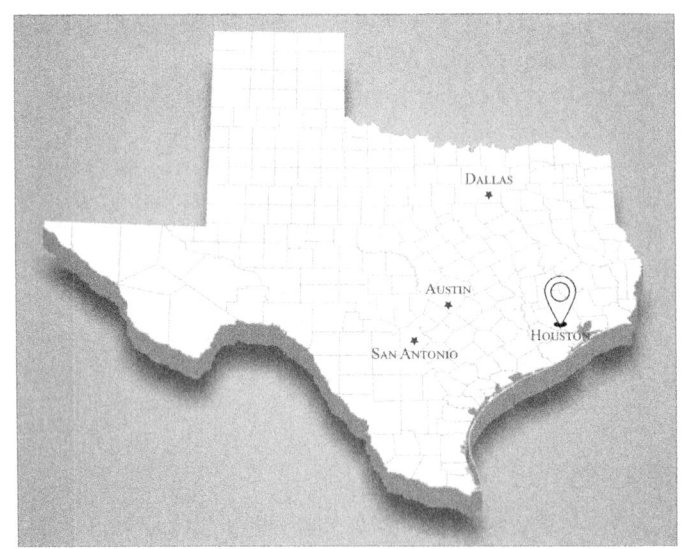

29.988916, -95.431221

WHAT'S ABOUT?:

The National Museum of Funeral History in Houston is a one-of-a-kind museum dedicated to the rich history and cultural significance of funerals and mourning traditions. It is a place where visitors can learn about the various customs and rituals that have evolved over time to help people cope with death and loss.

The museum's exhibits showcase various artifacts, including antique hearses, embalming equipment, and funeral attire from different cultures and periods. There are also interactive displays and multimedia exhibits that offer visitors an immersive and engaging experience.

One of the museum's most popular exhibits is the Presidential Funerals exhibit, which showcases the funerals of U.S. presidents from George Washington to George H.W. Bush. In addition, the exhibit features a replica of the horse-drawn caisson that carried President John F. Kennedy's casket during his funeral procession.

The museum also offers educational programs and workshops, providing visitors with a chance to learn about the history and significance of funerals and mourning traditions and the work of funeral directors and other professionals in the industry. Whether you are interested in the history of funerals or simply looking for an engaging and thought-provoking museum experience, this museum is well worth a visit.

WHERE IS?
The National Museum of Funeral History is in Houston, specifically at 415 Barren Springs Drive, Houston, TX 77090, USA. Houston is a large city in southeastern Texas, and the museum is in the northern part of the city, near the intersection of I-45 and Beltway 8. The museum is easily accessible by car, and ample parking is available on-site. The closest major airport for visitors flying into the area is the George Bush Intercontinental Airport, located approximately 12 miles northeast of the museum. Visitors can rent a car from the airport or take a taxi to the museum.

WHAT'S GOOD/WHAT'S BAD:
I highly recommend visiting this museum, with an interesting collection of funerary items and exhibits that honor the lives of people who have impacted US society. I wasn't sure what to expect, but all the exhibit areas were engaging and enlightening. The exhibits are not "funereal" at all, and I had a unique experience. I spent longer than I thought I would as the exhibits ranged from caskets, hearses, embalming, and cremation. I particularly enjoyed the presidential funeral section and the "Thanks for the Memories" exhibit. However, it's unsuitable for young children as they may find it boring, but not because of any gruesome content. If you have a couple of hours to spare and have already explored other museums and parks in Houston, it's definitely worth a visit.

DATE(S) VISITED:

WEATHER CONDITIONS:

ACCOMODATIONS:

WHAT WAS THE BEST PART OF TODAY?

SPECIAL MEMORIES:

OCEAN STAR OFFSHORE DRILLING RIG & MUSEUM

*90 TEXAS

Delve into the fascinating world of offshore oil exploration and drilling and learn about the technology and processes involved in this industry.

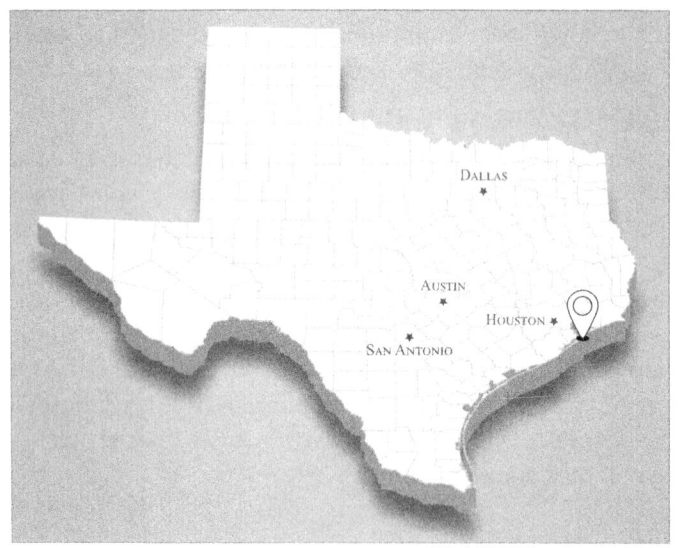

29.310331, -94.791761

WHAT'S ABOUT?:

The Ocean Star Offshore Drilling Rig & Museum is a unique and fascinating destination for those interested in the oil and gas industry.

The museum is housed in a retired offshore drilling rig in Galveston. It offers visitors an up-close look at the history and technology of the industry.

Visitors to the Ocean Star Offshore Drilling Rig & Museum can explore the rig's various decks and take in exhibits that showcase the drilling process, from the initial exploration to the final product.

The museum also includes a theater that shows films about the oil and gas industry and a gift shop where visitors can purchase industry-related souvenirs.

In addition to its exhibits and displays, the museum offers guided tours, providing a more in-depth look at the rig and the industry.

The tours are led by knowledgeable guides with firsthand experience in the oil and gas industry.

The Ocean Star Offshore Drilling Rig & Museum in Texas is a one-of-a-kind destination that offers visitors a unique and educational experience.

Whether you are interested in the history and technology of the oil and gas industry or simply looking for an offbeat and intriguing museum to explore, the Ocean Star Offshore Drilling Rig & Museum is a must-visit destination in Texas.

WHERE IS?
The Ocean Star Offshore Drilling Rig & Museum is at Pier 19 in Galveston. Visitors can take I-45 South to Galveston to reach the museum, then follow the signs to the historic Strand District. From there, visitors can park in one of the nearby public parking lots and walk to the museum, which is located just a short distance away. Additionally, visitors can take the Galveston Island Trolley, which stops near the museum as part of its route. The trolley runs daily from 10 a.m. to 10 p.m. during summer and on weekends during spring and fall.

WHAT'S GOOD/WHAT'S BAD:
I had a great time at this museum dedicated to offshore drilling. It was very informative, and everything I needed to know was covered. All of it happened on a retired drilling rig. I suggest you spend at least one to two hours getting the experience. I found the displays very detailed and educational and exploring the platform was fascinating. I opted for the audio tour, which cost an additional $5 per person. Still, it was worth it, significantly improving the overall experience. This museum might be more suitable for people with an engineering background since it has a slightly technical feel.

DATE(S) VISITED:

WEATHER CONDITIONS:

ACCOMODATIONS:

WHAT WAS THE BEST PART OF TODAY?

SPECIAL MEMORIES:

HOUSTON SPACE CENTER

The home of the Johnson Space Center offers a glimpse into the fascinating world of space exploration and showcases the achievements of human space flight.

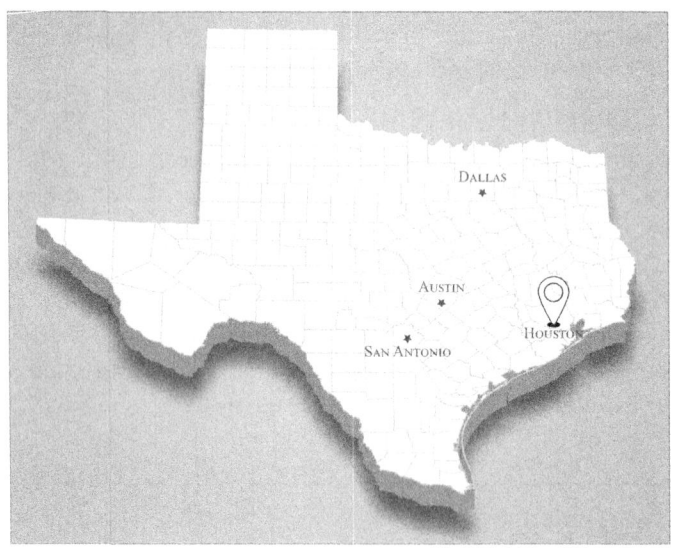

29.551465, -95.097763

WHAT'S ABOUT?:

The Houston Space Center is a must-visit destination for anyone interested in space exploration and technology and one of the city's most popular tourist attractions. Located in Houston, next to NASA's Johnson Space Center, it is the center of human space flight activities for NASA. It combines elements of a museum and an amusement park, offering a unique and thrilling experience.

Visitors can tour the facilities and learn about the fascinating history of space travel, from the Apollo missions to the International Space Station. You can see full-sized mockups of the Space Shuttle and see artifacts from space missions on display. There is also a planetarium show that provides a thrilling experience of liftoff and space travel. You can also learn about the science behind space travel, including the physics of rocket launches and the technology that astronauts use to live and work in space.

For those who dream of space travel, the Houston Space Center offers a unique opportunity to experience the thrill of space exploration. Also, learn about the fantastic technology behind it, and get a glimpse into the future of space travel. It's a place that will inspire, excite, and leave you in awe of the limitless possibilities of human endeavor.

This remarkable place has the power to amaze both kids and adults. It should not be missed by anyone traveling through Houston.

WHERE IS?
The address of the Houston Space Center is 1601 NASA Pkwy, Houston, TX 77058. It can be reached by car or by taking the METRO bus route 271 from downtown Houston. The center is about 20 miles southeast of downtown Houston, near the Johnson Space Center.

WHAT'S GOOD/WHAT'S BAD:
I had a fantastic time at Houston's Space Center; it's undoubtedly the best attraction in the city! I spent five hours there, and I could have stayed even longer. Even though I've been to the Space Museum in Huntsville, Cape Canaveral, and the Air Force Museum in Dayton, I think this one stands out the most. The price is affordable, and there's so much to learn and see. It's incredible to see what the space program accomplished. The children who visited with me were fascinated by the size of the shuttles and the engines. Although it was very crowded and seating was scarce, that's to be expected since it's such a popular destination. As a space enthusiast, I was in heaven, and there was plenty for those not as passionate about space to enjoy. The staff members were extremely helpful, and the place was very organized, with maps available.

DATE(S) VISITED:

WEATHER CONDITIONS:

ACCOMODATIONS:

WHAT WAS THE BEST PART OF TODAY?

SPECIAL MEMORIES:

MOODY GARDENS IN GALVESTON

Discover the wonders of nature and science in a tropical paradise offering a variety of attractions, including aquariums, rainforest pyramids, and IMAX theaters.

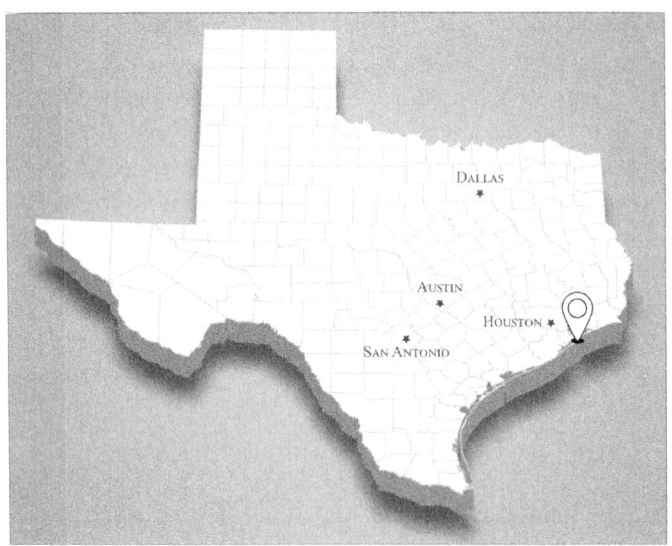

29.272784, -94.852570

WHAT'S ABOUT?:

Moody Gardens is a significant tourist complex located in Galveston and an exciting destination that offers a unique combination of educational and entertainment experiences. It features several attractions, including a 10-story glass pyramid showcasing a rainforest environment, an IMAX theater, a state-of-the-art 3D theater, a botanical garden with a lush rainforest habitat, a beach with a wave pool and lazy river, an aquarium with marine animals from all over the world, several other interactive exhibits, and much more.

The complex was opened in 1986 and has since become a popular destination for families and visitors to Galveston. At Moody Gardens, visitors can see various animals and plants, including exotic birds, sea otters, penguins, exotic fish, and over 200 species of plants in the rainforest pyramid.

One of the most fun and interactive attractions at Moody Gardens is the Aquarium Pyramid, which features a walk-through tunnel where visitors can observe sea creatures swimming above and around them. Another popular exhibit is the Discovery Pyramid, which features hands-on displays and educational exhibits about science and nature.Moody Gardens is a family-friendly destination, with attractions and exhibits designed to educate and entertain visitors of all ages. The complex is open year-round and offers a range of events and activities, from seasonal festivals to animal encounters and educational programs.

Whether you're a science enthusiast, nature lover, or just looking for a fun day out,

Moody Gardens has something for everyone. With its diverse attractions, interactive exhibits, and breathtaking views, visiting Moody Gardens will leave you feeling inspired, enlightened, and entertained. So, pack your sunscreen and prepare to be transported to a world of adventure and excitement.

WHERE IS?

Moody Gardens is located on scenic Galveston Island. The address is One Hope Boulevard, Galveston, TX, 77554. The easiest way to reach Moody Gardens is by car, about a 50-minute drive from downtown Houston. There is also a shuttle service available from various locations in Houston. If traveling by plane, the closest airport is the William P. Hobby Airport in Houston, approximately a 45-minute drive from Moody Gardens.

WHAT'S GOOD/WHAT'S BAD:

The Aquarium is fantastic! I was struck by the underwater MG-2017 watercraft and video when I walked through the front doors. It's an inviting and mesmerizing visual experience. The tanks and collections are immaculately maintained by the approachable and friendly staff. The shark exhibit was exciting, and I loved walking through the tube walkways with fish and mammals swimming overhead. I recommend exploring the other buildings on the property. The Arboretum was stunning and interactive, featuring various animals and bird species that wandered alongside you on the winding paths. It's a lot of fun and definitely worth a visit.

DATE(S) VISITED:

WEATHER CONDITIONS:

ACCOMODATIONS:

WHAT WAS THE BEST PART OF TODAY?

SPECIAL MEMORIES:

FORT WORTH MUSEUM OF SCIENCE AND HISTORY

★ 93 TEXAS

Explore the wonders of science, history, and technology, where interactive exhibits and hands-on activities make learning exciting and fun.

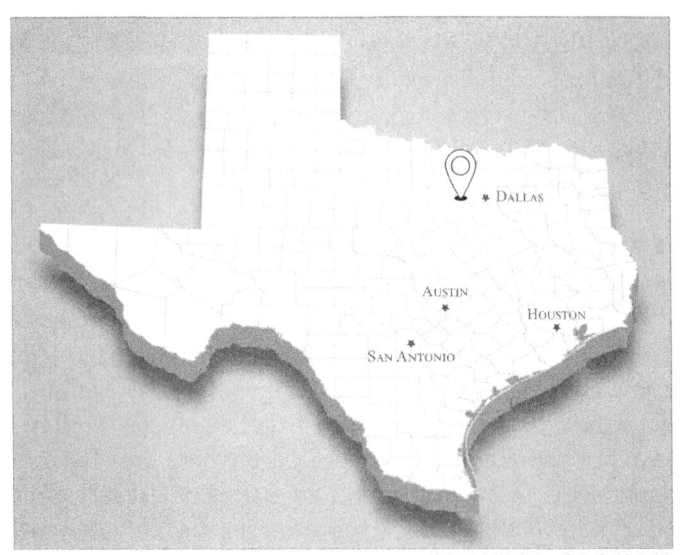

32.743927, -97.368542

WHAT'S ABOUT?:

The Fort Worth Museum of Science and History is a cultural and educational center in Fort Worth. With an extensive collection of interactive exhibits, immersive displays, and hands-on activities, this museum is an excellent place for families and individuals to explore and learn about science, history, and culture.

Visitors can delve into the mysteries of the universe in the Omni Theater. This dome-shaped IMAX theater offers stunning views of the stars and planets. The Energy Blast exhibit is another popular attraction where visitors can discover the science behind energy production and use.

The museum also has a dinosaur exhibit featuring life-sized models and interactive displays that bring these fascinating creatures to life.

The Fort Worth Museum of Science and History is also home to the Cattle Raisers Museum, showcasing the rich history of the cattle industry in Texas and the American West.

In addition, the museum offers a range of educational programs and events (from interactive workshops and demonstrations to science camps and special events), making it an ideal destination for families and school groups.

The museum also has a state-of-the-art planetarium, a hands-on children's museum, and a modern research library, making it a comprehensive resource for those interested in science, history, and culture.

WHERE IS?

The Fort Worth Museum of Science and History is located in Fort Worth at 1600 Gendy St, Fort Worth, TX 76107. It can be reached by car, with parking available on-site or via public transportation. The museum is a short walk from the Fort Worth Intermodal Transportation Center, which is served by local buses and the Trinity Railway Express.

WHAT'S GOOD/WHAT'S BAD:

This museum is often overlooked, but it's one of my favorites. Located just outside the Dickies Arena, this small venue packs a wealth of information on subjects related to American history. Although small, many interactive exhibits will pique the interest of science enthusiasts of all ages. As Fort Worth is the epicenter of stock shows and cattle ranching, the museum includes a fascinating exhibit dedicated to cowboy and cattle drives history. This museum is an excellent choice if you want to take a quick trip with the family or learn about basic science and cowboy history. Also, the Cowgirl Museum and Hall of Fame is located next door, so you can use ticket combinations.

DATE(S) VISITED:

WEATHER CONDITIONS:

ACCOMODATIONS:

WHAT WAS THE BEST PART OF TODAY?

SPECIAL MEMORIES:

HOUSTON ZOO

Discover exotic wildlife and exciting animal encounters, and immerse yourself in the vibrant cultures and habitats of creatures worldwide.

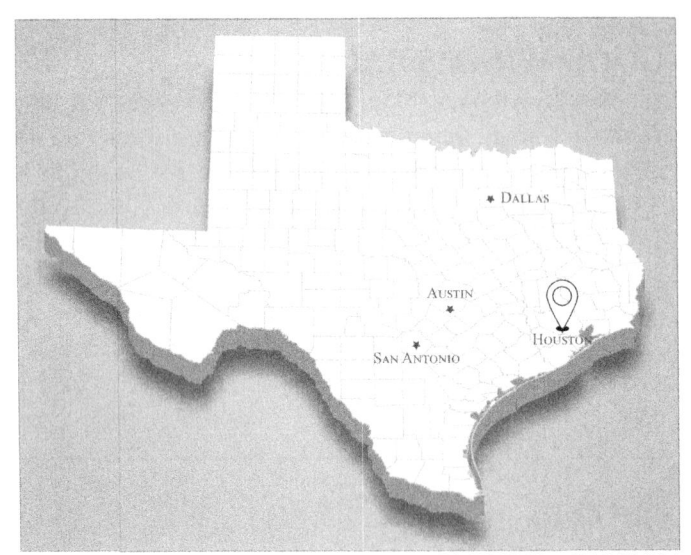

29.716069, -95.390394

WHAT'S ABOUT?:

The Houston Zoo is a 55-acre facility located in Hermann Park, Houston.

The zoo is home to over 6,000 animals representing over 900 species. It allows visitors to see and learn about diverse wildlife worldwide.

Visitors can walk through the African Forest exhibit to see elephants, giraffes, and other African wildlife.

They can also explore the Kipp Aquarium, which features diverse marine life, including stingrays, sea turtles, and other exotic species.

The McGovern Children's Zoo provides a fun and interactive experience for children, with a petting zoo, a farm exhibit, and a variety of hands-on activities.

The zoo offers educational programs and classes, including animal encounters and behind-the-scenes tours.

In addition, it has a train ride that provides visitors with a scenic tour of the zoo grounds.

The train ride is a popular attraction for children and families, offering a unique perspective of the animals and habitats at the zoo.

Whether you're a nature lover or simply looking for a fun and educational day out, the Houston Zoo is the perfect destination for families, animal enthusiasts, and anyone looking to experience the wonders of the animal kingdom.

WHERE IS?
The Houston Zoo is located at 6200 Hermann Park Drive in Houston. The best way to reach it is by car, with on-site parking. However, if you prefer public transportation, you can take METRORail's Red Line to the Museum District station, a short walk from the zoo.

WHAT'S GOOD/WHAT'S BAD:
This zoo was an impressive experience. Although I usually feel sad about animals in captivity, I couldn't help but notice that they seemed healthy and well taken care of. The zoo's display areas were adorned with sculptures and colorful designs. I was astonished at the range of animals that were there. Almost every animal was exhibited, and I got to see them all. The Aviary was particularly impressive, with various active tropical birds. The day we spent there was well worth it. The zoo had a good café that wasn't overpriced. I had pre-booked our tickets online. I traveled to the zoo by train from downtown but had trouble finding the front entrance. It was a long walk from the side entrance, around the golf course, to the front. I recommend getting clear directions on how to get there.

DATE(S) VISITED:

WEATHER CONDITIONS:

ACCOMODATIONS:

WHAT WAS THE BEST PART OF TODAY?

SPECIAL MEMORIES:

FORT WORTH ZOO

95 TEXAS

A thriving wildlife haven that offers a chance to get up close with exotic animals from around the world, an exciting experience for animal lovers of all ages.

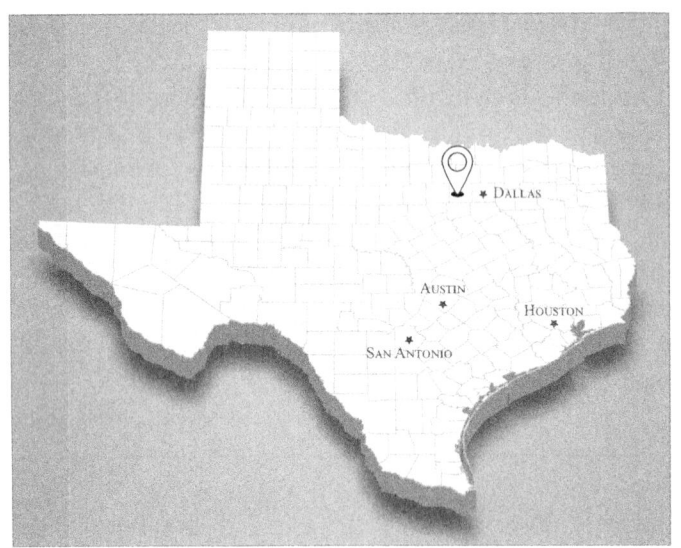

32.723296, -97.356331

WHAT'S ABOUT?:

The Fort Worth Zoo is one of Texas's oldest and largest zoos. Its world-class facility offers visitors a unique opportunity to experience wildlife worldwide. It covers over 64 acres of land and has over 5,000 animals representing nearly 500 species. It allows one to see creatures up close and personal in natural habitats.

The zoo is recognized for its broad range of animals, which comprise primates, reptiles, big cats, and birds, and its initiatives for protecting endangered species. Visitors can explore the African Savannah, Asian Falls, and Australian Outback exhibits. They can observe exotic animals like elephants, lions, kangaroos, and more. The zoo also features interactive exhibits that allow visitors to get hands-on with the animals and learn about their behavior and habitat. Children can also participate in educational programs and animal encounters, a fun and exciting way to learn about the natural world.

Visitors can explore the zoo on foot, but a monorail takes visitors through some of the zoo's habitats.

This is a must-visit for families, animal lovers, and anyone looking for an educational and enjoyable day out.

The zoo is open every day except Christmas Day and offers special events and exhibits throughout the year. Fort Worth Zoo was one of the first zoos in the country to participate in the Species Survival Plan, which helps to ensure the genetic diversity and viability of captive populations of endangered species.

WHERE IS?
The Fort Worth Zoo is located at 1989 Colonial Pkwy, Fort Worth, TX 76110, United States. It is located near downtown Fort Worth and can be reached by car or public transportation. If driving, there is ample parking available on-site. Alternatively, the Fort Worth Transit Authority operates several bus routes that stop near the zoo. The zoo is also accessible via bike, with several bike trails and bike racks available at the zoo entrance.

WHAT'S GOOD/WHAT'S BAD:
What a wonderful experience! The animals were very active, and all their enclosures were well-maintained, making it easy to see them. I visited on Wednesday when the admission was discounted, which was worth it. The zoo was clean and easy to navigate, and plenty of animals could be seen. I particularly enjoyed the new exhibits and the water park, where I interacted with stingrays. The construction didn't bother me, and I plan to return when it's finished. The Crocodile Cafe was a unique experience as I ate my delicious burgers and fries beside the tank. The prices were a little high, but the experience made it worth it. I highly recommend this place!

DATE(S) VISITED:

WEATHER CONDITIONS:

ACCOMODATIONS:

WHAT WAS THE BEST PART OF TODAY?

SPECIAL MEMORIES:

SAN ANTONIO BOTANICAL GARDEN

96 TEXAS

A picturesque haven of diverse flora where visitors can explore diverse landscapes and immerse themselves in a tranquil natural environment.

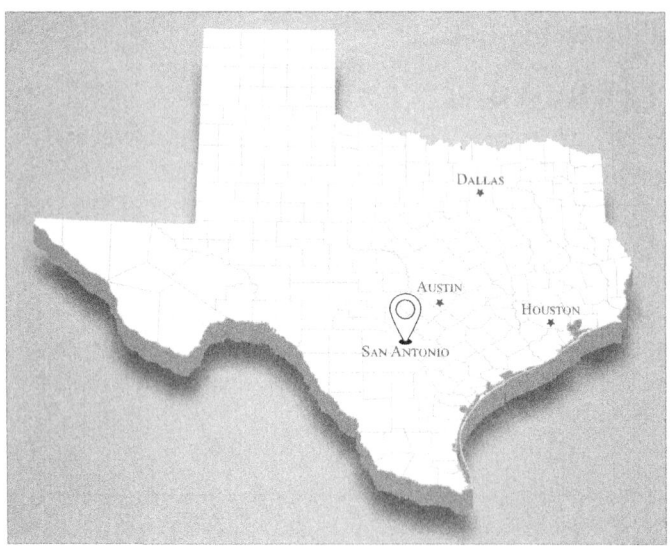

29.457439, -98.459037

WHAT'S ABOUT?:

The San Antonio Botanical Garden is a beautiful and peaceful oasis in the heart of San Antonio. Spread across 33 acres, the garden features a variety of landscapes, from lush gardens and tranquil ponds to desert landscapes and nature trails. Visitors can stroll through the garden's well-manicured paths and take in the sights and sounds of the plants and wildlife that call the garden home. One of the highlights of the San Antonio Botanical Garden is the lush Rose Garden, which features a wide variety of roses, from classic hybrid teas to modern shrub roses. Visitors can also explore the Desert Pavilion, which showcases a variety of desert-adapted plants, including cacti and succulents. Another must-see area is the Japanese Garden, which features a serene pond, a beautiful tea garden, and a traditional tea house. The San Antonio Botanical Garden also offers several educational opportunities for visitors of all ages. From guided tours to workshops and classes, visitors can learn about the many different types of plants, animals, and ecosystems that call the garden home. In addition, the garden hosts various events throughout the year, including festivals, concerts, and workshops, making it a fun and exciting place to visit for the whole family. Whether you're a plant enthusiast, a nature lover, or simply looking for a peaceful place to relax, the San Antonio Botanical Garden is a must-visit destination. With its stunning landscapes, diverse collection of plants and animals and educational opportunities, it's the perfect place to connect with nature and experience the beauty and wonder of the natural world.

WHERE IS?
The San Antonio Botanical Garden is at 555 Funston Place, San Antonio, Texas, 78209. It can be reached by car or public transportation, with the Botanical Garden being a short distance from several bus stops on the VIVA Culture route and parking available on site.

WHAT'S GOOD/WHAT'S BAD:
This place was a fantastic experience for me. The gardens are beautiful, and walking along the meandering paths was a great experience. I was pleasantly surprised by the indoor gardens, as they exceeded my expectations. The admission cost was worth it, and I loved every moment. The kids' area, walkways, big red chairs, and the tower were all amazing sights. Everywhere you turn, there are different plants and flowers, with signs to tell you about them. I wish they had more benches around to just sit on and relax. I especially loved the greenhouse area with its ferns and cactus buildings. The orchids in another building were simply stunning. It was a peaceful and beautiful place, and I could have spent hours exploring the different areas.

DATE(S) VISITED:

WEATHER CONDITIONS:

ACCOMODATIONS:

WHAT WAS THE BEST PART OF TODAY?

SPECIAL MEMORIES:

LANDA PARK

A natural oasis filled with lush greenery, scenic rivers, and opportunities for outdoor recreation for a tranquil escape from the hustle and bustle of city life.

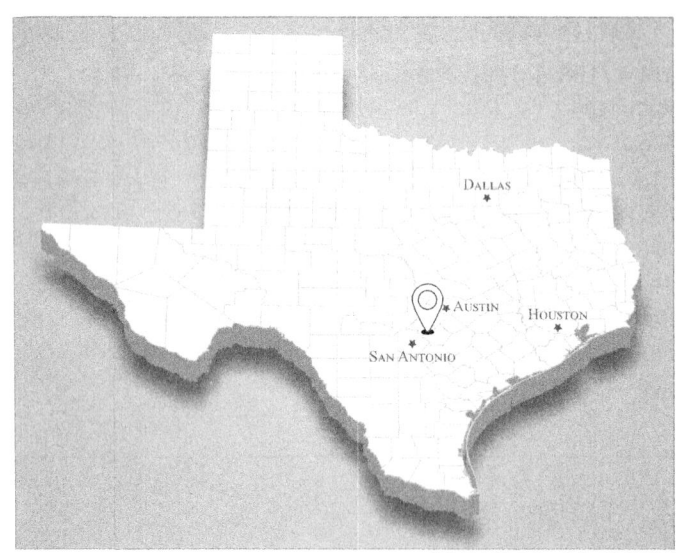

29.710016, -98.133595

WHAT'S ABOUT?:

Landa Park is a beautiful and scenic park located in the city of New Braunfels. With over 200 acres of land, the park offers a wide range of outdoor activities for visitors of all ages, making it an ideal destination for families and outdoor enthusiasts.

The park features a large lake with a natural spring-fed pool, perfect for fishing, swimming, boating, and sunbathing.

Landa Park also has several sports fields, including basketball, tennis, and volleyball courts for those who enjoy outdoor sports.

In addition to its outdoor activities, Landa Park is home to several historic landmarks, including a beautiful and well-preserved dance hall.

The park is also home to a miniature train ride, a popular attraction for children and families.

Landa Park offers several scenic walking trails, including the Panther Canyon Nature Trail, which winds through the park's beautiful woods and hills.

Whether looking for outdoor adventure, historical landmarks, or a scenic stroll, Landa Park is a picturesque and relaxing destination that offers something for everyone.

WHERE IS?
Landa Park is located in New Braunfels. It is situated just north of downtown, between Interstate 35 and the Guadalupe River.

To reach Landa Park, visitors can take Interstate 35 to Exit 189, then head west on Seguin Avenue until they get to the park. The park has ample parking, with several parking lots throughout the grounds.

Additionally, visitors can take public transportation to Landa Park. The Comal Transit bus service has a stop near the park's entrance, making it accessible to those without a car.

WHAT'S GOOD/WHAT'S BAD:
This park is one of the best in New Braunfels. There's always something to do, and I feel safe here. The trails are great, and you can see many birds and wildlife. They even have a train that runs through it which is always popular with kids and young parents. There's a nice pool and water feature too. They've labeled some of the plants and trees, which is interesting. The lake and stream water are so clear that I saw some fish. I had no trouble finding parking, but I think the $25 fee for a picnic space is ridiculous. It's only mentioned in the fine print of the rules and handouts.

DATE(S) VISITED:

WEATHER CONDITIONS:

ACCOMODATIONS:

WHAT WAS THE BEST PART OF TODAY?

SPECIAL MEMORIES:

PEROT MUSEUM OF NATURE AND SCIENCE

Unleash your curiosity and discover the thrill of science in this innovative, interactive, and engaging Museum.

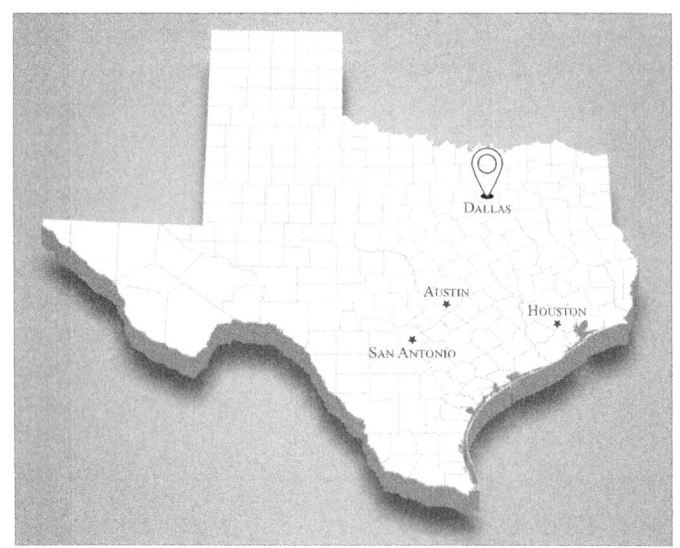

32.785624, -96.806840

WHAT'S ABOUT?:

The Perot Museum of Nature and Science, located in Dallas, is an exceptional destination for anyone interested in natural history and science. The museum offers various exhibits and interactive experiences that allow visitors to explore multiple aspects of the natural world, technology, engineering, and mathematics.

One of the museum's main attractions is the five exhibit floors that feature interactive and engaging experiences that will keep visitors entertained and informed for hours.

Some of the most popular exhibits include the Expanding Universe Hall, where visitors can explore the cosmos and learn about the wonders of space. Also, the Being Human Hall, which explores the complex and fascinating workings of the human body and mind. And the T. Boone Pickens Life Then and Now Hall features an impressive collection of fossils, including a complete dinosaur skeleton.

Other Perot Museum of Nature and Science exhibits include the Gems and Minerals Hall, which showcases beautiful specimens worldwide.

The Engineering and Innovation Hall features hands-on activities that allow visitors to explore the engineering world. Finally, the Energy Hall explores the science and technology behind energy production and conservation.

In addition to the exhibits, the Perot Museum of Nature and Science offers a range of programs and events, including lectures, workshops, and film screenings.

Visitors can also enjoy the museum's outdoor spaces, including a beautiful terrace with stunning views of the city.

A visit to the Perot Museum of Nature and Science is an excellent opportunity to explore and learn about the natural world. But also engage in fun and interactive experiences, and develop a new appreciation of science and technology.

WHERE IS?

The Perot Museum of Nature and Science is in Dallas. Its address is 2201 N Field St, Dallas, TX 75201, USA. The museum is conveniently located in the Victory Park neighborhood, just north of downtown Dallas. It can be easily reached by car, with paid parking available on-site. Visitors can also use public transportation, with several bus and light rail stations nearby. The closest DART (Dallas Area Rapid Transit) station is Victory Station, just a short walk from the museum.

In addition, the museum is located near several major highways, including I-35E and the Dallas North Tollway, making it easily accessible from other areas of the city and beyond.

WHAT'S GOOD/WHAT'S BAD:

This museum is enormous, is Texas-sized! And it has a massive collection of dinosaur bones. I think it's one of the best dinosaur museums in the United States. Five floors are filled with exhibits, ranging from dinosaurs to biology to history and innovation. Each exhibit hall has a different focus, and they all contain informative displays, which make the visit less tiring despite all the walking. I highly recommend checking out the minerals and gems exhibit. There are also many exciting things to see outside the museum. However, remember that the museum is very popular with children and can be noisy.

DATE(S) VISITED:

WEATHER CONDITIONS:

ACCOMODATIONS:

WHAT WAS THE BEST PART OF TODAY?

SPECIAL MEMORIES:

MCDONALD OBSERVATORY

Experience the wonder of the cosmos and witness the beauty of the night sky at a premier astronomical observatory in Texas.

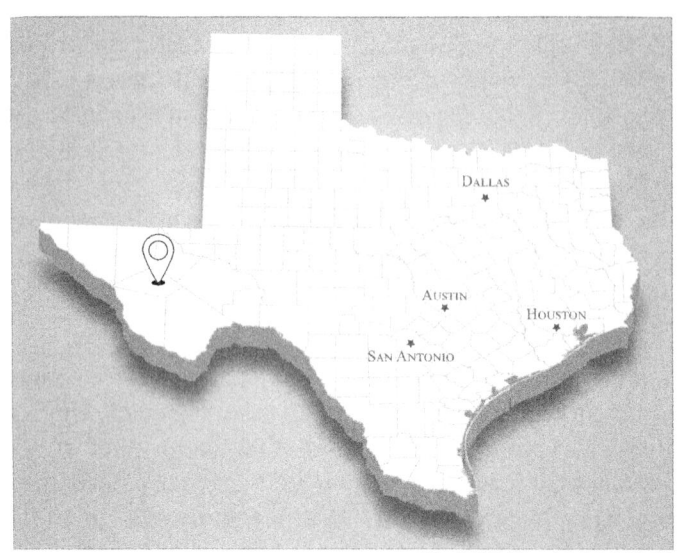

30.671869, -104.022062

WHAT'S ABOUT?:

The McDonald Observatory in the Davis Mountains of West Texas is a world-renowned astronomical research facility and a popular destination for stargazing and astronomy enthusiasts. The observatory is home to several powerful telescopes and other instruments, which astronomers from around the world use to study the universe and make groundbreaking discoveries.

Visitors can take guided tours of the facility, which provide an in-depth look at the telescopes and other instruments and the research being conducted at the observatory. Visitors can also attend star parties, held several times each week, and provide an opportunity to stargaze with the help of knowledgeable guides and powerful telescopes. In addition to the tours and star parties, the McDonald Observatory also offers a range of educational programs and events designed to help visitors of all ages learn more about astronomy and the universe. These programs include workshops, classes, and special events, which provide a fun and engaging way to explore the wonders of the cosmos. A visit to the McDonald Observatory can evoke a sense of awe and wonder as visitors are transported to the outer reaches of the universe and gain a deeper understanding of our place in the cosmos. The experience can be educational and inspiring as visitors learn about the latest discoveries in astronomy and gain a greater appreciation for the beauty and complexity of the natural world. Explore the mysteries and wonders of the universe and connect with one of the most fascinating and awe-inspiring destinations in Texas!

WHERE IS?

The McDonald Observatory is located in the Davis Mountains of West Texas, specifically at 3640 Dark Sky Drive, McDonald Observatory, TX 79734, USA. The observatory is about 450 miles west of Austin and 200 miles east of El Paso. Visitors can reach the observatory by car, with several major highways and roads in the vicinity, including I-10 and Texas Highway 118. In addition, the observatory is located about an hour's drive from the nearest town, Fort Davis, Texas.

The observatory also offers a shuttle service from Fort Davis, which runs several times daily, making it easy for visitors without transportation. However, the shuttle must be reserved in advance.

WHAT'S GOOD/WHAT'S BAD:

Fort Davis was an excellent family vacation spot; the highlight was McDonald's Observatory. The staff members are all dedicated individuals eager to share their knowledge and enthusiasm with visitors. It is recommended to plan ahead and reserve a spot early if you want to participate in one of the activities. If you do schedule and cannot make it, be sure to cancel since seats are limited. Driving or riding out to the observatory is worth taking in the surroundings even if you don't participate in any activities.

DATE(S) VISITED:

WEATHER CONDITIONS:

ACCOMODATIONS:

WHAT WAS THE BEST PART OF TODAY?

SPECIAL MEMORIES:

KIMBELL ART MUSEUM

Immerse yourself in a world of timeless beauty and artistic masterpieces, and experience the wonder of the world's great artistic traditions.

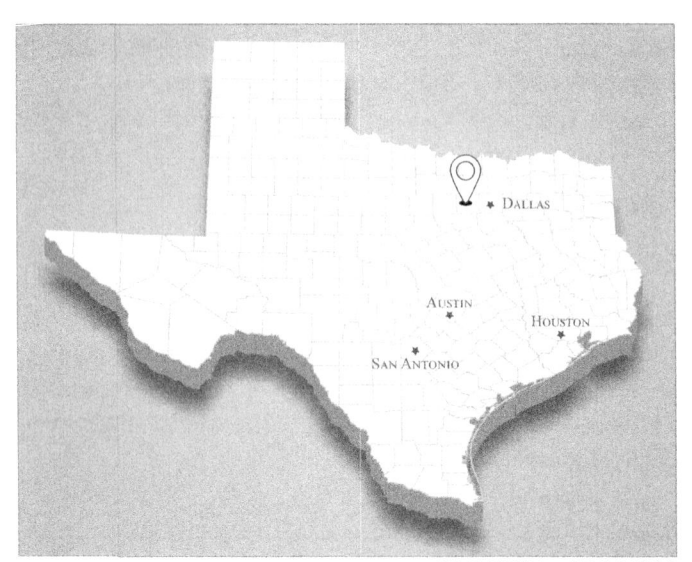

32.748604, -97.364829

WHAT'S ABOUT?:

The Kimbell Art Museum, located in Fort Worth, is one of the most renowned museums in the country, housing an exceptional collection of European, Asian, and African art. It was designed by the famous architect Louis Kahn and is known for its excellent design and beautiful natural lighting. Kimbell's collection includes pieces from a wide range of cultures and periods, with works by artists such as Michelangelo, Caravaggio, Monet, and Matisse, among many others. Visitors can explore the collection through guided tours, audio guides, or self-guided tours, all of which provide an in-depth look at the history and significance of each work.

In addition to its permanent collection, the Kimbell Art Museum hosts a range of temporary exhibitions throughout the year, featuring works from some of the most celebrated artists in the world. These exhibitions allow visitors to explore different artistic styles and cultures and gain a deeper understanding of the art world.

The Kimbell Art Museum also offers a range of educational programs and events, including lectures, workshops, and art classes, which allow visitors to engage with the collection and learn about the artistic process. The museum also features a beautiful outdoor space with a tranquil reflecting pool and lush gardens, providing visitors with a peaceful oasis in the city's heart.

Overall, a visit to the Kimbell Art Museum is an opportunity to explore some of the world's most exceptional works of art, learn about different cultures and artistic styles, and experience the transformative power of art.

WHERE IS?
The Kimbell Art Museum is located in Fort Worth, specifically at 3333 Camp Bowie Blvd, Fort Worth, TX 76107, USA. The museum is in the heart of the city's Cultural District, easily accessible by car, bus, or bicycle. The museum provides free parking in its own lot, and street parking is available nearby. Visitors can also use public transportation, with several bus routes serving the area. In addition, the museum is conveniently located near several major highways, including I-30 and I-35W, making it easily accessible from other areas of the city and beyond.

WHAT'S GOOD/WHAT'S BAD:
The museum is fantastic, and the architecture is impressive. The sculptures are ancient and date back to 1,000 B.C. They also have a great art collection, with the renaissance period being my favorite. The pieces were stunning, and seeing art students drawing sketches of the sculptures was fascinating. Even for someone who isn't art-savvy, it was a wonderful experience. The museum is well-designed and easy to follow, and it only took me two hours to explore, although I would have stayed longer if I could.

DATE(S) VISITED:

WEATHER CONDITIONS:

ACCOMODATIONS:

WHAT WAS THE BEST PART OF TODAY?

SPECIAL MEMORIES:

SUNDANCE SQUARE

101 TEXAS

Immerse yourself in the vibrant energy of downtown Fort Worth and discover a world of shopping, dining, and entertainment in the heart of Texas.

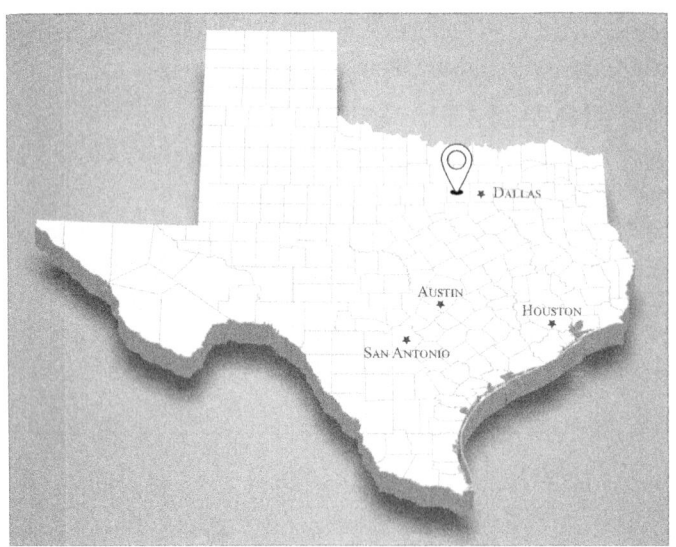

32.747715, -97.326592

WHAT'S ABOUT?:

Sundance Square, located in the heart of downtown Fort Worth, is a vibrant and bustling destination that offers visitors a chance to explore the city's best. The area is home to a wide range of shops, restaurants, and entertainment venues, making it a great destination for anyone looking to experience the energy and excitement of urban life. Visitors to Sundance Square can explore the area's many shops and boutiques, which offer a range of products, from unique artisanal items to high-end designer fashions. The area is also home to many great restaurants, cafes, and bars, offering a range of cuisines and dining experiences, from casual to fine dining. In addition to shopping and dining, Sundance Square offers a range of entertainment options, including live music, theater, and art galleries.

There are several fountains and water features in Sundance Square, which add to the charm and beauty of the area. The most iconic fountain is the "Jetted Geyser" fountain, which features a series of synchronized water jets that shoot up into the air at various heights, creating a mesmerizing and beautiful display. Several other smaller fountains and water features throughout the area provide a peaceful and relaxing atmosphere for visitors to enjoy. The water features in Sundance Square are trendy during the hot Texas summers, as they offer a refreshing respite from the heat and a fun place for children to play.

A visit to Sundance Square can evoke a sense of excitement and adventure as visitors explore the vibrant and dynamic cityscape.

WHERE IS?
Sundance Square is located in downtown Fort Worth, specifically in the area bounded by Houston Street to the east, Commerce Street to the south, 3rd Street to the north, and Throckmorton Street to the west. The area is easily accessible by car, bus, or train, and several public parking garages and lots are available for visitors wishing to drive. Visitors can also use public transportation, with several bus routes and the Trinity Railway Express serving the area.Sundance Square is located near several major highways, including I-30 and I-35W, making it easily accessible from other city areas and beyond.

WHAT'S GOOD/WHAT'S BAD:
Upon arriving in Fort Worth, I was surprised to find a more modern and fashionable town than I anticipated. Our main interest was Sundance Square, which I highly suggest exploring in the evening. We were able to enjoy the live music that could be heard from nearby restaurants, as well as the stunning fountains and lights with a mural as a backdrop. It was amusing for children to run around the fountains after they shut down. In addition, it was an excellent location for taking photos.

DATE(S) VISITED:

WEATHER CONDITIONS:

ACCOMODATIONS:

WHAT WAS THE BEST PART OF TODAY?

SPECIAL MEMORIES:

A JOURNEY THROUGH THE LONE STAR STATE: AN UNFORGETTABLE TEXAS ROAD TRIP

Are you ready for an adventure? Join me on a journey through the Lone Star State, where we'll discover some of Texas's best attractions.

This road trip itinerary is designed to showcase some of the State's most incredible sights and experiences. From the vibrant city of Austin to the rugged beauty of Big Bend National Park, this trip will take you on a whirlwind adventure through Texas's diverse landscapes and rich history. So buckle up and get ready for an unforgettable ride!

Embark on your Texas road trip by touching in Austin, the State's Capital.

Austin is the perfect starting point whether flying in or driving from a nearby state. The Austin-Bergstrom International Airport offers numerous rental car options for your convenience. Choose the vehicle that suits your needs best, and then set off to explore the city.

STOP 1: AUSTIN

Explore the vibrant capital of Texas, a city brimming with unique energy, music, and art. Austin's cultural scene has landed it a spot in the UNESCO Creative Cities Network, and it is known for its quirky vibe and diverse community. Immerse yourself in the local scene, from enjoying live music at famous venues to indulging in delicious food trucks. Stroll through sprawling parks, admire the street art, and experience the city's undeniable allure. Plan to stay at least one or two nights to fully embrace all Austin offers.

Experiences You Can't-Miss in Austin

- *Discover the Texas State Capitol*

Located in the heart of Austin, the Texas State Capitol is a must-see attraction for anyone visiting the city. Built of pink granite in 1888, it is a domed building taller than the U.S. Capitol in Washington, D.C.. Join a free guided tour to learn about the history and architecture of this beautiful building, and be sure to take in the stunning view from the observation deck.

- *Discover the Bob Bullock Texas State History Museum*

Immerse yourself in the history of Texas at the Bob Bullock Texas State History Museum.

Located in downtown Austin, this interactive museum tells the story of Texas from its earliest inhabitants to the present day. Exhibits include artifacts, multimedia displays, and hands-on experiences that will engage and educate visitors of all ages.

- *Visit the LBJ Presidential Library*

The LBJ Presidential Library in Austin is a must-visit attraction for anyone interested in American history and politics. This beautiful library is dedicated to the life and work of President Lyndon B. Johnson, who served as the 36th President of the United States from 1963 to 1969. The museum houses a collection of historical documents, photographs, and artifacts that offer a unique insight into President Johnson's life, presidency, and impact on American politics. The library is also home to a beautiful fountain, a replica of the Oval Office, and a gift shop where you can purchase presidential memorabilia.

- *Explore the Lyndon B. Johnson National Historical Park*

The Lyndon B. Johnson National Historical Park is located in the Texas Hill Country, about 50 miles west of Austin. It includes a visitor center, the LBJ Ranch, and the Texas White House, which was the residence of President Lyndon B. Johnson during his time in office. The park also has several walking trails that allow visitors to explore the ranch and the surrounding natural beauty of the area. Visitors can watch a short film about President Johnson's life and presidency at the visitor center and browse exhibits highlighting his achievements and the issues he faced during his office. The LBJ Ranch is a working ranch; visitors can see the longhorn cattle roaming the property. Overall, the Lyndon B. Johnson National Historical Park offers a fascinating look into the life of one of America's most influential presidents and the Texas Hill Country that he called home.

- *Swim at the Barton Springs Municipal Pool*

In Austin's Zilker Park, Barton Springs Municipal Pool is a favorite local spot for swimming and relaxation. The natural pool is fed by underground springs, providing a refreshing temperature year-round. The pool's clear, turquoise water and surrounding greenery create a beautiful and peaceful visitor environment. The pool also has a diving board and a grassy area for picnics and sunbathing. So whether you're looking for a place to cool off on a hot day or just want to relax in a beautiful natural setting, Barton Springs is a must-visit destination in Austin.

- *Immerse Yourself in Live Music*

Being the Live Music Capital of the World, catching some live music shows scattered throughout the city is a must during your visit. Indulge in a night of bar-hopping on Sixth Street and take in the energy of the live performances in each venue. Alternatively, you can visit the Moody Theater, which hosts the renowned Austin City Limits and has featured diverse musical artists over the years. If you're lucky enough to be in Austin at the right time, don't miss the opportunity to attend the South By Southwest music festival.

STOP 2: HAMILTON POOL PRESERVE

The beautiful Hamilton Pool Preserve is just a short drive outside Austin. This natural swimming hole was formed when the roof of an underground river collapsed. The result is a crystal-clear pool surrounded by lush greenery and a towering 50-foot waterfall. Make sure to dip in the refreshing water, but be aware that no lifeguards are on duty, so swim at your own risk. A beautiful carved-out cave behind the waterfall provides a shady spot to relax and enjoy the serene surroundings. You can also explore the hiking trails or picnic on the tables in the area. Don't forget to make an online reservation before your visit. Keep in mind that swimming may be prohibited if the bacteria levels in the water are too high. Timing your visit after rainfall will ensure the waterfall is flowing.

STOP 3: SAN ANTONIO

Leaving Austin, it will not be long before you reach San Antonio, a city with a wonderful mix of natural and historical wonders that cater to every traveler's preferences. Whether exploring historic battlegrounds or venturing into mysterious caverns, San Antonio has something to offer you. Founded in 1718 as a Spanish mission, San Antonio is the second-largest city in Texas. Its rich cultural heritage is evident throughout the city. With world-renowned sites like the Alamo and the San Antonio Missions National Historical Park being recognized as UNESCO World Heritage sites, the city attracts millions of visitors annually. Don't forget to savor the city's Spanish influences and culture that you can find around every corner.

Experiences You Can't-Miss in San Antonio

- *Visit The Alamo*

No Texas road trip would be complete without visiting the iconic Alamo in the heart of San Antonio. Once a Spanish mission, the Alamo was pivotal during the 1836 battle between Texans and Mexican soldiers in Texas history. Today, the Alamo stands as a symbol of Texas freedom and offers visitors a chance to step back in time and experience the events there. As you stand in the courtyard, you can almost hear the echoes of the past as you imagine the brave Texans who fought for independence. Take a self-guided tour of the grounds, explore the building's historical artifacts and exhibits, or opt for a guided tour to learn more about the Alamo's rich history. Admission is free for self-guided tours, while guided tours are available for a fee.

- *Discover the San Antonio River Walk*

The San Antonio River Walk is a must-see attraction in the city that should not be missed during your Texas road trip. This pedestrian walkway stretches 15 miles along the San Antonio River and provides a unique city perspective.

The downtown section is trendy, featuring a variety of restaurants, bars, shops, and museums to explore. Take a leisurely stroll along the River Walk to enjoy the ambiance and discover the hidden gems.
- *Visit San Fernando Cathedral and San Antonio Missions National Historical Park*

San Fernando Cathedral is a historic landmark in San Antonio and is located in the city center. The cathedral is the oldest standing church in Texas and is known for its stunning architecture and religious significance.

The San Antonio Missions National Historical Park is a UNESCO World Heritage site with four missions. The park preserves and showcases the Spanish colonial history of the region and offers visitors a glimpse into the past with its beautiful architecture and artifacts.
- *Explore the Natural Bridge Caverns*

For an exciting expedition to a natural wonder, go to the Natural Bridge Caverns located just north of the city. These caverns are the biggest commercial caverns in Texas and are truly remarkable. Descend 180 feet below ground to marvel at the stunning rock formations.
- *Tube The Comal River*

If you're looking for a fun water activity near San Antonio, tubing down the Comal River is a great option. New Braunfels, located about 30 minutes northeast of San Antonio, offers tube rentals for a relaxing float down the river. The Comal River is a popular spot for tubing, with its clear water and gentle rapids. This is a great activity for families and friends to enjoy on a hot summer day. Don't forget to pack sunscreen and snacks for the trip!
- *Experience Gruene Hall, Texas' Oldest Dance Hall*

Gruene Hall is a famous dance hall in the small town of Gruene, just a short drive from New Braunfels. It is the oldest dance hall in Texas and has been around since 1878. The hall is famous for its live music; many famous musicians have played there. In addition to the music, the hall also offers a unique shopping experience, with various vendors selling vintage and handmade items. If you're looking for a taste of Texas history and culture, visiting Gruene Hall is a must.
- *Discover the Cascade Caverns*

Cascade Caverns is a beautiful limestone cavern system located in the Texas Hill Country, just outside Boerne, approximately a 30-minute drive from San Antonio. The caverns are open for guided tours, and visitors can see a variety of geological formations, such as stalactites, stalagmites, and flowstones. The tours take approximately an hour and are suitable for all ages. The site also includes a gift shop, picnic area, and nature trails for visitors to explore.

STOP 4: BIG BEND NATIONAL PARK

Prepare for a long but rewarding drive on this Texas road trip to your next destination. Big Bend National Park is a must-visit place for those who love exploring the great outdoors and checking off U.S. national parks. The park is located on the Texas-Mexico border. It offers breathtaking desert and mountain landscapes perfect for camping, hiking, and wildlife watching. With its remote location and vast size, you can truly disconnect from the crowds and immerse yourself in nature. To fully experience the park, consider staying for one or two nights.

Experiences You Can't-Miss in Big Bend National Park

- *Discover the Santa Elena Canyon*

Explore the Santa Elena Canyon by hiking and admiring the beautiful natural rock formations carved out by the Rio Grande. The trail is less than two miles round trip, making it a manageable hike for most visitors. Along the way, you will be treated to breathtaking views that will leave a lasting impression. Don't forget to bring your camera to capture the stunning scenery!

- *Explore Boquillas Canyon*

Boquillas Canyon is located in the eastern section of Big Bend National Park, near the border with Mexico. The canyon features towering cliffs and a narrow gorge cut out by the Rio Grande. Visitors can hike the Boquillas Canyon Trail, which is approximately 1.5 miles round trip and offers stunning views of the canyon and surrounding landscape. It's an excellent bird-watching spot, with many species native to the area. Additionally, visitors can take a guided horseback or canoe tour through the canyon for a unique perspective of the area.

- *Experience Mexican Culture with a Day Trip Across the Border*

With your passport in hand, you can take a day trip to Mexico and explore its national parks and charming towns. You can cross the border at Boquillas and take a ferry ride across the Rio Grande. This is a great opportunity to experience the rich Mexican culture and witness breathtaking scenery. Don't forget to check the latest travel advisories before crossing the border.

- *Visit Fort Davis National Historic Site*

At the Fort Davis National Historic Site, you can step back in time to the days of the American Frontier. This former military fort protected settlers and travelers in the mid to late 1800s and has been well preserved, allowing visitors to experience what life was like in the Old West. With its scenic location in the Davis Mountains and its many exhibits, this historic site is a must-visit for anyone interested in the history of the American West.

STOP 5: EXPLORE TEXAS HILL COUNTRY

After exploring the beautiful landscapes of Big Bend, the next stop on your Texas road trip itinerary is the picturesque Texas Hill Country. Nestled between Austin and San Antonio, this region is known for its scenic rolling hills covered in beautiful wildflowers, including the famous Texas Bluebonnets.

With abundant state parks and scenic vistas, Texas Hill Country is the perfect destination for nature lovers and photographers alike. To fully experience all this area has to offer, plan to spend a few nights exploring the stunning scenery.

Experiences You Can't-Miss in the Texas Hill Country

- *Discover the Beauty of Bluebonnet Flowers*

The Texas Hill Country in the spring is picturesque, with vibrant bluebonnet flowers covering the rolling hills. The state flower of Texas blooms in abundance during this time, making it an excellent opportunity to witness and appreciate the region's natural beauty. Be sure to take plenty of photos as a keepsake of this enchanting sight.

- *Climb the Majestic Enchanted Rock*

Take a challenging yet rewarding hike up the iconic pink granite mountain at Enchanted Rock State Natural Area. With an elevation of 1,825 feet, the summit rewards visitors with breathtaking panoramic views of the Texas Hill Country, especially at sunset.

- *Paddle Along the Guadalupe River*

The Guadalupe River is a popular destination for outdoor enthusiasts, especially those who love water activities. A visit to the Guadalupe River State Park is a must-do for kayaking, tubing, swimming, or fishing. The scenic river also offers a chance to explore the park's hiking and mountain biking trails.

- *Drive along the scenic route Willow City Loop*

Willow City Loop is a scenic drive that winds through the heart of Texas Hill Country. The route is known for its stunning views of wildflowers, rolling hills, and rocky terrain. It's trendy when the bluebonnets and other wildflowers fully bloom in the spring. You'll see ranches, creeks, and historical sites as you drive along this scenic route. The road is also perfect for a leisurely bike ride or a picnic with a view.

Suggestions for Accommodations

Consider staying in Fredericksburg, a charming town in the heart of Texas Hill Country that provides the perfect base for exploring the region. Alternatively, you can stay in Austin or San Antonio, which are just a short drive away and offer plenty of accommodation options.

Whether looking for a cozy bed and breakfast, a luxurious resort, or a budget-friendly hotel, you will find something to suit your needs in these cities.
If your choice is to stay in Fredericksburg:

- *Visit The National Museum of the Pacific War*

The National Museum of the Pacific War in Fredericksburg is the only museum in the United States dedicated entirely to telling the story of the Pacific Theater battles of World War II. This museum spans six acres and includes an outdoor display of tanks, planes, and other vehicles from the war. Inside the museum, visitors can explore a variety of exhibits, including a recreated combat zone, which immerses visitors in the sounds and sights of the Pacific Theater. Additionally, the museum has a research library featuring extensive collections of photographs, maps, and documents. The National Museum of the Pacific War is a must-visit attraction for any history buff or anyone interested in World War II history.

STOP 6: DALLAS

No Texas road trip would be complete without a visit to Dallas, a modern and vibrant city with a rich history and plenty of exciting activities to explore. With so much to see and do, you could plan to spend at least a few days here. Dallas is also an excellent home base for exploring the surrounding area, with many fantastic day trip options.

Experiences You Can't-Miss in Dallas

- *Deepen the JFK Assassination at the Dealey Plaza National Historic Landmark District*

President John F. Kennedy was assassinated in Dallas in 1963 by Lee Harvey Oswald. History buffs will want to visit the Sixth Floor Museum in the former Texas School Book Depository building where Oswald had shot from. This museum offers a comprehensive look at the events leading up to the assassination, exhibits with photos and videos, information about conspiracy theories surrounding the shooting, and a preserved view of the spot where Oswald had fired his gun. Visiting this museum provides an engaging way to learn about this significant moment in U.S. history.

- *Admire The Dallas Arboretum and Botanical Garden*

The Dallas Arboretum and Botanical Garden is a must-visit attraction for anyone who loves flowers and gardens. The 66-acre garden is located on the shores of White Rock Lake and features a wide variety of plants and flowers from around the world. You can stroll through the gardens and admire the different landscapes, including a children's, rose, and vegetable garden. Don't forget to bring your camera as there are many picturesque spots for photos.

- *Discover Museums in Dallas*

Dallas is home to a diverse selection of museums catering to various interests. If you are interested in art, head to the Dallas Museum of Art, which has a collection of over 24,000 works of art from around the world. The Nasher Sculpture Center is a must-see for those who love sculpture, housing a collection of over 300 pieces of modern and contemporary sculpture. Finally, for those who love science and nature, the Perot Museum of Nature and Science is an interactive and educational museum offering various exhibits and activities.

While in Dallas, you may want to take a short trip to Fort Worth, a nearby city with plenty of attractions. Fort Worth is about 35 miles west of Dallas and a popular destination for art and history lovers.

- *Discover Fort Worth Stockyards*

The Fort Worth Stockyards is a historic district in Fort Worth that is worth a visit while you are in the Dallas-Fort Worth area. This district was once a hub for the cattle industry in Texas and is now home to various shops, restaurants, and entertainment options celebrating its Western heritage. You can watch a cattle drive down the main street, take a horseback ride, or even attend a rodeo at the Cowtown Coliseum. The Fort Worth Stockyards also has several museums that showcase the area's history, including the Texas Cowboy Hall of Fame and the Stockyards Museum. The distance from Dallas to Fort Worth is about 40 minutes, so it's an easy day trip from the city.

- *Visit the Kimbell Art Museum*

The Kimbell Art Museum is a world-renowned museum featuring a collection of art ranging from ancient to modern times. The museum's permanent collection includes pieces from renowned artists such as Monet, Picasso, and Matisse. The building is a work of art, with a design seamlessly integrating into the surrounding landscape. Admission to the museum is free, although some special exhibitions may require a fee. It is a must-visit for art lovers traveling to the Dallas-Fort Worth area.

- *Watch Animals at the Fort Worth Zoo*

If you have kids with you on your Texas road trip or love animals, you may want to visit the Fort Worth Zoo. It is a popular attraction established in 1909 and has since grown to become one of the top-ranked zoos in the country. The zoo has over 7,000 animals worldwide, including many rare and endangered species. Visitors can see animals such as lions, tigers, elephants, giraffes, and gorillas, among many others. The zoo also offers a variety of experiences, including animal encounters, behind-the-scenes tours, and educational programs for all ages.

STOP 7: HOUSTON

The next stop on your Texas trip is Houston, the State's largest city and the fourth largest in the U.S. Whether you have a weekend or just a short stop, Houston is a must-visit destination. It's a three-and-a-half-hour drive south fr
om Dallas, but the unique attractions and cultural experiences you'll find here make it well worth the trip. Known as Space City, Bayou City, and the Culinary Capital of the South, Houston is a global and diverse city with much to offer. Don't miss the Museum and Theater Districts, and try some mouth-watering Texas BBQ while you're here.

Experiences You Can't-Miss in Huston

- *Discover the Fascinating World of Space Travel at Space Center Houston*

For centuries, the mysteries of outer space have captured the imagination of people worldwide. If you are fascinated with space exploration, science, or NASA, visiting one of Houston's top tourist attractions is a must. The Space Center Houston boasts a wealth of exhibits, interactive displays, fascinating artifacts, and behind-the-scenes documentaries that offer a unique glimpse into the world of space travel. So step inside and immerse yourself in the world of NASA, where exploration and innovation are unlimited.

- *Explore Earth's History at the Museum of Natural Science*

Continuing on your educational journey, head to the Houston Museum of Natural Science to delve into the wonders of our planet. Admire impressive displays of precious gems and minerals, marvel at complete dinosaur skeletons, examine ancient Egyptian artifacts, and observe realistic wild animal dioramas.

- *Unwind at Hines Waterwall Park*

The main attraction of Hines Waterwall Park is an impressive 64-foot-tall fountain that resembles a waterfall. It's an iconic sight that's perfect for a photo opportunity. After capturing the moment, you can take a break and enjoy a picnic or relax on the lush green lawn in front of the fountain.

- *Visit the San Jacinto Monument*

The San Jacinto Monument is a 567.31-foot tall monument in La Porte, Texas, just outside Houston. It is a popular tourist destination and a great place to learn about Texas's history. The monument commemorates the Battle of San Jacinto, fought on April 21, 1836, and resulted in Texas gaining its independence from Mexico. Visitors can take an elevator to the top of the monument for a panoramic view of the surrounding area. The monument also houses a museum, theater, and gift shop. It is possible to take a field trip to the San Jacinto Monument from Houston. The distance between the two is approximately 25 miles, translating to a 30-minute drive under normal traffic conditions. However, traffic can be heavy during peak times, so it is best to plan accordingly.

- *Explore the Hermann Park*

Hermann Park is a 445-acre urban park located in the heart of Houston. The park was named after George Hermann, a wealthy Houstonian who donated land in 1914. It features a variety of attractions and amenities, including gardens, trails, playgrounds, a golf course, a miniature train, and the Houston Zoo. One of the park's most popular attractions is the McGovern Centennial Gardens, which features 15 acres of beautifully manicured gardens and an interactive family garden. Hermann Park is also home to the Miller Outdoor Theatre, which annually hosts free performances and events.

- *Get up close with wildlife at Houston Zoo*

Houston Zoo is a popular attraction in the heart of Houston's Hermann Park. It houses over 6,000 animals representing over 900 species from around the world. Visitors can see a wide variety of animals, including elephants, giraffes, gorillas, lions, tigers, bears, reptiles, and birds. The zoo is dedicated to animal conservation and education. Many programs and events are focused on teaching visitors about wildlife and their habitats. It is a great destination for families, animal lovers, and anyone interested in learning more about the world's diverse animal populations.

STOP 9: GALVESTON: A FUN BEACH TOWN TO WIND DOWN FROM YOUR TEXAS ROAD TRIP

Galveston is a coastal city located just a few minutes southeast of Houston. It's a fun beach town on a long island connected to the mainland by causeways. Whether you have time for a day trip from Houston or want to explore more in-depth by staying in the small city, Galveston is the perfect place to wind down from your Texas road trip.

Experiences You Can't-Miss in Galveston

- *Explore the Historic Bishop's Palace*

Although it is called Bishop's Palace, this stunning architectural masterpiece was built as a private mansion for a wealthy couple in 1892. It stands tall as a historic landmark and is a remarkable example of Victorian-era design. Go on a tour of the exquisite mansion and immerse yourself in the rich history of the place while admiring its intricate details and craftsmanship.

- *Visit the Moody Gardens*

The Moody Gardens consist of three contemporary glass pyramids, each dedicated to a unique theme. The Aquarium Pyramid, the Rainforest Pyramid, and the Discovery Pyramid each offer a different experience. Together, they provide a blend of a zoo, park, and museum.

- *Enjoy the Ocean View from the Seawall*

The Seawall is a 10-mile-long seawall built to protect Galveston Island from the devastating effects of storms and hurricanes. It is now a popular attraction for visitors to Galveston as it offers stunning views of the Gulf of Mexico and is a great place to walk, jog, or bike. You will find numerous restaurants, shops, and hotels along the Seawall, making it a great place to spend an afternoon or evening.

- *Discover the Ocean Star Offshore Drilling Rig and Museum*

The Ocean Star Offshore Drilling Rig and Museum is a fascinating place to visit in Galveston, especially if you are interested in the history of offshore drilling. This retired drilling rig has been transformed into a museum where visitors can learn about the drilling process, the life of offshore workers, and the environmental impacts of offshore drilling. The museum features exhibits, artifacts, and interactive displays that offer a unique and educational experience.

- *Simply Relaxing on the Beach*

After an exciting Texas road trip, it's time to relax and unwind at one of Galveston's seven beautiful beaches. So set up a beach towel, grab a chair with an umbrella, and let the sound of the waves lull you into a peaceful state. There's no better way to end your Texas adventure than by enjoying the sun, sand, and sea.

End Your Texas Adventure by Departing from Houston

As your Texas road trip ends, head back to Houston from Galveston, drop off your rental car, and check in for your flight at the airport. If you arrive by car, it's time to begin your journey home. With its diverse landscapes and rich history, Texas offers a unique travel experience that the whole family will surely enjoy!

Note:

Please note that this itinerary covers a lot of ground, so it may be best to add additional days to spend more time in each location. Additionally, it's important to check park hours and road conditions before embarking on any trip. Keep in mind that this itinerary is just a suggestion and can be adjusted based on personal preferences and time constraints.

CONCLUSION

After listing the 101 best things to see and do in Texas, I can confidently say that the biggest attraction of Texas depends on what you are looking for.

For me, the Hill Country is an absolute favorite, with urban areas like Austin and San Antonio and areas with no cell phone reception just an hour's drive away.

Another favorite childhood spot was Big Bend, where we visited Fort Davis, Fort Stockton, The McDonald Observatory, Balmorhea, Marfa, and many other interesting places. I have family in Nacogdoches and spend some quality time in east Texas, where the slower pace and historic significance make for a great visit. West Texas and the Panhandle offer some great, wide-open spaces where you can really breathe, and then there's the Gulf Coast and all it has to offer.

To me, the biggest attraction in Texas is the friendliness of most people. The quality of life is also impressive. As well as the laid-back way of life that's much more relaxed than in the northeast.

Living near the Gulf Coast, I can attest to the numerous free or low-cost activities for adults and children; it includes cultural opportunities, parks, nature reserves, and churches, all within a short drive. And, of course, I cannot forget to mention the Bluebonnets, which are breathtaking in season.

You won't find huge buses shuttling tourists around Texas from point A to point B. You'll need your car and be expected to chart your course, which is honestly the best part. Regardless of what you're looking for, you'll find it in Texas, along with awesome food and friendly people who are always happy to show out-of-towners how awesome our state is.

Texas truly has something for everyone! So, as I close this guide, I hope it has inspired you to explore and discover all this great state has to offer.

May your travels be filled with wonder, joy, and unforgettable experiences here in Texas and beyond. Happy exploring!

A SPECIAL REQUEST

I really appreciate your support! A short, simple review on the Amazon page for this book will be very helpful for me. Thank You for choosing my book!

Forrest R. Cowan

TEXAS REGIONS MAP

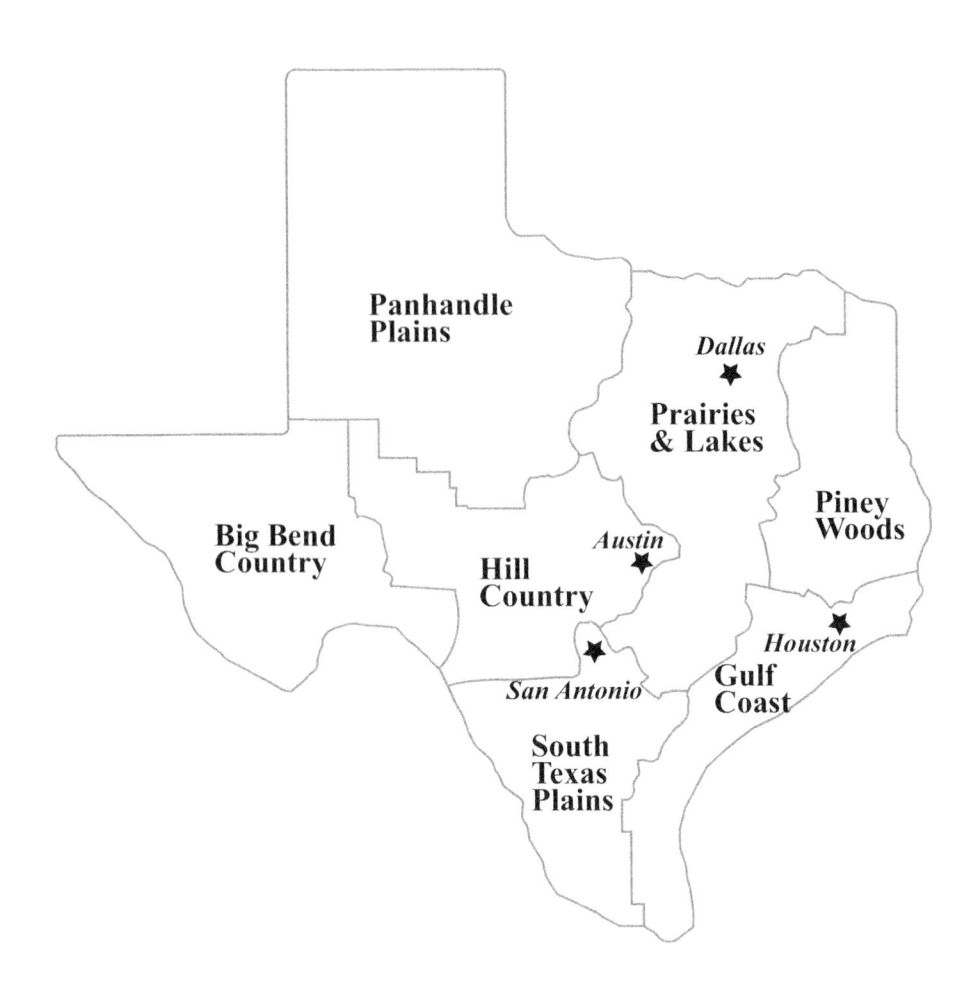

Panhandle Plains

Dallas ★

Prairies & Lakes

Big Bend Country

Austin ★

Hill Country

Piney Woods

Houston ★

San Antonio ★

Gulf Coast

South Texas Plains

PLACES BY REGION AND ALPHABETICAL ORDER

PANHANDLE PLAINS page

10.	Buddy Holly Museum	28
83.	Cadillac Ranch - Amarillo	174
41.	Lake Meredith National Recreation Area	90
9.	National Ranching Heritage Center	26
4.	Palo Duro State Park Canyon	16

PRAIRIES & LAKES

42.	Cedar Hill State Park and Lake Joe Pool	92
6.	Dallas Arboretum and Botanical Garden	20
21.	Dallas Museum of Art	50
64.	Dealey Plaza National Historic Landmark District	136
93.	Fort Worth Museum of Science and History	194
7.	Fort Worth Stockyards	22
95.	Fort Worth Zoo	198
47.	Fossil Rim Wildlife Center	102
73.	Grapevine Historic Main Street District	154
100.	Kimbell Art Museum	208
28.	Nasher Sculpture Center	64
98.	Perot Museum of Nature and Science	204
61.	President George H. W. Bush Museum in College Station	130
101.	Sundance Square	210
69.	Texas Ranger Hall of Fame and Museum	146
65.	Top O'Hill Terrace	138
50.	White Rock Lake Park	108

HILL COUNTRY

22.	Austin City Limits Music Festival - ACL	52
43.	Balcones Canyonlands National Wildlife Refuge	94
45.	Barton Springs Pool	98
12.	Bat Watching in Austin Under Congress Bridge	32
74.	Blue Hole in Wimberley	156
60.	Bob Bullock Texas History Museum in Austin	128
51.	Cascade Caverns	110
86.	Cathedral of Junk in Austin	180
71.	Caverns of Sonora	150
75.	Devil's Sinkhole State Natural Area in Rocksprings	158
30.	Enchanted Rock State Park and Natural Area	68

31.	Garner State Park	70
76.	Gorman Falls	160
20.	Gruene Hall - Texas' Oldest Dance Hall	48
27.	Inner Space Cavern	62
79.	Jacob's Well in Wimberley	166
44.	Lady Bird Lake Hike-and-Bike Trail	96
97.	Landa Park	202
63.	LBJ Presidential Library	134
46.	Longhorn Cavern State Park	100
70.	Lost Maples State Natural Area	148
59.	Lyndon B Johnson National Historical Park	126
37.	Natural Bridge Caverns	82
52.	Pedernales Falls State Park	112
39.	South Llano River State Park	86
85.	Sparky Pocket Park in Austin	178
8.	Texas State Capitol	24
62.	The National Museum of the Pacific War	132
11.	Tube the Comal River	30
77.	Westcave Preserve	162
25.	Willow City Loop Near Fredericksburg	58

BIG BEND COUNTRY

3.	Big Bend National Park	14
33.	Boquillas Canyon	74
32.	Chisos Mountains	72
34.	Fort Davis National Historic Site	76
35.	Guadalupe Mountains National Park	78
88.	Hueco Tanks in El Paso	184
82.	Marfa Lights Viewing Center	172
81.	Marfa Prada Store in Valentine	170
99.	McDonald Observatory	206
48.	Santa Elena Canyon	104
26.	Scenic Drive - Overlook	60
84.	The Ghost Town of Terlingua	176

SOUTH TEXAS PLAINS

36.	Amistad National Recreation Area	80
87.	Barney Smith's Toilet Seat Art Museum in San Antonio	182
55.	Goliad State Park & Historic Site	118
80.	Japanese Tea Garden in San Antonio	168
67.	King Ranch Visitor Center	142
68.	King William Historic District	144

66.	Majestic Theatre in San Antonio	140
58.	McNay Art Museum	124
96.	San Antonio Botanical Garden	200
54.	San Antonio Missions National Historical Park	116
53.	San Fernando Cathedral	114
1.	The Alamo	10
2.	The San Antonio River Walk	12

PINEY WOODS

40.	Big Thicket National Preserve	88
13.	Nacogdoches Visitor's Center	34
23.	Texas Rose Festival in Tyler	54

GULF COAST

19.	1892 Bishop's Palace in Galveston	46
29.	Gerald D. Hines Waterwall Park	66
72.	Eight Wonders of Port Aransas	152
16.	Herman Park in Houston	40
17.	Houston Museum of Natural Science - HMNS	42
91.	Houston Space Center	190
94.	Houston Zoo	196
18.	Huston Museum of Fine Arts - MFAH	44
78.	Malaquite Beach	164
14.	Menil Collection in Houston	36
92.	Moody Gardens in Galveston	192
89.	National Museum of Funeral History	186
90.	Ocean Star Offshore Drilling Rig & Museum	188
49.	Rockport Beach	106
15.	Rothko Chapel in Houston	38
56.	San Jacinto Monument	120
38.	Sea Rim State Park	84
5.	South Padre Island National Seashore	18
24.	The Seawall in Galveston	56
57.	USS Lexington in Corpus Christi	122

Printed in Great Britain
by Amazon